a writer's guidebook

FREW, GUCHES, MEHAFFY

A PEEK PUBLICATION

CORRECTION SYMBOLS

Agr	Agreement faulty
Awk	Awkward sentence
Cap	Capitalization faulty
C-S	Comma-splice
[ ]	Delete or move
Dev	Lacks development
X	Obvious error
Frag	Sentence fragment
Logic	Logic faulty
∧	Something missing
MM	Misplaced modifier
Num	Error in use of numbers
Order	Sentences not in most effective order
¶ or *no* ¶	Begin or do not begin new paragraph
Paral or //	Parallel construction faulty
Pass	Passive instead of active verb
Pers	Person of verb not correct

a writer's guidebook

Robert Frew
Richard Guches
Robert Mehaffy

American River College
Sacramento, California

Peek Publications • P.O. Box 50123 • Palo Alto, California 94303

PE
1408
.F592
1982

Manufactured in the United States of America
213353

Preface

A Writer's Guidebook is for students who must learn to write. And that is every student. Of course, some students think "must learn to write" refers only to mastering enough composition skills in order to earn a passing grade. Not so. As our world becomes more and more complex each year, writing becomes increasingly important. Indeed, our society expects educated people to be able to write well.

Some students reading this book will have relatively good backgounds in writing when they start; others will not. Similarly, some students will find the assignments easy while others will struggle. No matter how different students are at the beginning and during the semester, however, all will share one thing when they have completed the text: a good working knowledge of sentence, paragraph, and essay structure.

This book contains only that material which the authors have found to work best, after teaching thousands of students. As an individual using this book, you can expect it to cover only the concepts you need to succeed as a writer. That is, you will not be assigned endless exercises that have no purpose. Each exercise is specially designed to help you understand a specific concept. Each sentence and paragraph you are asked to write will make it that much easier to write with confidence in the future. Because A Writer's Guidebook does not contain extra, unneeded material, it is smaller than many similar books.

You may also notice another difference. Guidebook deliberately builds your overall writing skill one step at a time. You are asked to understand the simple sentence before the compound sentence, and the paragraph before the essay. The organization has been tested in the classroom again and again until it almost guarantees success. This sequential arrangement makes the writing of an essay a logical, step-by-step procedure rather than a tedious, mysterious ordeal. By the end of the course, you will have acquired the confidence you need to tackle future writing tasks without trauma. Writing may still be hard work in the future—that is to be expected. But the knowledge and skills you pick up from this book will give you the positive attitude you will need to complete those future assignments.

A Writer's Guidebook is divided into four basic parts: sentence writing, paragraph writing, essay writing, and the handbook. In the sentence writing portion, you will move from a review of basic sentence patterns to the more complex revision of sentence errors. You will write many sentences of your own and revise poorly written sentences written by others.

The second part of the book covers the writing of paragraphs. You will learn how to organize paragraphs, from topic sentences to support sentences to concluding sentences. When you have mastered the structure, you will then learn how to write several types of paragraphs. You will write introductory paragraphs, a variety of body paragraphs, and concluding paragraphs.

When you completely understand the paragraph, you will then move on to the third part of the book: the complete composition. In this portion, you will write a variety of short papers, putting to use everything you have learned to date. You will write expository, argumentative, autobiographical, and research papers.

Every exercise in *A Writer's Guidebook* has only one purpose: to help you become an effective writer. When you have completed this book, you will be able to write with confidence. But possibly even more important, when you have completed this book you will be able to communicate clearly with anyone.

Contents

1

Simple Sentences

This chapter is designed to help you recall what you have already learned about basic sentences. At one time or another, you have studied almost everything presented in this chapter. Your goal now is to remember it all. Depending on how long it has been since you last studied basic sentence structure, your review may be easy or difficult.

Although reviewing sentence structure is time consuming, it is worth it. You are going to write many paragraphs and essays as you work through this book. Knowing correct sentence structure will make your writing easier and more effective. As you begin to understand how sentences are put together, you will feel more at ease when you write. You will also be able to edit and revise your sentences faster and more competently than ever before. You *can* write well. But first you must take the time to review what you may have forgotten about sentence structure.

LESSON ONE—Writing Simple Sentences

Complete Subjects and Complete Predicates

The basic unit in writing is the **simple sentence**. Usually a simple sentence contains a **subject** that is followed by a **predicate**. The topic of a sentence—who or what is being written about—is the **complete subject** of the sentence. By the end of this chapter you will be able to identify the subject and the predicate in any sentence you write.

WHO OR WHAT DOES WHAT?

Often a sentence can be divided into its complete subject and complete predicate by asking *who* or *what does what?* By asking *who* or *what* does what, you can find the subject being written about; by asking *what does* the subject do, you can locate the predicate. In this type of sentence the subject performs an action.

Examples

COMPLETE SUBJECT (Who or What?)	COMPLETE PREDICATE (Does What?)
Piranhas	bite.
The hairy, foamy-mouthed monster	loved the beautiful young maiden.

WHAT HAPPENS TO THE SUBJECT?

Sometimes, however, the complete predicate answers the question, *What happens to the subject?* In this type of sentence the subject does not perform an action. Instead, the subject is acted upon by someone or something else.

Examples

COMPLETE SUBJECT (Who or What?)	COMPLETE PREDICATE (What Happens to the Subject?)
The books	have been returned to the library.
The deer	were often seen in the meadow at dusk.
The new design of Carl's	will be tested many times.

Thus, in the above examples, the subjects do not do anything. The books do not return themselves, the deer do not see themselves, and the design does not test itself.

WHAT CONDITION IS THE SUBJECT IN?

At other times the complete predicate tells in *what condition the subject is, was, or will be* — the subject's state of being.

Examples

COMPLETE SUBJECT (Who or What?)	COMPLETE PREDICATE (Condition of the subject)
The avocado	is *soft*.
The clerks in the Housewares Department	looked *exhausted* at the end of the sale.

In what condition is the *avocado?* It is *soft*.
How did the *clerks* look (what was their condition)? They looked *exhausted*.

WHO OR WHAT IS THE SUBJECT?

The complete predicate may also tell *who* or *what* the subject is, was, or will be. The subject is *who?* A complete predicate that answers this question identifies or renames the subject.

Examples

COMPLETE SUBJECT (Who or What?)	COMPLETE PREDICATE (The Subject is Who?)
Our teacher	is a photographer.
The reduced price	seems to be a real bargain.
The pilots	were experienced combat fliers.
Ugly caterpillars	become pretty butterflies.

In each case a noun (or pronoun) in the complete predicate renames the subject. The *teacher* and the *photographer* are the same person. The noun *photographer* is another name for the *teacher.*

(noun that renames)
teacher = photographer

Similarly, the *reduced price* seems to be a *bargain.* In other words, *bargain* renames *price* in the sentence.

(noun that renames)
price = bargain

Who were the *pilots?* They were experienced *fliers.*

(noun that renames)
pilots = fliers

What do ugly *caterpillars* become? They become pretty butterflies.

(noun that renames)
caterpillars = butterflies

Copy the last word from the complete subject and the first word of the complete predicate onto notebook paper. Then place a virgule (slash) between them.

Example: The birds fly south for the winter.
birds / fly

1. The subway train rolled to a stop.

2. He should have waited for the rain to stop.

3. A stubborn high-pressure ridge kept the winter rains away from the entire region.

4. The worst time of year for some people is Christmas.

5. She bought her boyfriend a gold ring for his birthday.

Simple Subjects and Simple Predicates

The **simple subject** in a sentence is the subject that is left after all of the modifying words and word groups (adjectives, adverbs, prepositional phrases, etc.) have been removed. The simple subject is usually a noun or pronoun.

Examples

COMPLETE SUBJECTS	SIMPLE SUBJECTS
Piranhas	piranhas (noun)
The hairy, foamy-mouthed monster	monster (noun)
The books	books (noun)
The clerk in the Housewares Department	clerk (noun)
They	they (pronoun)

The simple subject is never part of a prepositional phrase.

Example

	PREPOSITIONAL
SUBJECT	PHRASE
The flock	(of birds) was flying south for the winter.

The **simple predicate** of a sentence is the central verb—the **key verb**—found within the complete predicate. The simple predicate may also include one or more other verbs called **helping verbs**.

Some Helping Verbs							
am	are	is	was	were	be	been	being
have	has	had	having				
do	does	did	done	doing			
can	must						
about to	keep on	to be	to see (to + any verb)				

A verb accompanied by helping verbs is called a **verb phrase.**

Examples

> is going
> have known
> are being built
> will have finished

The *simple predicate* is the key verb, or verb phrase, stripped of all objects and modifying words.

Examples

COMPLETE SUBJECT	COMPLETE PREDICATE	SIMPLE PREDICATE
Sally	soaked in her redwood hot-tub every evening.	soaked
The four scientists	had worked on the formula for ten years.	had worked
John	is buying new tires for his car.	is buying

The simple subjects and simple predicates can be difficult to find in the following special situations:

LINKING VERBS

When you have difficulty finding the key verb in a sentence, it could be because that verb is a **linking verb**. Action verbs are easily identified because they show some kind of action. But linking verbs are different. Rather than showing action, linking verbs connect two parts of the sentence. Compare the following sentences:

Examples

> ACTION VERB
> The football players **lost** the game last night.
> LINKING VERB
> The football players **were** tired and discouraged.

The most common linking verbs are the forms of the verb *to be: am, is, are, was, were, be, been, being.* You should learn to recognize these words automatically because they are the most commonly used verbs in our language. (Do not confuse these linking verbs with helping verbs. The same words serve in both situations, but they function differently.)

Examples

Porsche *cars* **are** sleek and expensive.
The *girl* with the blue *eyes* **was** the winner.
The jury *members* **were** tired.

COMMANDS

In **commands** the simple subject is the pronoun *you*, in spite of the fact that the "you" is not stated in the sentence.

Examples

UNSTATED SIMPLE SUBJECT	SIMPLE PREDICATE
(You)	*Quiet* down now!
(You)	*Take* the third seat in row four.

QUESTIONS

The simple subject and simple predicate may be harder to find in a **question** if the simple predicate is a *verb phrase* (a verb with helping verbs in front of it) and part of the phrase comes before the subject. Rewriting the question as a statement may help you find the helping verbs.

Example

Will *Charlie* **see** Betty today? = *Charlie* **will see** Betty today.

When you have to identify the verb phrase in question, you will find it easier if you separate the parts of the sentence.

Examples

HELPING VERB	SIMPLE SUBJECT	HELPING VERB	VERB
Is	she		working today?
Should	they	have	bought the house?
Are	schools	going to	begin a new semester?

The simple subject may also be hard to find in sentences that begin with *question words* such as the following:

Some Question Words				
who	*whom*	*whomever*	*what*	*whatever*
which	*whichever*	*when*	*whenever*	
where	*wherever*	*how*	*however*	
why	*whyever*			

Examples

SIMPLE SUBJECT	SIMPLE PREDICATE	
Who	has	the time?
Which *room*	will be	available?

	HELPING VERB	SIMPLE SUBJECT	VERB	
Where	will	*they*	eat?	
Why	doesn't	*he*	want	to go?

In the third sentence the simple predicate is the verb phrase *will eat*. In the last sentence the verb phrase *to go* is not part of the simple predicate.

THERE IS, HERE IS

In sentences that begin ''There is'' and ''Here is,'' the subject always comes *after* the predicate. The word *there* or *here* is never the subject. (This type of sentence is more acceptable in conversation than in compositions or essays. Always use this type of sentence sparingly.)

Examples

	SIMPLE PREDICATE	SIMPLE SUBJECT	
There	is	Helen.	

	SIMPLE PREDICATE	SIMPLE SUBJECT	
Here	is	the best way	to work this problem.

Writing the sentence in reverse order may help you find the subject. For example, *There is more room in the garage.* = *More room is there in the garage.*

-ING VERBS USED AS SUBJECT

A *verb* ending with **-ing** may function as the simple subject of a sentence.

Examples

SIMPLE SUBJECT | SIMPLE PREDICATE
Skiing   in the Sierras   **was delayed**   this year.

      SIMPLE SUBJECT   SIMPLE PREDICATE
Her   *cooking*   **is**   the great joy of her life.

Note that an *-ing* verb is never used as a verb unless it has a helping verb. "Marcia writing in her book" is an incomplete sentence (a fragment) because the helping verb has been omitted. To complete the sentence, the verb "is" or "was" must be added. "Marcia is writing in her book."

EXERCISE 1.2

Number your paper from 1-10. Then copy the simple subject and the simple predicate from each of the following sentences.

Example: Skiing in the Sierras was delayed this year.
Skiing / was delayed

1. The horned owl glided over the rooftops of the subdivision.
2. The boat on the horizon was a schooner from Boston.
3. The grass had been piled in the street.
4. The battery was very weak.
5. When will the second movie begin?
6. There is no safe place in the city.
7. Stay until five o'clock.
8. Hang-gliding is not a sport for the timid.
9. The old locomotive refused to pull the ore cars up the grade.
10. Does the seller want to receive a large down payment?

EXERCISE 1.3

Write two of each of the kinds of sentences required below.

1. a simple sentence in which the subject does something
2. a simple sentence in which something happens to the subject
3. a simple sentence in which the complete predicate tells what condition the subject is in

8

4. a simple sentence in which the complete predicate tells who or what the subject is

5. a simple sentence in which a verb phrase is used as a simple predicate

6. a command

7. a question

8. a simple sentence in which an **-ing** verb functions as the simple subject

Compound Subjects and Predicates

Use a simple sentence with a compound subject when you want to say the same thing about two or more things or people.

Examples

SIMPLE	SIMPLE	SIMPLE
SUBJECT #1	SUBJECT #2	PREDICATE

1. *Frankie*   and   *Andy*   **were**   partners.

SIMPLE SUBJECT #1
2. The *Kennedy Marching Band*   from Cleveland and the
SIMPLE SUBJECT #2   SIMPLE PREDICATE
Regimental Drum and Bugle Corps   **marched**   together.

In each of the sentences above, the two subjects have something in common. Because of the relationship between the subjects in each sentence, only one predicate is needed to make a statement about both subjects. Even though both sentences have more than one subject, they are still simple sentences.

In the *simple sentence* with *compound predicate*, two or more predicates work together to make a statement about the subject of the sentence.

Examples

SIMPLE	SIMPLE		SIMPLE
SUBJECT	PREDICATE #1		PREDICATE #2

1. *Writers*   **edit**   and   **revise**   their work.

SIMPLE   SIMPLE
SUBJECT   PREDICATE #1
2. The *ferryboat*   **gained**   some time on the trip
                       SIMPLE
                       PREDICATE #2
   to Tiburon but   **lost**   it on the trip back.

SIMPLE   SIMPLE
SUBJECT   PREDICATE #1, #2,   #3
3. *Sue*   **dieted**,   **jogged**, and **danced** to lose weight.

Compound subjects and compound predicates may be hard to find, especially when separated by other words or phrases. Look closely at the second example above.

NOTE: Look carefully at any sentence that appears to have a compound predicate. What looks like a pair of verbs may be a pair of adjectives or nouns. Only two or more verbs in the predicate produce a compound predicate. The following sentences do not contain compound predicates:

Examples

	SIMPLE PREDICATE	2 ADJECTIVES
The organic apple	is	*pale and wormy.*
	SIMPLE PREDICATE	3 ADJECTIVES
The new electric heater	was	*big, expensive, and unreliable.*
SIMPLE PREDICATE	3 NOUNS	
He was	a *beggar,* a *thief,* and a *liar.*	
SIMPLE PREDICATE	2 -ing VERBS USED AS NOUNS	
She continued	*swimming* and *diving* after the accident.	

If you become confused in cases like these, it is probably because the adjectives and nouns in the predicates seem to say something about the subjects. For example, in the sentence *The organic apple is pale and wormy*, the adjectives do indeed modify the subject.

pale and *wormy* organic apple

Nevertheless, they are adjectives and not verbs; therefore, the predicate is not compound. When you are analyzing a predicate, make certain you are counting the verbs and not the adjectives and nouns.

EXERCISE 1.4

Number your paper from 1-10. Make two columns beside the numbers; write SUBJECT over the first column and PREDICATE over the second column. Write simple or compound under each heading to indicate whether the following sentences have simple or compound subjects and predicates.

Example: The shaggy little dog barked at the child and wagged its tail.

SUBJECT	PREDICATE
simple	compound

1. Trees bent and broke in the storm.

2. Apricots and prunes are dried in the sun.

3. The last game of the season was boring and anticlimactic.

4. John and Paula fight and make up daily.

5. Rats often grow to be large and mean.

6. Money and fame gave him all of his pleasure and caused all of his problems.

7. The biggest white pine in the country was left uncut.

8. Guam and Tinian are beautiful islands.

9. The sports editor read and reread the article.

10. Jackson first played for Oakland and then played for New York.

The simple sentence with all of its variations is the most basic sentence pattern in English. You will use it every time you write. However, one danger exists. You may find that your writing will become boring if you use this pattern too much. To avoid this problem, use all variations of the simple sentence. Try also to vary the length of your sentences. Too many short sentences, like too many long ones, can produce dull writing.

EXERCISE 1.5
_____

Write *two* each of the following simple sentence variations listed below.

1. simple subject and compound predicate

2. simple subject and simple predicate

3. compound subject and compound predicate

4. compound subject and simple predicate

5. a simple sentence with either two adjectives or two nouns placed after the simple predicate

LESSON TWO—Some Punctuation Principles

Now that you have practiced writing simple sentences, it is time to consider how to punctuate them properly. Punctuating most sentences is easy, especially when you are writing isolated sentences like those in the last lesson. When you write simple sentences in paragraphs, however, punctuation becomes more challenging. To write smooth paragraphs, you will need to use transitions, coordinate adjectives, and items in a series. You will also want to use commas to create emphasis. All of this is easy and natural, if you learn the rules governing such punctuation.

Setting Off Introductory Words and Phrases

An **introductory word** or an **introductory phrase** needs a comma if it is followed by a *pause*. Your ear will prove the most trustworthy guide if you read the sentence aloud. However, avoid reading pauses where there are none, or where they are not desirable.

INTRODUCTORY TRANSITIONAL WORDS AND PHRASES

Use **transitional words** and **phrases** to carry the reader smoothly from one sentence to another. Such words and phrases are used to connect thoughts and to show the relationship between separate statements. The italicized transitions in the list below are the ones used most often; you should memorize them.

Some Introductory Transitional Words and Phrases

Accordingly	Granted (If followed by a pause)	Obviously
Afterward	Hence	*Of course*
Afterwards	Hereafter	On the whole
All in all	Heretofore	Otherwise
Also (If followed by a pause	*However*	Second
As a matter of fact	*In addition*	Similarly
Clearly, then	In fact	Still (If followed by a pause)
Consequently	In general	*Then*
Finally (If followed by a pause)	In other words	To make matters worse
First	In particular	To be sure
For instance	In short	*Therefore*
For example	In summary	Thereupon

12

For one thing	Indeed	Third
Fourth	Likewise	*Thus*
Furthermore	*Moreover*	*Unfortunately*
	Nevertheless	Worst of all

When one of these transitonal words or phrases is placed at the very beginning of a sentence, the word or group of words should be separated from the rest of the sentence with a comma, if you want the separation to be read as a pause.

Examples

> *However*, very few people knew about her sister. (*However* is always followed by a pause and a comma)
>
> *Then* the trouble began. (*Then* and *other short transitional* words are not usually followed by a comma — no pause)
>
> *First*, assemble the shed frame. *Second*, attach the roof pieces. *Third*, screw on the siding panels. (Using commas after these short transitional words places the emphasis on the order in which things are to be done — the commas produce pauses.)
>
> *First* assemble the shed frame. (no comma — less emphasis on *first*)

EXERCISE 1.6

Number your paper from 1-8. Write each of the introductory transitional words and phrases after the appropriate number. Place a comma after each if necessary.

Each time a large ship travels along the East Coast, an ecological disaster is imminent. *For example* (1) a number of accidents on the Atlantic coast have involved huge oil tankers which have collided with other ships, broken in half, or spilled oil during loading or unloading. The damage that occurs with each spill takes place in predictable stages. *First* (2) thousands or even millions of gallons of oil spill into the ocean or harbor. *Then* (3) the winds and currents spread the gooey slick for dozens of miles, fouling the water and shores. *In addition* (4) terrible damage is done to wildlife and marine life, such as ducks and shellfish. The damage done to boats, marinas, docks, and other structures, and the expenses involved in clean-up efforts may cost millions of dollars. *However* (5) the cost of the deaths of thousands of birds and fish is inestimable. *For instance* (6) in the case of one seven-million-gallon spill near Maryland, thousands of birds died within a few hours. Many more died in the weeks that followed due to drastic changes in their shore environment. *Moreover* (7) Chesapeake Bay was declared off limits for shell fishermen for months after because of sludge sinking to the bottom. This sludge contaminated the breeding grounds of the clams and mussels. *Unfortunately* (8) more of these disasters are almost certain to occur.

INTRODUCTORY WORDS AND PHRASES THAT MODIFY

Many **introductory words and phrases that modify** should be set off with commas. A comma separating the introductory part gives it emphasis by creating a pause that keeps readers from misreading the sentence. In some sentences the need for a comma is obvious.

Example

> MISLEADING
> *Disgusted* Edna quit the committee.
> CLEAR
> *Disgusted,* Edna quit the committee.

However, in other sentences a comma after an introductory word or phrase is optional—a matter of style. The current style is to read without pausing through most introductory adverbs and short prepositional phrases that tell where or when. In these instances the need for commas is thereby eliminated.

Examples

> *There* they found the table they wanted. (adverb)
> *Before noon* it began to rain. (prepositional phrase—adverbial)
> *Underneath the dashboard* is a fuse panel. (prepositional phrase—adverbial)

Other *introductory words and phrases* may or may not need commas after them, depending on the sentence and the emphasis desired.

Examples

> *Later* he was very sorry about his decision. (no pause)
> *Later,* her whole world crumbled. (pause)
> *Just after twelve,* three trucks arrived at the store. (pause keeps numbers separated)
> *Obviously,* satisfied customers were more common than dissatisfied ones. (pause—prevents *obviously* from being read as an adverb modifying *satisfied*. In this sentence *obviously* functions as an introductory transitional word)
> *Obviously* satisfied customers outnumbered the dissatisfied ones. (no pause —adverb modifying the adjective *satisfied*)
> *Running down the stairs,* he fell and broke his arm. (pause—phrase—always separate introductory -ing and -ed phrases from the main sentence)

A comma is always needed after a long introductory phrase or when two or more phrases appear before the independent clause. (Any introductory phrase five words or longer is considered long enough to require a comma after it.)

Examples

> On the way to the Senate meeting, he stopped by the gym.
> Throughout the long, painful ordeal, she never complained.

INTERJECTIONS AND NOUNS-IN-DIRECT ADDRESS

Introductory **interjections** and **nouns-in-direct-address** are marked by commas although they are neither transitional words nor modifiers. (Interjections are seldom used in academic writing.)

Examples

Good grief, where have you been? (Interjection)
Yes, the answer is correct. (Introductory)
Carl, please mow the lawn now. (Noun-in-direct-address)

EXERCISE 1.7

Number your paper from 1-15. Write the introductory word or phrase in each of the following. Place a comma after any word or phrase needing one.

1. After the meeting they stopped for dinner.
2. Excited Dick went to see his new boat.
3. To most people conservation of gas means cold homes, bulky sweaters, and wood or coal-burning stoves.
4. However most of the gas consumed in American homes is used wisely.
5. In the next five years strict conservation methods by industry could reduce consumption of gas by twenty-five percent.
6. For example industrialized nations such as Sweden use only sixty percent of the energy for industry that the United States uses.
7. Before dawn it began snowing.
8. Frustrated George took a break from his math homework.
9. Slowed by machinery breakdowns the company was unable to meet its contracted deadlines for product deliveries.
10. George see if the stove has been turned off.
11. In August the executive council will meet in Seattle.
12. Seeing their chance the three women ran for the woods.
13. Afterwards the meaning of what had happened hit him all at once.
14. Thursday we will meet ten minutes before class.
15. Just beyond the mouth of the bay the glass-bottom boat struck a jagged reef and sank.

COORDINATE ADJECTIVES

An **adjective** is a word that modifies a noun or pronoun.

Examples

	ADJECTIVE	NOUN
Roger negotiated a	*huge*	*settlement.*

	NOUN	ADJECTIVES	
The	*castle,*	*dark* and *dreary,*	stood on a high cliff.

Often, two or more adjectives are placed before or after a noun or pronoun. When each adjective modifies the noun or pronoun equally, the adjectives are called **coordinate adjectives**. In other words, such adjectives modify the noun or pronoun equally but separately, as if the other adjective or adjectives were not there.

A simple way to determine whether adjectives are coordinate is to reverse their order. If the adjectives and noun (or pronoun) still make sense together after the order has been switched, the adjectives are coordinate. Occasionally, you will find it difficult to be sure the words "sound right" when reversed. For a second check, place *and, but,* or *or* between the two adjectives. If the modifying words are *not* coordinate adjectives, the conjunction will sound awkward.

Examples

COORDINATE ADJECTIVES	NOT COORDINATE
brisk, bright day	raw silk tie
bright, brisk day (reversed)	silk raw tie (cannot be reversed)
brisk and bright day (conjunction)	raw and silk tie (awkward)

Place a *comma* between *coordinate adjectives* unless the adjectives are already separated with a conjunction such as *and, or* or *but.* After reversing the adjectives and reading the sentence to see if it still makes sense, read the sentence again in its original order. The comma separating the coordinate adjectives should mark a pause or break in speech.

Examples

COORDINATE ADJECTIVES	NOT COORDINATE
a hot, burning sensation	the suspicious private detective
a soiled, ragged sail	a serious superior court judge
the tired, hungry hunters	a tiny blue porcelain dish
the stern, fair captain	
the stern but fair captain (conjunction)	

WORDS AND PHRASES IN A SERIES

Use a comma to separate each word or phrase in a series; also, use a comma before the conjunction that separates the last two items in the series. Some teachers consider the comma immediately before this conjunction optional. In most sentences, however, the series is made clearer by the use of the comma before the conjunction.

Examples

> The flag is red, white, and blue. (series of words)
> The crew checked the tires, filled the gas tank, and washed the windows. (series of phrases)
> Without clearer objectives, better coordination, and more adequate funding, the new association will not be very efficient. (word groups)

Whenever you want to emphasize the individual words or word groups of a series, you can place conjunctions between each of the items. When doing so, *never* separate the items with commas.

Examples

> While in the army, we marched and marched and marched. (no commas)
> The moon rose clear and bright and full. (no commas)

Avoid placing a comma in front of the first word or after the last word in a series, except when required by the structure of the sentence (see the last example below).

Examples

> NO   YES   YES
> The team was tough, disciplined, and enthusiastic.
> YES   YES   NO
> They were tired, broke, and discouraged by the time they got to Paris.
> YES YES   YES   YES   YES
> The seasoning, salt, pepper, garlic, and paprika, was included in a foil packet.

EXERCISE 1.8

Number your paper from 1-10, skipping every other line. Copy all incorrectly punctuated sentences in this exercise and properly punctuate each. Write **C** after the number of any sentence that needs no punctuation.

1. Carol preferred a light moist cake.

2. The little boy was given a big happy puppy for his birthday.

3. Grandmother is a humble lovable person.

4. The sailboat is thirty-six feet long sloop-rigged and designed for racing.

5. John was shy and frightened and not at all sure he wanted to go through with the interview.

6. With an improved gasoline-mileage rating sleeker body lines and more leg room, the automobile will appeal to more American buyers.

7. The crowd, rowdy belligerent and mean, began to set fires in the bleachers.

8. The cold clear fast-moving stream tumbled down the mountain.

9. The research project involved hundreds of tape-recorded interviews with persons in politics governmental administration and criminal justice.

10. John Foley will formally accept the nomination today or tomorrow.

Enclosing Words and Phrases That Interrupt Sentences

TRANSITIONAL WORDS AND PHRASES THAT INTERRUPT

Transitional words and **phrases** are enclosed by commas when they are placed in the middle of a sentence. (See the complete list of these words and phrases on pages 12-13.) In fact, placing the transitional word or phrase inside the sentence rather than at the beginning often creates a more graceful transition from a previous sentence.

Examples

Some education experts, *however,* are reluctant to use standardized tests to measure writing competency.

The latest treaty, *for example,* guarantees all airline pilots emergency landing rights.

She was shocked, *nevertheless,* at what had happened.

ESSENTIAL VS. NON-ESSENTIAL

An interrupting word or phrase should be set off with a pair of commas when the interrupting part is not an essential part of the sentence. That is, the material enclosed by commas may give additional information but is not essential to the basic meaning of the sentence. The test for commas around phrases in sentences, such as this phrase which interrupts this sentence, is whether the material is essential or non-essential.

Examples

The student, wishing more information, wrote to the scholarship director. (non-essential: *wishing more information* is additional information which, if removed, would not change the basic meaning of the sentence or cause problems in identifying which student is meant)

The student wishing more information wrote to the scholarship director. (essential: no commas indicates that there are other students in the writer's mind and that this one is being identified as *the student wishing more information*)

PARENTHETICAL WORDS AND PHRASES

Enclose parenthetical words and phrases with commas. If the interrupting word or phrase could be placed in parentheses, it should also be set apart from the rest of the sentence with commas.

Examples

His performance, *to tell the truth*, was poor.
His performance (to tell the truth) was poor.

John's friend, *a former navy pilot*, wants to hike from Mexico to Canada.
John's friend (a former navy pilot) wants to hike from Mexico to Canada.

CREATING PAUSES

If you want readers to *pause* briefly at the beginning and the end of an interrupting word or phrase, enclose the expression with commas. Test the effect of using or not using the commas by reading the sentence aloud several times. Your voice will drop slightly when you read the part of the sentence enclosed in commas.

Examples

        PAUSE   VOICE DROPS   PAUSE
The primitive tribe   ,   *unknown except to a few anthropologists* ,
lived deep in the Amazon rain forest.
              VOICE
       PAUSE DROPS PAUSE
The project   , *in general* , is proceeding on schedule.
       PAUSE   VOICE DROPS   PAUSE
Mary Chavez   , *a fourth-year medical student* , planned to set up
her practice in Akron, Ohio.

CREATING EMPHASIS

You might want to enclose words or phrases in commas for **emphasis**. When commas are used this way, the expression is marked by a pause at the beginning and at the end, emphasizing the enclosed word or phrase.

Examples

             PAUSE   EMPHASIZED PAUSE
He realized   ,   *much too late*   ,   that the plane had left without him.
        PAUSE   EMPHASIZED   PAUSE
And   ,   *suddenly*   ,   she found the missing keys.
           PAUSE   EMPHASIZED   PAUSE
The elephants   ,   *half crazed with fear*   ,   stampeded.
          PAUSE   EMPHASIZED   PAUSE
George   ,   *thinking that Martians were invading Earth*   ,   began blazing away at the helicopter with his shotgun.

PREVENTING MISUNDERSTANDING OR AWKWARDNESS

Sometimes you will need to enclose interrupting words and phrases in commas to prevent the sentence from being *misread* or sounding *awkward*. These commas help readers to separate words that might otherwise be mistakenly run together with confusing results.

Examples

        PAUSE   PAUSE
Carl   ,   *Frank's brother*   ,   wrote the script. (prevents misunderstanding)

            PAUSE   PAUSE
The seasoning   ,   *salt, pepper, garlic, and paprika*   ,   was included in a foil packet. (prevents awkwardness)

EXERCISE 1.9

Number your paper from 1-12, skipping every other line. Copy any of the following sentences that need punctuation and place commas wherever needed. If a sentence does not need any commas, do not copy it but place a **C** after its number.

(1) Frank a former businessman from San Francisco bought a choice lot in Honolulu. (2) The brush-covered steep lot had a dramatic ocean view. (3) Planning to build a large house with three levels Frank consulted an architect. (4) His request was simple: he wanted a beautiful home. (5) The architect talked with Frank measured the lot and developed rough drawings immediately. (6) The plans were instantly accepted. (7) In fact Frank asked the architect to develop final plans as soon as possible. (8) The young enthusiastic architect blurted out her happiness. (9) At that point Frank however re-

membered to ask about costs. (10) He was given an unbelievably high estimate. (11) Taken aback he told the architect he needed one week to consider the project. (12) Disappointed Frank later told the architect to design a smaller two-level house.

Separating Words and Phrases at the Ends of Sentences

Occasionally you will need to set off a word or phrase at the **end** of a sentence. Using a comma this way will create an emphatic pause, prevent misreading, or keep the sentence from sounding awkward.

Examples

Drug abuse is on the decline among college students; it is epidemic among the general population, *however*. (transitional word, pause)

Sally hit a grand-slam home run, *her first*. (emphatic pause)

The group performed in many small towns all over the country, *in Michigan, Ohio, Kentucky, Missouri, and Montana*. (to prevent misreading)

Then the allied army retreated without warning, *causing panic and anarchy among the soldiers and the citizens*. (pause, to prevent misreading)

It was a lively debate, *to say the least*. (pause, keeps sentence from sounding awkward)

EXERCISE 1.10
_____

Number your paper from 1-10, skipping every other line. Copy each sentence that needs punctuation. If the italicized word or phrase *at the end of the sentence* should be set off from the rest of the sentence, punctuate it with a comma. If a comma is not needed, write **C** after the number.

1. She should apply for the job *nevertheless*.

2. Sam failed his science test *as expected*.

3. She arrived at the airport thirty minutes *before boarding time*.

4. The researcher isolated the virus *a real breakthrough in efforts to find a cure for the disease*.

5. Shirley's doctor said she was suffering from fatigue *caused by months of overwork*.

6. Look in the closet *behind the vacuum cleaner*.

7. The recommendations for water rationing were passed *including the controversial water-meter regulation*.

8. Next time, make sure there is water in the pool *before you dive*.

9. He wanted to hire Sam *Phillip's brother*.

10. He became a king with no power *stripped of his lands and armies*.

Write and correctly punctuate the following kinds of sentences on notebook paper.

1. simple sentence with compound subject and simple predicate
2. simple sentence with simple subject and compound predicate
3. simple sentence with introductory transitional word or phrase
4. simple sentence with interrupting transitional word or phrase
5. simple sentence with transitional word at the end
6. simple sentence with coordinate adjectives before the subject
7. simple sentence with a series needing commas
8, simple sentence with a series needing no commas
9. simple sentence with interrupting parenthetical phrase
10. simple sentence with group of words at the end set off by a comma

Chapter One Review

PART ONE

Copy sentences 1-4 onto your paper. Place a slash between the *complete subject* and the *complete predicate* in each.

1. The small submarine descended rapidly to the sunken freighter.
2. The strange cries were often heard by tenants in the old building.
3. The man on the corner is actually an undercover police detective.
4. The ecological problems of the proposed project became a political issue.

PART TWO

On your paper, write the *simple subject* and *simple predicate* from each of the following sentences. Underline the simple subject once and the simple predicate twice.

5. The little red plane with the twin engines is, according to the experts, very fast.
6. Why does she have to have this report now?
7. Hold this package for me for a few minutes.
8. During her last buying trip in England, France, and Germany, she bought sixty crates of antiques.

PART THREE

Identify the subject and predicate in the following sentences. On your paper, write *simple subject* or *compound subject* and then write *simple predicate* or *compound predicate* to identify each part of the sentences.

9. The excited soccer fans shoved and pushed one another.
10. The lunches in Honolulu were leisurely and filling.
11. His teachers and his counselor mean well but do not understand his problem.
12. One of the last bobcats in the swamp was shot by a rabbit hunter last winter.

PART FOUR

On your paper, write the kind of simple sentence requested. Be sure to punctuate your sentences properly.

13. Write a simple sentence in which the subject does something.
14. Write a simple sentence in which something happens to the subject.
15. Write a simple sentence in which the complete predicate tells what condition the subject is in.
16. Write a simple sentence in which the complete predicate tells who or what the subject is.

PART FIVE

On your paper, write one of each pattern of simple sentence as directed. Be sure to punctuate your sentences properly.

17. Simple subject and compound predicate.

18. Simple subject and simple predicate.

19. Compound subject and compound predicate.

20. Compound subject and simple predicate.

PART SIX

Copy any of the following sentences that needs punctuation onto your paper. Insert commas wherever needed as you do so. If a sentence needs no commas, do *not* copy it onto your paper; instead, write **C** after the number of that sentence.

21. Therefore the problem can be solved.

22. Mr. Hardgrass the last farmer in the county with horse-drawn equipment had vowed never to buy a tractor.

23. After the fall he took fewer chances.

24. The new ranch foreman to the old cowboy's astonishment was a woman.

25. Betty was looking for a responsible knowledgeable partner to help her with the buying for her business.

26. Jackie believing nobody refused to see the truth about her lover.

27. He is pale and sickly and weak.

28. Dreaming of conquest and power the dictator planned to invade the small helpless country of Navarre.

29. The Highway Department will receive bids for the last section of freeway the link between Sacramento and Stockton.

30. With the wind in her favor that morning Fatima was able to fly the Cessna at a steady 185 miles per hour.

2

Compound and Complex Sentences

This chapter continues your review of sentence construction. In this chapter you will learn about and practice writing compound and complex sentences. You will also learn to revise sentences to eliminate three kinds of sentence construction errors: fragments, run-ons, and comma splices.

In this chapter you will develop confidence in using many kinds of sentence patterns. Not only will this practice provide you with a wide variety of sentence structures to draw from later, but it will also show you that by deliberately choosing your sentence patterns you can develop your ideas with greater precision and style.

LESSON ONE—Compound Sentences

Often you will be faced with the choice of either writing two short sentences or combining them in a single, longer sentence. When you decide to form a single sentence from the two, you are choosing to write a **compound sentence.**

Example

The wind blew steadily from the north. (First Sentence)

+

The smog disappeared. (Second Sentence)

becomes

The wind blew steadily from the north, and the smog disappeared. (Compound Sentence)

25

You might decide to combine two sentences in one compound sentence for two reasons. First, the close relationship between two ideas might be communicated more clearly in a compound sentence. Second, the longer, compound sentence might sound smoother than the two short sentences would.

Frequently you will write a longer sentence and wonder if it is a compound sentence. You will need to know when you have written one because a compound sentence requires different punctuation from other sentences. The decision as to whether a sentence is or is not a compound sentence has to be made before you can check the punctuation.

How can you tell a compound sentence from one that is not? Usually it will be a conjunction (*and, but, or, for, yet*) or a semicolon (*;*) that will catch your attention.

Examples

1) We drove to Seattle *and* later took the ferry to Vancouver. (Compound Sentence??)
2) We drove to Seattle, *and* later we took the ferry to Vancouver. (Compound Sentence??)
3) We drove to Seattle; later we took the ferry to Vancouver. (Compound Sentence??)

When identifying a compound sentence, the first step is to ask yourself if the part to the left of the conjunction or semicolon could be a sentence. That is, if the part to the left stood by itself—marked at the end by a period—would it be a sentence? Does the part on the left have a subject and a predicate, and does it contain a complete thought? If it does have all of those, could it stand alone, as long as it remained in its same position in the paragraph? If the answer to these questions is *yes*, then one of the requirements for a compound sentence has been met.

In each of the three examples above, the answer is *yes*. The part on the *left* could be a sentence. But you must check further.

SUBJECT   PREDICATE
We   **drove**   to Seattle. (YES)

The second step in identifying a compound sentence is to ask if the part to the right of the conjunction or semicolon could be a sentence by itself. If the answer is *yes* again—if both the parts on the left and the right could be complete sentences—you have written a compound sentence. The part on the *right* in the *first* example could not be a sentence by itself.

PREDICATE
Later *took*   the ferry to Vancouver. (NO)
(In this part the subject, *we*, is missing. Thus, this group of words cannot be a sentence. It is the second half of a compound predicate in a simple sentence. We / drove and *took*.)

In the examples above, only the last two sentences pass the test.

26

```
                SUBJECT    PREDICATE
        Later we        took        the ferry to Vancouver. (YES)
```

Another Example

Sentence to be Analyzed

The school had an honor code, but it was not working.

Clues

1) a longer sentence that seems to be divided into two parts
2) the conjunction *but* (usually preceded by a comma)

Analysis Breakdown

```
        SUBJECT    PREDICATE
The school        had        an honor code. (Left Part)
SUBJECT    PREDICATE
It        was        not working. (Right Part)
```

Analysis Decision

Both parts are sentences. Therefore, the whole sentence (the part on the left plus the part on the right) is a compound sentence.

EXERCISE 2.1

Write the answers to the following questions.

1. How do you write a compound sentence?

2. What are the two reasons for combining two sentences?

3. What is the procedure for testing a sentence to see if it is a compound sentence?

EXERCISE 2.2

Number your paper 1-10. Using the testing procedure explained in this lesson, decide which sentences are compound sentences. Write COMPOUND or NOT COMPOUND for each sentence.

1. The steak was burned, and the salad was soggy.

2. Joey complained to the waiter, but the waiter did not care.

3. The sky grew dark; the wind began to blow fiercely.

4. Most students have no trouble writing compound sentences; however, they do have trouble punctuating them.

5. Seven candidates for Vice President were considered, but only one was satisfactory.

6. They boarded the plane in Pittsburgh and flew to Boston.

7. The band members were excited about their road trip; nevertheless, they were not looking forward to performing several times each day.

8. The crop-dusting plane swooped down behind the barn and reappeared beyond the row of trees.

9. The space mission was delayed, however, for serious problems with the onboard computers developed.

10. Mr. Castillo grew squash, tomatoes, lettuce, and corn in his garden.

Independent Clauses

A **clause** is a meaningful group of words that contains both a *subject* and a *predicate*. An **independent clause** is a meaningful group of words with a subject and a predicate that can stand alone as a sentence. The fact that an independent clause can stand alone is what distinguishes it from a **dependent clause**. A dependent clause also contains a subject and a predicate, but it cannot stand by itself as a sentence (covered in detail on pages 38-40).

Examples

      SUBJECT   PREDICATE
John   went   to the library (Independent Clause)
        SUBJECT   PREDICATE
after *John*   **went**   to the library (Dependent Clause)
        SUBJECT   PREDICATE
that *she*   **wanted**   for her room (Dependent Clause)

When you analyze a sentence to determine whether the parts to the left and right of the conjunction or semicolon could be complete sentences, you are checking whether they are *independent clauses*.

Examples

PART ON THE LEFT		PART ON THE RIGHT
Juanita took Bus 81 to work	, but	her husband rode his bike.
Africa is in a state of political transition	, and	governments quickly rise and fall.

The two examples above are compound sentences because each contains two independent clauses. Observe that each pair of independent clauses is joined by a comma *and* a conjunction. The only other way to join two independent clauses is to use a semicolon.

Example

      SUBJECT   PREDICATE
The *vice president* of the company **was**   in charge of six regions;
SUBJECT PREDICATE
she   **was**   also responsible for new product design.

A compound sentence may also contain one or more dependent clauses.

Sometimes this type of compound sentence is referred to as a *compound-complex sentence*. To have a dependent clause in it and still be a compound sentence, however, the sentence must still pass the "sentence on the left / sentence on the right" test. In this book any sentence that passes this test will be called simply a *compound sentence*, even if one or more dependent clauses are found in it.

Example

DEPENDENT CLAUSE INDEPENDENT CLAUSE #1
After he ate dinner,   Fred went to the library,
INDEPENDENT CLAUSE #2
but he was too tired to study.

Analysis

After he ate dinner, Fred went to the library. (*Yes*, there is a sentence on left.)

He was too tired to study. (*Yes*, there is a sentence on the right.)

Conclusion

Even though the sentence contains a dependent clause, it is a compound sentence.

EXERCISE 2.3

Number your paper 1-5. Write COMPOUND or NOT COMPOUND according to which each of the sentences below is.

1. Before Rita could move, the dog jumped off the pickup truck and started chasing the children.

2. The car that he wanted was hard to find, but he kept looking.

3. I had some second thoughts about my plan, but I decided to go through with it since my brothers and sisters were counting on me.

4. I knew that the teacher would be late but not exactly how late.

5. Joann Zelinski, who lived in back of us, had an irritating habit; in spite of our protests, she always threw any snails she found into our yard.

Connectors in Compound Sentences

The independent clauses that are combined to form a compound sentence must be properly connected. Three types of connectors may be used:

> 1. A comma + a conjunction
>
> 2. A semicolon
>
> 3. A semicolon + a conjunctive adverb + a comma

1. A COMMA PLUS A CONJUNCTION

A **conjunction** is a connector word used to join words and groups of words. The conjunctions most commonly used to connect the independent clauses in a compound sentence are listed below:

Conjunctions

and
but
or
yet (meaning *but*)
so (meaning *therefore*)
for (meaning *because*)

When a conjunction is used to join independent clauses, a **comma** (,) should be placed in front of the conjunction. The comma and the conjunction are a team— one cannot be used without the other to join independent clauses.

Examples

The teacher was late, **and** the class became restless.

Victoria ordered more French fries, **but** the waiter never brought them.

The winter rains must begin soon, **or** water shortages will occur next summer.

They ordered the automobile in February, **yet** it still had not been delivered in May.

Marilyn's wheelchair would not fit through the door, **so** she could not rent the apartment.

The divers looked around carefully, **for** the area was a favorite for sharks.

Choosing the Appropriate Conjunction

When connecting two independent clauses with a comma and a conjunction, always choose the conjunction that best expresses the relationship between the clauses.

Examples

The automobile flipped over, **and** the driver was thrown out onto the busy street.

> The conjunction *and* is used to explain that *in addition* to what happened to the automobile, something happened to the driver.

The driver was not hurt badly, **but** he was scraped and bruised.

> *But* shows a contrast between what is said in the first and second independent clauses. The conjunction *but* can also be used to show opposition: "The witness called me reckless, *but* actually I was driving very carefully."

The driver skidded across the busy right-hand lane like a rag doll, **yet** two cars, a bus, and a cement truck managed to miss him.

> *Yet* like *but* is used to show contrast or opposition. However, *yet* is more specific and is normally used to stress that what the second clause describes is not what most readers would expect after reading the first clause.

He can ride to the hospital for a checkup, **or** he may see his own doctor later.

> *Or* shows the alternate possibilities of the first and second independent clauses.

The wrecker towed the man's automobile away, **for** the damaged vehicle could no longer be driven.

> *For* should be used as a conjunction when a connector that means *because* is needed (when *for* sounds better than *because*). The conjunction *for* should not be confused with the preposition *for*, as in the sentence "He began to look *for* a new car."

His car will be in the repair shop for a week, **so** he will take a bus to work until the car is ready.

> To test the word *so* to see if it is a conjunction, see if it can be replaced by *therefore*. If it can, as in the example above, you are looking at a compound sentence. If, on the other hand, the *so* means "so that," as in the sentence "She joined the club *so* she could meet some people with similar interests," you are not dealing with a compound sentence.

EXERCISE 2.4

Number your paper 1-10. Choose the conjunction that most accurately relates the second sentence to the first.

1. After the dance they may stop for a pizza, (*and but yet*) they may stop for hamburgers instead.

2. The Coast Guard report blamed the captain of the tanker for running aground, (*and but or*) the captain claimed his navigation instruments were faulty.

3. Someone should tell him to come to class more regularly, (*and for or*) he will fail the course.

4. The sea was calm, (*and but yet*) the sky was blue and cloudless.

5. He purchased the antique sword, (*and but for*) he thought it was a good investment.

6. Harold rehearsed for the interview for three days, (*and so but*) he was well prepared for the Personnel Director's questions.

7. She will look for a job, (*and but or*) she will go to school instead.

8. Carmelita and Nadia cannot come to practice next Saturday, (*and but yet*) they will come the Saturday after.

9. The holdup occurred at noon on the busy street, (*and but yet*) no one tried to help the victim.

10. Her lease is up, (*so but for*) she plans to move her shop.

EXERCISE 2.5

For each conjunction listed, write *three* sample compound sentences. Remember to use both the comma and the conjunction.

1. and
2. but
3. or
4. yet (meaning *but*)
5. so (meaning *therefore*)
6. for (meaning *because*)

2. THE SEMICOLON

A **semicolon** (;) can be used to combine two closely related independent clauses. A better name for the semicolon might be "semiperiod" since the period can be used anywhere a semicolon can be used.

Example

Walking is good for your health. You should do more of it.

becomes

Walking is good for your health; you should do more of it.

Use the semicolon as a connector in a compound sentence when you want the reader to move rapidly through the connection. The semicolon tells the reader to pause less between the two connected independent clauses than if a period had been used. The semicolon also emphasizes the close relationship between the two independent clauses that are joined. Use the semicolon occasionally to give variety to the flow of thought. Do not overuse any one connector.

Example

Bret and Meloney made the fateful decision on Tuesday. They could wait no longer; they knew it. The snow had been falling on the mountain all night, and by noon the wreckage of the plane would be completely covered. Meloney had to hike down the mountain for help; no one would see them from the air.

Write five compound sentences in which you use semicolons for connectors.

3. A SEMICOLON PLUS A CONJUNCTIVE ADVERB (AND A COMMA)

A **semicolon and a conjunctive adverb** (followed by a comma) can be used together very effectively to join two independent clauses. The compound sentence that results emphasizes the unity of the thought, and the connection receives more attention than if a less emphatic conjunction, such as *and* or *but*, or a semicolon alone were used.

Example

> The students were given only fifteen minutes to complete the fifty-question test; *however*, most of them were able to finish it.

The word *conjunct* means "cojoined," or "bound in close association"; a *conjunction* is a connective used to "link" or "join." Thus, *conjunctive adverbs* are adverbs and short adverb phrases used as connectors instead of modifiers.

Some Conjunctive Adverbs

;afterwards,	;hence(,)	;obviously(,)
;all in all,	;hereafter,	;of course,
;also(,)	;however,	;on the whole,
;as a matter of fact,	;in addition,	;otherwise,
;as a result,	;in fact,	;second(,)
;consequently,	;in general,	;still,
;finally(,)	;in other words,	;then(,)
;first(,)	;in summary,	;thereafter,
;for instance,	;indeed,	;therefore,
;for example,	;likewise,	;thus(,)
;furthermore,	;moreover,	;to be sure,
;granted,	;nevertheless,	;unfortunately,

Correct Punctuation

Always place a *semicolon* in front of a conjunctive adverb. The semicolon takes the place of the period that would be there if the two sentences (independent clauses) had not been joined. Moreover, it is customary to place a comma immediately after most conjunctive adverbs. The comma makes the reader pause briefly before going on with the rest of the compound sentence.

Example

> World weather patterns will undergo major changes in the near future; *therefore*, agricultural expansion is not advisable.

Be aware of some exceptions to the rule that a comma should be placed immediately after the conjunctive adverb. Do not follow *then* with a comma unless a pause to emphasize the *then* is desired.

Example

> Oil will soon become too expensive to be used for marine fuel; *then* huge computer-controlled sailing ships will be built. (normal)

> First you must prove that you own the automobile and that you have paid the fine; *then*, you may reclaim it. (emphasis on *then* created by pause)

Other short conjunctive adverbs may or may not need commas after them. Decide in each situation whether or not you need a pause. (In the list on the previous page the optional commas have been placed in parentheses.)

Examples

> Aretha did not go back to work until she was forty-two; *thus* she was determined to earn promotions as rapidly as possible. (no pause)

> Revenue will be down this year; *thus*, the following budget cuts are necessary. (pause)

EXERCISE 2.7

Write compound sentences using the following conjunctive adverbs. Punctuate the sentences correctly.

1. also
2. consequently
3. for example
4. furthermore
5. however
6. moreover
7. nevertheless
8. of course
9. then
10. therefore

Choose the Appropriate Conjunctive Adverb

Although more than one conjunctive adverb may be correct for combining a particular pair of independent clauses, one is usually a better choice than the others. The one to choose is the conjunctive adverb that makes the logical connection between the two sentences the clearest. The following table illustrates the proper function for the most commonly used conjunctive adverbs:

Relationship To Be Established	Conjunctive Adverb To Use
addition, comparison	moreover, furthermore, in addition, also
contrast, difference, opposition	however, nevertheless
as a result, conclusion	therefore, thus, consequently
concession to opponent	of course, granted
emphasis	indeed, unfortunately
illustration	for example, for instance

EXERCISE 2.8

Copy the sentences below, using the appropriate conjunctive adverb to join each of the two independent clauses. Punctuate each compound sentence correctly.

1. The road between Pollock Pines and Omo Ranch was quite rough _____ we found it more comfortable to drive slower than usual.

2. In the spring the tiny streams become roaring rivers _____ in the summer the rivers dry up into little rivulets.

3. Their boat became becalmed near Martha's Vineyard _____ they spent the night waiting for the wind to return.

4. Kent seldom bothers to attend class or read his assignments _____ he has not even taken the first test.

5. "Heart of Darkness" is undoubtedly one of Conrad's best short stories _____ "The Secret Sharer" is also one of his better stories.

6. Fewer people are reading fiction this year _____ non-fiction has become much more popular than before.

7. More students are enrolling in college _____ they are taking fewer courses each semester than in the past.

8. The commentator named the five great threats to humanity _____ none of the listeners seemed to care.

9. She is teaching some unusual home economics courses _____ one of them is called "Brown Bag Gourmet."

10. His test grades in algebra were bad _____ he decided to look for a good tutor.

Conjunctive Adverbs and Transitional Words

The words and phrases listed in this lesson as *conjunctive adverbs* are also listed in Chapter One. There they are called either *introductory transitional words and phrases* (see page 12) or *interrupting transitional words and phrases* (see page 18). These same words and phrases can be used in three different positions for three different purposes. You need to understand each of the purposes and the proper punctuation to use when one of these words or phrases is used in a particular position.

1. At the beginning of a sentence as an *introductory transitional word or phrase*

   Example

   > Many of the students had part-time jobs in the afternoon. *Consequently,* they refused to enroll in classes after twelve o'clock.

2. In the middle of a sentence as an *interrupting transitional word or phrase*

   Example

   > Many of the students had part-time jobs. They refused, *consequently,* to enroll in any classes after twelve o'clock.

3. To connect two independent clauses (sentences) as a *conjunctive adverb*

   Example

   > Many of the students had part-time jobs; *consequently,* they refused to enroll in any clases after twelve o'clock.

EXERCISE 2.9

Number your paper 1-5. Write the letter that correctly identifies the type of word or phrase italicized in each sentence.

   A. introductory transitional word or phrase
   B. interrupting transitional word or phrase
   C. conjunctive adverb

1. People make a mistake when they assume creativity deals only with writing, art, and music. *For example,* a computer programmer can be as creative as a musical composer.

2. *Moreover,* a creative person does not have to be suffering or unstable.

3. After a good night's sleep most people are energetic and efficient; *however,* after a poor night's sleep people are usually slow and ineffective.

4. George was, *to be sure,* an old-fashioned boss who believed in treating his son like a regular employee. The son, *however,* wanted to "step into his father's shoes" immediately.

5. The company was so bound up in rules, regulations, and other red tape that the managers did not really lead the employees; *in fact,* a real leader would have been resented by the other executives.

36

Number your paper 1-3. Write the type of sentence requested.

1. a simple sentence with an *interrupting transitional word or phrase*
2. a simple sentence with an *introductory transitional word or phrase*
3. a compound sentence with a *conjunctive adverb*

LESSON TWO—Complex Sentences

A **complex sentence** is a sentence that includes one independent clause and one or more dependent clauses. In contrast to a compound sentence, a complex sentence never contains more than one independent clause.

Examples of Complex Sentences

INDEPENDENT CLAUSE	DEPENDENT CLAUSE
1. They wanted to buy the restaurant	*although they had no restaurant experience.*

DEPENDENT CLAUSE	INDEPENDENT CLAUSE
2. *As the men rowed across the inlet,*	they could see the fortress.

SUBJECT OF IND CLAUSE	DEPENDENT CLAUSE
3. Zachary,	*who had cheated through the entire test,*

PREDICATE OF INDEPENDENT CLAUSE
later complained that the test was not fair.

Dependent Clauses

You will remember from the last lesson that an *independent clause* is a group of words that can stand alone as a sentence. Because it is a *clause,* an independent clause has both a subject and a predicate. Having a subject and a predicate is the main characteristic of any clause.

A **dependent clause** is different from an independent clause because a dependent clause is not a sentence. A dependent clause must always be connected to an independent clause. Usually the dependent clause will be connected to a sentence with a single independent clause. Occasionally, however, a dependent clause will be found in a compound sentence (see *compound-complex sentence* on page 29).

Examples

DEPENDENT CLAUSE	INDEPENDENT CLAUSE
1. *Before she met Jim,*	she thought she would never marry. (Complex)

DEPENDENT CLAUSE	INDEPENDENT CLAUSE #1
2. *Before she met Jim,*	she thought she would never marry,

INDEPENDENT CLAUSE #2
but she quickly changed her mind. (Compound-complex)

How to Recognize a Dependent Clause

A dependent clause includes three main parts:

1. A signal word or signal phrase
2. A subject
3. A predicate

Any independent clause (or sentence) has a subject and a predicate, but in

38

addition to the subject and predicate, a dependent clause has a signal word or phrase at the beginning.

Examples

    DEPENDENT CLAUSE

    Signal Word   Subject   Predicate

1. **Before**   the *terrorists* **could grab** their weapons,

    INDEPENDENT CLAUSE

    the commandoes burst into the airport lounge.

    DEPENDENT CLAUSE

    Signal Word & Subject   Predicate

2. The terrorists, **who**   **were caught** by surprise,

    fought back furiously.

                             DEPENDENT CLAUSE

    INDEPENDENT CLAUSE   Signal Word

3. Three of the hostages were found dead **after**   the

    Subject   Predicate

    shooting **stopped**.

Signal Words and Signal Phrases

The following words and phrases often signal the beginning of a dependent clause:

Some Common Signal Words and Phrases

after	once	when
although	provided that	whenever
as	since	where
as long as	so long as	whereas
because	so that	wherever
before	than	whether
but that	that	which
except	though	while
how	unless	who
in case	until	whoever
in order that	what	whom
in which	whatever	whomever
if	what if	whose
now that	whatsoever	why

Upon encountering one of the signal words or signal phrases, check further to see if the signal word or phrase is followed by a subject and a predicate. If it is the group of words is a dependent clause. (If the signal word or phrase is not followed by a subject and a predicate, the word group is a *phrase*.)

Examples

SIGNAL WORD	SUBJECT	PREDICATE
after	*we*	**sat** down
because	*Sue*	**wanted** a milkshake
which	*she*	**found** at the auction
whom	*Lee*	**had met** in Tampa

Relative Pronouns as Signal Words

Signal words include all words known as **relative pronouns**. A relative pronoun is a word that refers back to another word in a sentence (back to an antecedent).

Relative Pronouns

that
what
which
who
whom

ANTECEDENT	RELATIVE PRONOUN	
The *car*	**that**	Carlos bought was a lemon.

When a relative pronoun is used as a signal word, it often does double duty. It serves as the signal word and the subject or the object of the dependent clause. Sometimes these relative pronouns will be followed by a subject, but not always.

Examples

SIGNAL WORD & SUBJECT	PREDICATE
that	**burns** too much gasoline
who	**ate** and **drank** too much

For the different usages of *that* and *which* see page 45.

Phrases

A **phrase** is a meaningful group of words that does not contain a subject and a predicate.

Examples

PHRASE

Bill *had earned* a fortune.

PHRASE

The boy dove *into the river*.

PHRASE

Roaring by the spectators, the race car was a blur.

PHRASE

The explorers, *confused by the many tunnels*, soon became lost.

PHRASE

She hoped *to win a scholarship*.

PHRASE

The Ploughboys, *a much feared street gang*, terrorized the citizens.

A phrase may contain a noun or a pronoun, and it may contain a verb; it may even contain both a noun and a verb.

Examples

NOUN

under the *tree*

VERB   NOUN

fighting against impossible *odds*

But a phrase does not contain a *subject* and a *predicate*. There is often a difference between saying a group of words includes a noun or a verb and saying it includes a subject and a predicate. Thus, you must look carefully at a word group if you are to decide whether it is a phrase or a dependent clause.

Elliptical Dependent Clauses

Some dependent clauses look like phrases because they are incomplete—*elliptical*. In **elliptical dependent clauses** something has been left out; nevertheless, they are considered to be dependent clauses. You have to imagine that what has been left out is still there. There is nothing wrong with elliptical dependent clauses; in fact, they are more concise than the complete versions. You do need to recognize them, however, so that you will use them more effectively.

Examples

ELLIPTICAL
1. *While eating*, he read a magazine.
COMPLETE
While (he was) eating, he read a magazine.

ELLIPTICAL

2. The apartment *Sue wanted to rent* was very expensive.

COMPLETE

The apartment (*that*) *Sue wanted to rent* was very expensive.

ELLIPTICAL

3. That room is larger *than the other one.*

COMPLETE

That room is larger *than the other one* (*is large*).

At first glance you may not see how an elliptical dependent clause differs from a phrase that begins with a word ending with *-ing* or *-ed*. The phrase (called a *participial phrase*) lacks the signal word found at the beginning of the dependent clause.

Examples

ELLIPTICAL DEPENDENT CLAUSES

after driving downtown
when finished with her dinner

PARTICIPIAL PHRASES

driving downtown
finished with her dinner

EXERCISE 2.11

Number your paper 1-20. Identify the word or word group by writing one of the following labels: INDEPENDENT CLAUSE, DEPENDENT CLAUSE, ELLIPTICAL DEPENDENT CLAUSE, PHRASE, SIGNAL WORD, SIGNAL PHRASE.

1. in the second box

2. after the dance ended

3. so that

4. the movie was a huge success

5. which the menu included

6. driving carefully

7. whenever it rained

8. the plans were complete

9. if

10. while driving carefully

11. we went to the hockey game

12. before morning

13. before

14. on a bench under a tall elm

15. although

16. who stood beside him through the crisis

17. feeling good

18. The job *Marleen wanted* was still open. (Identify the italicized part.)

19. Priscilla ate corn chips *while studying her Spanish.* (Identify the italicized part.)

20. It was I *who told you.* (Identify the italicized part.)

Number your paper 21-25. Copy the following sentences. Underline all of the dependent clauses. Some sentences contain more than one.

21. Although Weldon's friends all jog, he insists that he does not need to exercise.

22. Veronica was not afraid of the growling dog because she had her can of dog repellent ready.

23. The people who knew her thought Katrina was well qualified for the position.

24. When Molly saw the computer print-out, she knew that the company was finally making a profit.

25. If the bus was late, Mel always ate part of his lunch while he waited.

EXERCISE 2.12

Add a signal word or signal phrase that will convert each independent clause to a dependent clause. Underline the simple subject *once* and the simple predicate *twice*; draw a box around the signal word or phrase.

1. _____ the earthquake rattled the whole building

2. _____ they painted their dorm room

3. _____ six hundred students attended the concert

4. _____ the committee held its last public hearing

5. _____ Carmen flew to Phoenix

Convert each of the following word groups to a dependent clause by adding a *relative pronoun* for a signal word.

6. _____ she used on her hair

7. _____ Tom bought for his car

8. _____ Sheila knew in Evansville

9. _____ worked very well

10. _____ managed the cafeteria

Dependent Clauses Are Used To Introduce, To Interrupt, and To Conclude

A dependent clause in a complex sentence may appear at the beginning, in the middle, or at the end of the sentence. Think about where you want to position a dependent clause in a sentence; try moving the dependent clause around to see where it will sound best.

Examples

beginning   *Although the dog looked like a mongrel*, it was actually very rare and expensive.

middle   The dog, *although it looked like a mongrel*, was actually very rare and expensive.

end   The dog was actually very rare and expensive *although it looked like a mongrel*.

When To Use Commas in Complex Sentences

INTRODUCTORY DEPENDENT CLAUSES

When you *introduce* a sentence with a dependent clause, set the clause apart from the rest of the sentence with a comma. Without this separation the reader may not realize the dependent clause has ended, and may have to reread the sentence several times to understand it. Keep your readers from having to puzzle over the sentence structure. Remember to insert a comma at the end of a dependent clause placed at the beginning of a sentence.

Example

CONFUSING
When she taught history was her favorite subject.
CORRECTED
When she taught, history was her favorite subject.

The comma after the introductory dependent clause also creates a pause needed to make the sentence read properly.

Examples

PAUSE
When Beth typed her term paper,   she forgot to include her footnotes.
PAUSE
After jogging,   Flo always takes a shower and a nap. (Elliptical Dependent Clause)

INTERRUPTING DEPENDENT CLAUSES

If a dependent clause that *interrupts* the independent clause is essential to the sentence, do not set it off with commas. But if the interrupting dependent clause is not needed, enclose it with a pair of commas.

To see if the two commas are needed, block out the dependent clause and read the sentence. If the sentence makes sense when it is read without the dependent clause, the commas should be used. If, on the other hand, the meaning of the sentence is changed or if the meaning is no longer clear, do not use commas.

The *Two-Or-Nothing Rule* should guide you in your decision. According to the rule, use either two commas or none at all. The first comma marks the beginning of the interrupting dependent clause, and the second marks the end.

The *Pause Test* is also useful. Read the sentence (aloud if possible) to determine if readers should pause at the beginning and end of the interrupting dependent clause.

Examples

All automobiles *that have bad brakes* should be banned from the streets.

>In the above example the dependent clause is essential. Without it the sentence would read, "All automobiles should be banned from the streets." Since the dependent clause is definitely necessary, no commas are used.

Eleanor Martinez, *who lives down the block from me*, is one of the best volleyball players in the country.

>Whenever a dependent clause follows someone's name, the dependent clause is considered non-essential. Because it is not needed, it is set off with commas.

The American history class *that Joan wanted very much* was closed.

The American history class *which Joan wanted very much* was closed.

>In both of the examples above the dependent clauses are essential; thus, they are not set off with commas. The writer, in each case, is talking only about the American history course that Joan wanted to take.
>
>Note that the use of the relative pronoun *that* is preferred to the use of the relative pronoun *which* when no commas are used. Both of the above examples are acceptable, but the first example shows the preferred practice of using *that*.

The American history class *Joan wanted very much* was closed.

>In this example the dependent clause is needed, so no commas are used. This dependent clause is different from those in the previous examples because in this case the relative pronoun has been left out, making it an *elliptical* dependent clause.

The American history class, *which Joan wanted very much*, was closed.

>In this version the dependent clause is non-essential, so the pair of commas is used. The fact that Joan wanted very much to take the class is extra information; the main point is that the American history class was closed, not that Joan wanted to enroll in it. The commas tell the readers to pause at the beginning and end of the non-essential information.

non-essential	Sheri, *whom we saw last night*, works in the library.
essential	The girl *whom we saw last night* works in the library.
essential	The girl *we saw last night* works in the library. (Elliptical Version)
non-essential	Dessert, *which John likes best*, will be served later.

CONCLUDING DEPENDENT CLAUSES

In general, a dependent clause that *follows* an independent clause should not be set off with a comma. When you place a dependent clause at the beginning of a sentence, you *do* set it off with a comma. But when you *end* a sentence with a dependent clause, do not separate it from the rest of the sentence with a comma unless you have a very good reason for doing so.

Most writers rarely set off a dependent clause placed after an independent clause. Do so only to achieve clarity or a desired effect that cannot be accomplished without the comma.

Examples

He will attend the university *if he is accepted as a transfer student.*

She worked on her paper *until she had to leave for work.*

They knew *that the situation was hopeless.*

Is she more afraid of flying *than you?* (Elliptical Dependent Clause)

Rod worked as a real estate appraiser *before he married Jody*, working in San Jose and Walnut Creek. (Dependent clause follows independent clause; a phrase follows the dependent clause.)

The following are cases when you *should* place a comma between an independent clause and the dependent clause that comes after it.

1) Use a comma to prevent confusion or misreading.

Examples

Carrie was happy *as she drove to work.*

> In the above example no comma is used because the sentence is perfectly clear without the comma.

Carrie was happy, *as she knew her promotion was near.*

> In this example a comma *is* used. It keeps readers from being confused when they come to the dependent clause.

2) You may use a comma to create a pause between the independent clause and the dependent clause that concludes the sentence. The effect of this comma is to make your readers stress the dependent clause, to give it drama and suspense.

Examples

> He will attend the university, *if he is accepted.*
> Marlene passed the test, *although she came very close to failing it.*
> José felt great, *until he heard the news.*

3) You may also use a comma to show that the concluding dependent clause states extra, non-essential information.

Examples

> The news angered the old soldier, *as most news* did.
> Carol insisted on looking for a new job, *although she admitted that her social life was the real cause of her dissatisfaction.*

4) A comma separating the dependent clause from the independent clause may prevent the sentence from sounding awkward.

Examples

> The history book described Chief Joseph as being very noble and wise, *which he was.*
> Sharon understood that theory, *that each student has a unique learning style.*

EXERCISE 2.13

Copy the following sentences, punctuating each one correctly. If the sentence needs no commas, write CORRECT next to the number.

1. Although the weather forecast predicted rain the sky was clear and blue.

2. The sky was dark and threatening although the weather forecast called for clear skies.

3. The snack bar was always crowded when the main cafeteria served Spam stew.

4. When the semester was almost over Freddie decided it was time to start studying.

5. The pants she purchased Saturday were marked down for sale on Monday.

6. The raft trip which he thought about during lectures seemed a long way off.

7. Ralph knew that he had made a mistake that he had made a terrible mistake.

8. As far as they could tell the car was not seriously damaged.

9. As predicted Arnold Ramirez who had coached the basketball team for twenty-seven years announced his retirement.

10. The settler who built the cabin never did farm the land after clearing it.

Copy the following sentences. Punctuate them correctly. A few sentences do not need commas. To the the left of the number identify the sentence as being SIMPLE, COMPOUND, or COMPLEX.

_____ 1. When we returned home her father was waiting at the door.

_____ 2. While the snow was falling no traffic moved.

_____ 3. We rode snowmobiles during the morning and went skiing in the afternoon.

_____ 4. Jan and Rick when they were much younger were always in trouble.

_____ 5. She kept entering million-dollar contests but she never won.

_____ 6. We will leave whenever you are ready.

_____ 7. The girl with sad eyes looks very lonely.

_____ 8. When our group was asked for our report we could only laugh.

_____ 9. Geometry which is not my favorite subject is the only class I hate to attend.

_____ 10. Although it was fall everyone seemed to have spring fever.

_____ 11. The woman who lives behind my house grows beautiful roses.

_____ 12. Avery Anderson who delivers our mail is getting married next Saturday.

_____ 13. However the automobile was not for sale.

_____ 14. The frightened horse moreover stepped on the fallen rider.

_____ 15. Furthermore the yelling grooms made the horse more excited and he ran into the side of a car.

EXERCISE 2.15

Follow the same directions given for the previous exercise.

_____ 1. Jaguars which I like better than Corvettes are fine sport cars.

_____ 2. Joe is excited about the trip he thinks that it will be the best week of the year.

_____ 3. While we were in Ireland last summer it rained and rained and rained.

_____ 4. Au Sable River canoe trips produce sore muscles sunburned skin and many happy memories.

_____ 5. We knew of course that exploring the caves was dangerous nevertheless we entered the cave without food rope or flashlights.

_____ 6. They could have taken the bus downtown but chose to take a taxi instead.

_____ 7. Chuko a guy we met at the bottom of the canyon joined us for a campfire dinner.

_____ 8. We had been told that snakes come out for warmth at night.

_____ 9. When Jane and I hiked closer to the falls the noise became so loud that we had to shout to hear one another.

_____ 10. He was happy to be home after having a problem-filled day at work but he found more problems awaiting him there.

Subordination

In a compound sentence ideas of equal importance are **coordinated** by joining two independent clauses. In a complex sentence the main idea of the sentence is communicated in the independent clause, and the lesser ideas are **subordinated** in dependent clauses. Signal words, because they connect this less-important information to the sentence, are sometimes called *subordinating conjunctions*.

Example

INDEPENDENT CLAUSE
The glider soared up and away from the cliff
DEPENDENT CLAUSE
as soon as it hit the updraft.

The main idea in the above sentence is that the glider soared up and away from the cliff. This idea is stated in the independent clause. The *subordinate idea* is stated in the dependent clause. Note that although it is not as important as the main idea, the subordinate idea does add a significant detail. The dependent clause tells WHEN the glider was able to sail beyond the cliff.

Example

INDEPENDENT CLAUSE
Sue wanted to fly the huge orange sail kite
DEPENDENT CLAUSE
that her brother had built.

The main idea is that Sue wanted to fly the orange sail kite. The fact that her brother built it is not as important as the main idea. By telling WHICH kite Sue wanted to fly, the dependent clause only modifies the meaning of the independent clause.

As you become a more experienced writer, you will find yourself using more and more complex sentences. With complex sentences you can express your ideas accurately and smoothly. Although you will mix simple, compound, and complex sentences, you will rely more on the dependent clauses within the complex sentences. Not only will you use dependent clauses to subordinate ideas—

to clarify and qualify—but you will use them to give your sentences variety and rhythm.

EXERCISE 2.16

Write complex sentences according to the following directions. Punctuate each sentence correctly.

1. Write a complex sentence *beginning* with a dependent clause.

2. Write a complex sentence with a dependent clause that *interrupts* the independent clause. In this sentence make the interrupting dependent clause *essential*.

3. Write another complex sentence with an *interrupting* dependent clause. In this sentence make the interrupting dependent clause *non-essential*.

4. Write a complex sentence in which the independent clause is *followed* by a dependent clause. Do not set off the dependent clause with a comma.

5. Write another complex sentence that *ends* with a dependent clause. This time write a sentence in which the concluding dependent clause needs to be set off with a comma.

6. Write a complex sentence that contains an *elliptical dependent clause*.

7. Write a complex sentence with a *relative pronoun* for a signal word.

8. Write another complex sentence that *begins* with a dependent clause.

9. Rewrite the sentence you wrote for item 8, placing the dependent clause in the middle.

10. If possible, rewrite the sentence again, this time placing the dependent clause at the end of the sentence.

EXERCISE 2.17

Write a paragraph that is five to twelve sentences long, telling about something that happened to you recently. *Use only simple and compound sentences.* Then rewrite the composition. *In the second version use as many complex sentences as possible.*

LESSON THREE—Avoiding Sentence Fragments, Run-on Sentences, and Comma Splices

Sentence Fragments

A **sentence fragment** is a part of a sentence placed by itself and punctuated with a period. Professional writers sometimes use sentence fragments very effectively. But you should not use them in your school writing. Most teachers automatically see them as serious writing errors. Your teacher, seeing the fragment, may think you do not understand how to write complete sentences. Keeping this problem in mind, you should avoid all sentence fragments. *They will be marked as errors in any writing you do for the assignments in this book.*

Dependent Clause Fragments

The most common kind of fragment error is the **dependent clause fragment**. By its very definition, a dependent clause is a clause that cannot stand by itself. It must be attached to an independent clause. The fragment error occurs when a writer does not realize that a group of words is a dependent clause, capitalizes the signal word, and puts a period at the end of the clause.

Examples

> When we returned at two in the morning.
> Which was the kind they wanted.
> Who always criticizes the manager's policies.
> Where the action is.

Notice that in many cases by merely dropping or changing the signal word the dependent clause becomes an independent clause. Just one word can make the difference between a dependent clause and a simple sentence.

Examples

> *When* we returned at two in the morning. (Fragment)
>
> > *becomes*
>
> We returned at two in the morning. (Sentence)
>
> *Who* always criticizes the manager's policies. (Fragment)
>
> > *becomes*
>
> He always criticizes the manager's policies. (Sentence)

Any dependent clause fragment can be corrected easily. Simply attach it to an independent clause to create a complex sentence, or convert the dependent clause to an independent clause. To create a complex sentence, attach the dependent clause fragment either to the sentence before it or to the sentence after it, depending on which has the closer relationship.

If neither strategy works, revise the dependent clause fragment so that it becomes a complete sentence, between the two sentences to which you tried to connect it.

Examples

WRONG	CORRECTED
We stayed out much later than we planned. *When we returned at two in the morning.* We were surprised to see the lights on.	We stayed out much later than we planned. *When we returned home at two in the morning,* we were surprised to see the lights on.

The dependent clause has been attached to the sentence that follows it because the two parts fit together smoothly. They form one complex sentence. The dependent clause would not fit well with the sentence in front of it.

WRONG	CORRECTED
They bought an old Wurlitzer juke-box. *Which was the kind they had been looking for.* They placed it in the basement recreation room.	They bought an old Wurlitzer *juke-box, which was the kind they had been looking for.* They placed it in the basement recreation room.

In this example the sentence fragment error has been corrected by joining the dependent clause to the sentence in front of it. The dependent clause cannot be connected to the sentence that follows it. Put together, the two parts would not make sense.

WRONG	CORRECTED
With frightening speed the passenger express thundered on through the night. *Although the bridge ahead had been swept away by the flood.* No one aboard knew what awaited them around the bend.	With frightening speed the passenger express thundered on through the night. *However, the bridge ahead had been swept away by the flood.* No one aboard the train knew what awaited them around the bend.

In this case the writer chose to convert the dependent clause fragment to a sentence. This was accomplished by changing the signal word *Although* to the transitional word *However*.

Copy the following sentences, correcting the *dependent clause fragments*.

1. The young couple were unable to buy a house when they got married. Although they wanted to very much. They decided to rent an apartment until they could save enough money for a downpayment.

2. When the game was over, we all stopped for pizza. Because we did not have to get up early the next day. We were in no hurry to leave the restaurant.

3. Although the locomotive was forty years old. It still worked like new. Three times each day it pulled the antique passenger cars over the mountain.

4. Jonsie had two young children to support. She wanted to find a job. As soon as she finished two years of college.

5. Rudy was in an industrial accident. In which his back was broken. For more than a year he was unable to work.

Phrase Fragments

A phrase—a meaningful group of words without a subject or a predicate—must always be part of a sentence. Either a phrase or a series of phrases mistakenly placed by itself is a *sentence fragment*. **Phrase fragments** can be corrected by using the same methods used to repair dependent clause fragments.

Examples

WRONG	CORRECTED
The new subdivision will be located across the river. *On the Sullivan Ranch Property.*	The new subdivision will be located across the river *on the Sullivan Ranch Property.*
WRONG	CORRECTED
Nadar was in the library. *Working on a research paper.*	Nadar was in the library, *working on a research paper.*
WRONG	CORRECTED
Martin hitchhiked to Portland. *To find a job.*	Martin hitchhiked to Portland *to find a job.*
WRONG	CORRECTED
Marsha had a dog. *A large English sheepdog.*	Marsha had a dog, *a large English sheepdog.*

53

Copy the following sentences, correcting the *phrase fragments*.

1. They continued on their hike. Undefeated by the rain. They felt quite soggy when they arrived at Camp Williams.

2. He wanted to do his homework. After the movie. His mother thought he should complete the work first.

3. The widow built a home on the edge of the mountain lake. A huge stone castle. It resembled a Viking fortress.

4. Sharon welcomed the opportunity. To show her father that she could handle the responsibility. She thought he still treated her like a child.

5. Brad continued. Teasing his little sister. His mother told him repeatedly. To stop.

6. The old pine tree fell. Crashing into the cabin roof. Snow and splintered lumber littering the floor.

7. The President made his decision. Not to run for re-election. Serving just one term.

8. He took the job. With the understanding that he would not receive a vacation the first year.

9. The job provided a challenge. More of a challenge than he expected.

10. Feeling good, she looked forward to work that morning. In spite of the busy day ahead of her.

Copy the following sentences, correcting all sentence fragments.

1. Hundreds of homes were damaged. By the tornado. An unexpected tragedy.

2. The class was told to read at least five books. During the semester. Too many for some.

3. Team spirit has been very high. Since she began playing third base. Because she always peps up the rest of the team with her laughter, jokes, and chatter.

4. The trouble with Jordon's theory is that he has failed to take human nature into account. Fear of change. People resisting chances to improve their lives.

5. Although she could not stay. She visited for a few minutes. Meeting Bill's aunt and uncle from Dallas.

Run-On Sentences

A **run-on sentence** is two or more independent clauses, or sentences, that have been connected without any punctuation. Readers will have difficulty trying to make sense of the run-together ideas. All run-on errors must be corrected.

Examples

(run-on error)	She called a taxi she had always wanted to ride through Manhattan in a cab.
(corrected—two sentences)	She called a taxi. She had always wanted to ride through Manhattan in a cab.
(corrected—one sentence)	She called a taxi; she had always wanted to ride through Manhattan in a cab.

Comma Splices

A **comma splice** is another kind of faulty connection. Two independent clauses, or sentences, are mistakenly joined with a comma but no conjunction. In a comma splice the comma is inserted between the two independent clauses, but the conjunction is left out. The comma splice is a serious writing mistake, but it is one of the most common errors made by the beginning writers.

Examples

(comma-splice error)	He never seems to answer *questions, when* asked one, he replies with a question of his own.
(corrected—two sentences)	He never seems to answer questions. When asked one, he replies with a question of his own.
(corrected—conjunction added)	He never seems to answer questions, and when asked one, he replies with a question of his own.

Correcting Run-Ons and Comma Splices

Run-on and comma-splice errors may be corrected by any of *six* different methods. Choose the method that appears to be best in a particular situation.

1. USE A SEMICOLON:

Example

(run-on error)	The hawk swooped down upon the *mouse she* then flew back to her nest.
(comma-splice error)	The hawk swooped down upon the *mouse, she* then flew back to her nest.
(revised)	The hawk swooped down upon the mouse; she then flew back to her nest.

The independent clauses are correctly joined by a semicolon in the revision. This method is especially effective when the clauses are closely related.

2. USE A COMMA AND A CONJUNCTION:

Example

(run-on error)	The band played a three-hour Halloween *concert most* of the audience thought it was their best concert in years.
(comma-splice error)	The band played a three-hour Halloween *concert, most* of the audience thought it was their best concert in years.
(revised)	The band played a three-hour Halloween concert, *and* most of the audience thought it was their best concert in years.

Be careful! Many writers remember to use the comma, but they neglect to place a conjunction after it. The comma and the conjunction work together as a team.

3. REDUCE THE SECOND INDEPENDENT CLAUSE AND MAKE IT PART OF THE FIRST ONE:

Example

(run-on error)	Ukio studied for his math *test then* he worked on a lab report.
(comma-splice error)	Ukio studied for his math *test, then* he worked on a lab report.
(revised)	Ukio studied for his math test and then worked on a lab report.

The second independent clause has been condensed by dropping the subject *he*. It was then combined with the first independent clause. The result is a simple sentence with a compound predicate.

4. SUBORDINATE ONE OF THE INDEPENDENT CLAUSES:

Example

(run-on error)	Mr. Herder surprised his *class he* gave the chapter test a day early.
(comma-splice error)	Mr. Herder surprised his *class, he* gave the chapter test a day early.
(revision #1)	Mr. Herder surprised his *class when* he gave the chapter test a day early.
(revision #2)	*When* Mr. Herder gave the chapter test a day early, he surprised his class.

In the first revision the second independent clause has been converted to a dependent clause. To do this, the signal word *when* was added. In the second revision the second independent clause was converted to a dependent clause and then moved to the front of the sentence.

5. USE A SEMICOLON AND A CONJUNCTIVE ADVERB:

Example

(run-on error)   As the night wore on, they became less and less interested in *fishing they* were still determined to stay until dawn.

(comma-splice error)   As the night wore on, they became less and less interested in *fishing, they* were still determined to stay until dawn.

(revised)   As the night wore on, they became less and less interested in fishing; *nevertheless,* they were still determined to stay until dawn.

The conjunctive adverb *nevertheless* make the logical connection between the two independent clauses clear. None of the other revision methods would work as well; the conjunctive adverb is needed. Remember that whenever two independent clauses are joined with a conjunctive adverb, a semicolon is placed in front of the conjunctive adverb, and a comma is usually placed after it.

6. MAKE TWO SENTENCES:

Example

(run-on error)   Sue wanted to become an airline pilot after she finished *college she* already had a license to fly multi-engined planes.

(comma-splice error)   Sue wanted to become an airline pilot after she finished *college, she* already had a license to fly multi-engined planes.

(revised)   Sue wanted to become an airline pilot after she finished *college. She* already had a license to fly multi-engined planes.

In the above revision, dividing the faulty sentence into two separate sentences works well. The second sentence expresses an idea that is not easily coordinated with or subordinated to the idea of the first sentence. This method of correction is not advisable if the division creates short, choppy sentences.

When To Break the Rules

A comma splice is sometimes acceptable in a sentence containing a series of three or more independent clauses. In such cases the last two independent clauses must be joined by a conjunction (*and, or, but, yet, so, for*).

Examples

The bargain was made, the date was set, *and* the contract could not be altered.

He saw the problem, he knew better, *but* he did it anyway.

57

Copy each of the following, correcting the *run-on* or *comma-splice* error.

1. Two dozen chocolate cookies were in the jar at lunchtime only six cookies were left at nine o'clock that evening.

2. The road became too steep for the car to continue, therefore, we walked the rest of the way to the firetower.

3. The manned space missions most often discussed are space stations orbiting the earth and a permanent moon base, more spectacular plans for space cities are also being planned.

4. The thunder and lightning became worse, the dog became frightened he crawled under the bed.

5. The Western Desert covers more than two thirds of Egypt its surface is crossed by belts of sand dunes, including the great Sand Sea.

6. Standard auditing procedures fail to stop computer crime, the criminals program the computers to erase all incriminating evidence.

7. An original Beatles 45 rpm single record is worth more than one hundred dollars Beatles' pens cost $17.50 each.

8. The Type A person is always worried about not having enough time to finish something, the Type B person is rarely worried about running out of time.

9. Carol told all of her friends that she was on a strict diet, however, they noticed that she still ordered French fries and a double-thick banana shake for lunch every day.

10. During the Second Battle of Somme the British first used their new offensive weapon, the tank however, the machine was still in the experimental stage and, therefore, not effective.

Chapter Two Review

PART ONE

1. Define the term *compound sentence.*

2. Write a compound sentence, using *and, but,* or *or* for a conjunction. Punctuate the sentence properly.

3. Copy the following sentence, choosing the most effective conjunction.

> He had traveled Riverlane Boulevard for fifteen years, (*and but yet*) he still could not remember where to turn to get to his sister's house.

4. Write a compound sentence, using only a semicolon for a connector. (Do not use a conjunctive adverb.)

5. Write a compound sentence, using *consequently* as a conjunctive adverb. Punctuate the sentence correctly.

6. Copy the following sentence, using the most effective conjunctive adverb.

> In the past, legislative bills to place strict controls on strip mining had been defeated; (*therefore, however, in addition,*) this week the House voted for a bill requiring restoration of all land strip mined in the future.

7. (Write the letter of the correct answer.) The italicized word in the following sentence is used as

   a. an INTRODUCTORY TRANSITIONAL WORD

   b. an INTERRUPTING TRANSITIONAL WORD

   c. a CONJUNCTIVE ADVERB

> The city plans to hire high school students for summer vacation jobs; *however,* most of the jobs will require hot, dirty manual labor.

PART TWO

8. Define the term *phrase.*

9. Define the term *clause.*

10. Define the term *independent clause* and write an example.

11. Define the term *dependent clause* and write an example.

12. Define the term *elliptical dependent clause* and give an example.

13. (Write the letter of the correct answer.) The following word groups are

   a. INDEPENDENT CLAUSES

   b. DEPENDENT CLAUSES

   c. PHRASES

   d. SIGNAL WORDS or SIGNAL PHRASES

> *after the game*
>
> *to see her cousin*
>
> *turning the corner*
>
> *powered by a gas turbine*

14. Convert the following independent clause to a dependent clause.

   she studied for her geometry test

15. Copy the following sentence; then underline the dependent clauses in it.

   The dam, which had been weakened by the earthquake, suddenly crumbled after heavy rains filled the lake behind it.

16. The sentence below is a compound sentence. Convert it to a complex sentence by subordinating one of the independent clauses.

   Death ray weapons are being developed by the superpowers, and they will make anti-ballistic missiles obsolete.

17. Write a complex sentence in which the independent clause is *followed* by a dependent clause. Punctuate the sentence correctly.

18. Punctuate the following sentence correctly.

   The Starview Inn which Ramon and Marie had stayed in for the last three years was booked six months in advance.

PART THREE

19. Define the term *sentence fragment*.

20. Copy the following passage, correcting the phrase fragment.

   The rapid deforestation of the Amazon Basin may result in world-wide climate changes. Causing droughts in some areas and floods in others. Never before has such a drastic environmental change occurred so rapidly.

21. Copy the following passage, correcting the dependent clause fragments.

   Rod could not attend the party. Although he wanted to go. He had to work. Because no one would take his place.

22. Define the term *run-on sentence*.

23. The structure of the sentence that follows is faulty. Revise it to correct the run-on error.

   Maude planned to travel in six weeks she would visit twelve countries.

24. Define the term *comma splice*.

25. Revise the following sentence to correct the comma-splice error.

   Her reading speed increased dramatically, however, her improvement in comprehension was even more dramatic.

person, depending on your purpose and your audience. You can tell a *first-person narrative* by the use of *first-person* pronouns, such as *I, me, we, us,* and *our.*

Examples

> *I* was amazed to see . . .
>
> The strange man walked toward *me* . . .
>
> It did not take long for *us* . . .
>
> *We* reluctantly left *our* . . .

You can tell a *second-person narrative* by the use of the pronoun *you.*

Examples

> When *you* were a child, *you* drove *your* mother crazy with *your* endless questions.
>
> Upon entering the castle, *you* will see . . .

Second person narrative must be avoided in academic writing. Most writers and teachers believe that it should be used only for letters, directions (including textbooks), and speeches where the speaker can maintain eye contact with the audience.

You can tell a *third-person narrative* because it refers directly to people, places, and events by using a name or description. Third-person pronouns are *he, she, it, they, them, their,* etc.

Examples

> *The group* was disappointed to find . . .
>
> *The countryside* was parched during the drought . . .
>
> *Harriett* knew that . . .
>
> *She* hunted crayfish . . .
>
> *It* came running . . .
>
> *Their* boat finished last.
>
> *He* was alone.
>
> Three of *them* . . .
>
> How is *one* to know when . . .

The distinction between first, second, and third person may not seem important to you at this point, but most teachers will require you to choose either *first* or *third person* and then *use it consistently* throughout a single composition. Study the following examples; they provide longer illustrations of first- and third-person writing.

Example

First Person

Knowing little about the dangers involved, I climbed on my half-submerged log and proceeded to row with homemade paddles from one island to the next. The distance between was about two miles, but I failed to consider the fact that I was crossing open ocean water. Luckily, the water and weather were quite calm! Halfway between the islands, however, I was reminded that my legs hung into the water below the log when I saw a number of fins coming toward me. Thinking of the sharks behind me and paddling furiously toward the island I had left, I began a short but hopeless race. I had covered no more than fifty feet when the great finned creatures were upon me. One brushed against the log while another brushed my leg. Expecting to feel teeth in my leg at any moment, I increased my paddling. Suddenly, the threatening fish began to leap completely out of the water, obviously enjoying playing "cat and mouse" with their noon meal. Just as suddenly, I realized that sharks do not jump out of the water. The realization that I was surrounded by a group of playful porpoises flooded my heart with happiness.

Third Person

Knowing little about the danger involved, Bob climbed on his half-submerged log and proceeded to row with homemade paddles from one island to the next. The distance between the islands was about two miles, but he failed to consider the fact that he was crossing open ocean water. Luckily, the water and weather were quite calm! Halfway between the islands, however, Bob was reminded that his legs hung into the water below the log when he saw a number of fins coming toward him. Thinking of the sharks behind him and paddling furiously toward the island he had left, he began a short but hopeless race. He had covered no more than fifty feet when the giant finned creatures were upon him. One brushed against the log while another brushed his leg. Expecting to feel teeth in his leg at any moment, he increased his paddling. Suddenly, the threatening fish began to leap completely out of the water, obviously enjoying playing "cat and mouse" with their noon meal. Just as suddenly, Bob realized that sharks do not jumped out of the water. The realization that he was surrounded by a group of playful porpoises flooded his heart with happiness.

Newspapers use first- and third-person narrative every day. The story of an accident, for instance, will almost always be in third person (unless the reporter was involved in the accident). An article in which the reporter describes personal experiences during a demonstration would be in first person. Some magazines try to present a balance of first- and third-person narratives; others, such as travel magazines, nearly always print first-person accounts when they use narratives. Also, those magazine articles that tell the reader how to do something are usually written in second person.

more effective, and the development of the idea remains straightforward and interesting. The resulting paragraph stands by itself as a complete unit.

What to Write About?

You can write a narrative about any experience, but your most memorable experiences will be the best to write about. Your interest will keep the reader interested. Consider the following list of topics as you search for possible events to narrate:

1. An incident which caused you to be directly affected by a political or social problem (for example, women's rights, welfare, drug abuse, etc.).

2. The most important thing that has happened to you during the past two or three years.

3. The most important decision in your life, and how and why you made it.

4. An experience which caused your basic beliefs to be challenged.

5. When you learned to confront fear.

Establishing a Purpose

As you begin developing a topic into a narrative paragraph, you must communicate to your reader what you want to say. You may lose readers with the first sentence unless you include a *purpose sentence*. This sentence will inform readers of your aim in writing. Do not be overbearing. Beginning with *"I am going to tell you about . . ."* or *"My purpose is . . ."* will make the paragraph sound weak. A more subtle approach should be used. Begin with a sentence that introduces the subject and draws attention to a particular aspect of it at the same time.

Carefully read the following paragraph. Notice that the writer is only concerned with telling about the "inspiring place" found in the mountains.

Example

I discovered the most beautiful, inspiring place in my world once while I was hiking in the mountains during a summer rainstorm. Gradually, I had become aware of a loud, roaring sound coming from deep within the canyon ahead. I knew at once that when I got to the bottom I would find a swelling stream rushing along its banks. It was only a few minutes later that my guess became reality. There I was, standing face to face with the most beautiful series of intricately carved waterfalls I had ever seen. The rain had begun to subside, and I had an uncontrollable urge to strip to the skin and bathe in the churning waters. Soon, I was romping and splashing in the icy stream; for a minute, I stood beneath one of the many waterfalls and received an invigorating, natural shower. I have never been to a place that gave me such a voluptuous, lusty feeling. It is a place that I have returned to uncountable times, feeling just as excited as when I accidentally stumbled onto it several years ago.

Make a list of five memorable experiences from your life about which you might like to write.

Chronological Order

To avoid confusing readers, you need order in your writing. For a narrative, the most commonly used and easiest technique is **time** (chronological) **ordering**. While there are other types, they are seldom used in narrative writing, so you do not need to be concerned with them at this point.

Chronological ordering requires that you tell what happened *first, second, third*, etc., in the order that things took place. In telling your tale this way, readers become aware of the passing of time. Notice the order the author of the following paragraph has used to tell a story:

Example

I have my routine for leaving the house in the morning down so well, that if I want to, I can lounge in bed until my "snooze" alarm has gone off so many times that the space between buzzes has shortened to thirty seconds. On those extra sleepy days, I turn my body onto automatic and put my system into high gear. I toss the covers back, roll out of bed, blindly head through my bedroom door, and stumble into the bathroom. A very fast shower is always next as it is my hope the shock of water will catapult me closer to consciousness. I have no time to wash my hair on these days; a quick toweling while I'm reaching for my toothbrush and then the tingle of "Ultrabright" to wake up my mouth is it. I run a comb through my hair, but even if I had time to spend in front of the mirror, my eyes are not usually open enough yet to see much of anything. There is no time to be fussy about clothes, so I grab whatever is hanging closest and hope everything matches. I have found, too, that if I cannot find my keys, my wallet, or my shoes, I only have to make time to pause for thirty seconds, inhale a few deep breaths, and the information regarding their whereabouts usually pops right into my head. The last thing I do is put on my watch and often realize that I have only two minutes to go from my room, through the kitchen, out the back door, and down the street to the corner bus stop. I shift into overdrive, pause long enough to grab an apple, wave over my shoulder at whoever is eating breakfast, and race the bus to see which of us will reach the corner first. As I sit panting at the window, I often smile to myself and remember how only ten minutes before I was so tired I could hardly move, and now I am sitting there with all my energy juices flowing and my eyes wide awake.

From the list you prepared for Exercise 3.5, choose one experience and write a narrative paragraph that is in chronological order. (Do not forget your purpose sentence.)

LESSON TWO—Description

Narration and description go together like sailboats and wind. Narrative writing can stand alone just as a sailboat can exist without wind, but both are most impressive when they work together. Sailboats without wind merely bob uncomfortably on the water's surface, and narrative writing without description sits dully upon the page. By adding the counterparts, however, both sailing and narrating become spirited and exciting.

Take a look at the example in which the narrator tells of experiencing a rock concert (page 66). This narration includes description because the writer wants readers to visualize what happened. In the second sentence, the writer might have simply stated "More people came and made the crowd larger." However, in order to be more graphic, the writer has written, "*As I drew closer to the main gate, the crowd took on the appearance of a giant amoeba, with each new group of people adding to the enormous mass of the thing.*"

Description is particularly effective in certain kinds of narrative writing. **Report writing** depends upon good description. Without it, for example, an accident report can never be adequate. The following examples illustrate the importance of description in narrative writing. Each report narrates the same incident, but the second is far more useful because the description elaborates upon the event.

Examples

Accident Report

The accident occurred at 10:15 a.m. on March 23, 1981. Ten crew members were working with a crane and a front-end loader to lift and stack large concrete blocks when the crane's boom broke and fell across the front-end loader. The operator of the loader was struck by the boom as it fell. The boom was removed, and the operator taken to a hospital by ambulance.

Accident Report

The accident occurred at 10:15 a.m., March 23, 1981, behind warehouse #154. Ten crew members were working with a crane and front-end loader to lift and stack large concrete blocks which had been poured the previous day. Because the blocks had stuck to the concrete surface upon which they had been poured, the crane operator was experiencing serious difficulty. lifting some of them. Consequently, the back of the crane was lifted free of the surface each time the operator attempted to lift those which were struck. After working for some time on those blocks that seemed to be stuck fast, a loud "crack" was heard from a point midway up the crane's boom. The boom swerved suddenly to the right and fell directly across the cockpit of the front-end loader with a loud crash. Unfortunately, the loader operator did not have time to escape from the cockpit before the boom hit. The operator did, however, have time to crouch down as low as possible. When the 6,000 pound boom struck, the operator was forced down into the cockpit with such violence that his face and shoulder were severely injured. Blood was everywhere in the cockpit, and the rest of the crew instantly assumed the operator had been killed by the crushing weight of the boom. The crew members immediately gathered together in a heroic but futile attempt to lift the boom from the operator's shoulders; it was hopeless, however, and someone was dispatched to summon a lift-truck which was used to raise the boom. Moments later the ambulance arrived, and the loader operator was carefully removed from the cockpit. Upon close inspection, the ambulance attendants determined that the operator, although badly injured, was still alive, and they left for a hospital at top speed.

In the second example, good description helps the narration produce an account that is more interesting and far more detailed. For anyone who did not see the accident, the first report, although accurate, does not clearly explain what happened.

Sometimes good descriptive writing is used without narration. You may, for instance, be asked to describe something or someone completely. The following paragraphs are *descriptive*. As you read them, notice that the authors try to create word images of what they experience: a dog, a man, a shower. They explain what things look like and how they are arranged in relationship to one another. Notice that the writers communicate what they see, feel, hear, smell and taste. These paragraphs illustrate the most important characteristic of descriptive writing: "creating a clear image with words."

Examples

1

Black is a beautiful color, especially if the black thing has big brown eyes, a pink tongue and a big, bushy, wagging tail. His name is "Le Bête Noir de Loca Bleu," the "Black Beast of Blue Lake," but I call him Buddy. Originating from Belgium, this sheepdog is a direct descendant of the European wolf. His breed was first used for herding sheep and later for tracking and *schützen*, which is a German word for protect. Buddy's eyes are keen so he can protect and be watchful. He is graceful and agile; his energy is boundless. The black dog's ears are fairly small and pointed upward so that he can catch any sounds an enemy might make. A long and pointed snout helps him track. The jaws of this loving and loyal friend are able to overpower and hold down a full-grown person. For this reason, and because of the Belgium Sheepdog's characteristic black color, the breed was used during World War II for night-maneuvers. The black coat is like down next to the skin, with very long hair covering the rest of the body. Buddy is naturally aloof and arrogant to most people and can be ferocious, but he is humble and loving to one person—me.

2

I first met Charley Crenshaw about three years ago while I was doing some first-hand research on the effects of cheap wine on the central nervous system. He was casually leaning against a soot-covered brick building, grinning at the rush-hour traffic. He wore an almost-black navy blue pea coat that had obviously at one time belonged to someone of twice Charley's stature. His dark green wool pants were almost as ill-fitting as his coat; indeed, they had apparently at one time in their long life been altered to fit a very short-legged man, which Charley was not. About five inches below these pants, Charley's ankles plunged into a pair of black, steel-toed work shoes. The bulbous toes of the work shoes gave Charley an unmistakable

Bozo-the-Clown image of which I was sure he was very proud. To remember Charley's humorous blue eyes and his genuine laughter makes me recall the old cliché "You can't tell a book by its cover."

3

One of the greatest joys of my childhood was when I was allowed to take a shower rather than the usual nightly dip in the tub. I would stand in the steamy, warm tub enclosure letting the water cascade over my back and sometimes image that I was not really in our surburban home but that this moist heat was tropical. Surrounded by the lush greenery of the Congo or the Amazon, I would let the mist fall in droplets on my tongue, and the taste would change from city-chlorinated to mountain-pure. The water would crash over rock ledges that spread out hazily below my feet and disappear in a mysterious dark pool that rather resembled the bathtub drain. Voices in another room became the cawing of gloriously colored birds, hidden amongst the foliage of the shower curtain. The water and the images would pummel my shoulders and my neck, and together they would ease some of the pain of growing up.

A famous poem by Robert Browning, "Meeting at Night," contains some very fine descriptive lines. After reading the poem for its overall meaning, go back and look closely at the *description* conveyed in the individual lines. The images appeal to the reader's senses of sight, hearing, smell, and touch. Furthermore, the description clearly arranges the sea, the land, and the sky. Readers understand what lies at a distance and what is close at hand. Browning communicates motion, direction, and distance as he tells the story of the lovers' meeting. The poem communicates the joy of the lovers. Note how finely tuned the narrator's senses are. Under the influence of heightened expectation, perception is intensified.

MEETING AT NIGHT

I

The gray sea and the long black land;
And the yellow half-moon large and low;
And the startled little waves that leap
In fiery ringlets from their sleep,
As I gain the cove with pushing prow,
And quench its speed i' the slushy sand.

II

Then a mile of warm sea-scented beach;
Three fields to cross till a farm appears;
A tap at the pane, the quick sharp scratch
And blue spurt of a lighted match,
And a voice less loud, thro' its joys and fears,
Than the two hearts beating each to each!

Find several examples of vividly descriptive writing in magazines or newspapers. Cut out or copy down three paragraphs that describe an experience, a person, a place, or an object.

Write a paragraph in which you vividly describe an experience, a person, a place, or an object.

LESSON THREE—Longer Narration and Description

You can effectively combine *narrative* and *descriptive* writing, especially in papers longer than one paragraph. You will use this kind of writing throughout your life. Letter writing, of course, requires you to combine narration and description, but report writing also presents you with an opportunity to use both. Here are three examples that tell stories (narratives) and describe the settings and events effectively. Each was written by a person who wanted to narrate, in detail, a memorable event from the past.

Examples

1

As a result of never attending school, I was sent to juvenile hall where I learned a lesson that no school could provide. At this time in my life I looked up to people who tried to get something for nothing. I found a great number of these people in juvenile hall.

One of the most popular pastimes at the juvenile hall was formulating plans of escape. The inmates stood around in groups talking and planning. The leader of our particular group was a black man by the name of Al. Al was quite tall, had a massively strong build, and his face reflected a very hard life. Contrary to his appearance, however, he was very well-adjusted. Al's almost religious attitude towards escape seemed to be the only flaw in his character. Although we participated in the discussions of escape, no one really seemed to take them seriously. Unfortunately, a new arrival eventually did. The new inmate's name was Joe. Joe also had a massive build. His presence made it apparent that he would not take guff from anyone. Joe's appearance and gruff personality made him a not very likeable person; nevertheless, we invited him into our group.

Al's most recent plan was quite simple. The escape was to take place in the recreation area. Someone was supposed to knock out the guard with a cuestick and take his keys, which, of course, were the keys to freedom. The only drawback to his plan was that there were no volunteers to knock out the guard—that is, no volunteers until Joe came along. Joe absorbed Al's every word. At the end of the discussion, Joe spoke without any hesitation. He said that he would "knock the guard's lights out."

The guard was working his first day on the job. Unwittingly, he was reading a book and was completely unaware of the different activities going on in the room. I was shooting pool as the most tragic experience I had ever encountered, or will probably ever encounter, was about to take place. Joe walked up and grabbed my opponent's cuestick. He clutched it as if he were holding a baseball bat by the small end. The guard looked up from his book just as Joe swung the stick with blinding speed. The shattering impact caved in the left side of the guard's head, and blood spurted out of his right ear. My mind screamed with terror. I was completely incoherent. A fellow inmate's fruitless efforts to stop Joe only resulted in him being knocked to the floor. Joe's second swing caved in the right side of the guard's head. As the cuestick smashed into his head, it made a sickening crunching sound that seemed to open up a reservoir of blood. Joe's third swing had more velocity than either of the first two. The guard was hit with such force that the cuestick broke in two about twelve inches from the top at the big end. This final blow sent a lifeless form slowly falling to the floor. I felt like I was going to vomit. Joe and everyone else stood in complete disbelief, staring at the gory spectacle. The sight of the guard lying lifeless in the sickening pool of blood was incomprehensible. It was so horrible that no one would go near the guard to retrieve the keys. Then, suddenly, someone pushed the ALERT button. The guards were upon us instantly. They immediately rushed us off to our individual cells without making any effort to find out who was guilty. Then the guards rushed their comrade off to the hospital. But their hurried efforts were useless. The guard was pronounced dead on arrival at the hospital.

Later, the guards began questioning the inmates one by one about the killing. When it came to my turn to be questioned, I replied that I had not seen or heard anything until after I was rushed off to my cell. Approximately ten minutes later, a guard opened my cell door. I was still sick to my stomach at the thought of the blood. When I was outside the door of my cell, the guard began shoving me around. He informed me that I would have to clean up the mess. The guard then handed me some towels. I started cleaning up the blood. I could not hold the sickness back any longer. I vomited all over the place.

About two days after the incident I was released from juvenile hall. I dreamed about the murder every night for about two weeks. Even now it occasionally haunts me. The whole thing had such an impact on me that I can still remember it vividly.

2

Another routine flight was about to begin; each aircraft flew about three a day, and I was launching my last mission. The only difference was that this mission required the jet engines to be started with explosive charges called starter carts. The starter carts were installed in the starter breech, and I double checked to ensure that the breech was firmly secured to the starter. I hated these missions; the possibility of injury was always present, and that thought would chill my spine. After the pilot was complete with his preflight checks in the cockpit, he asked the crew chief if he was clear to start number one engine. As I made the final adjustments on my headset and extended the communication line to its maximum length, I crossed my fingers and gave him clearance. Immediately, from the left side of the aircraft, a large black stream of smoke came bellowing out of the engine exhaust port as the whine of the engine became increasingly louder. The smoke soon consumed the whole aircraft from the cockpit to the tail. This much smoke should have alerted anyone, anywhere, to call the fire department. The smell of the burning sulphur was in the air; it irritated my eyes and the pungent fumes burned my nostrils. Yet, over the noise of my coughing, I heard the pilot report to the tower that number one engine had a normal start.

The roar of the exhaust on engine number two was almost simultaneous with my clearance. The pilot's impatience perturbed me. I looked behind me to make sure the fifty gallon fire bottle was in easy reach. Suddenly, the bellowing smoke turned into roaring blue flames that reached from the belly of the aircraft to the ground below it. It was probably a hundred times larger than a welder's torch with the crackling electrostatic sound proportional to its size accompanying it. The sound alone had the same effect on me as fingernails being scratched on a chalkboard. I noticed the chalky white patch the torch was making as it seared the concrete. As I looked at the ground, pieces of metal were suddenly scattered around where the torch had just exhausted itself. I felt shock waves ripple through the ground past my boots, and another set of waves rushed past my face. My eyes focused on the fuel flowing from the open bowels of the aircraft. I stood frozen in my stance, and I was confused; why didn't I hear the explosion?

The jet fuel flowing from a ruptured line ignited when it contacted a piece of half-molten metal. I regained my composure in an instant and raced for the fire bottle and extended the hose. I ran underneath the aircraft to fight the spreading fire as I swore a long string of profanities under my breath — I hated this job.

My first aim was upwards into the engine bay; however, the nozzle was faulty, and a small leak in it shot backwards into my eyes. I screamed. The chemical agent, which has the same effect on skin as sulfuric acid, was eating my eyes. My panic-stricken impulse was to turn and run. With the second step, I caught a jagged edge of the airplane skin with my scalp. Every muscle in my body flexed as hard as possible trying to stop the pain, but the scorching shock of pain reached deep through to my groin. I was completely without sight and direction; I knelt and supported myself on a tube-shaped rail. I heard the pilot's boots land on the concrete then race away from the aircraft. As the footsteps faded away, I realized how alone I was. A chill covered my body when a breeze touched my sweat-soaked shirt. I could hear no one near by; my immediate impression was that no one even knew what was happening here. I felt afraid and abandoned. Determined to live, I committed all my energy to fight. I could hear the fire behind me as I searched with my hands for the fire bottle nozzle. I faced the smell and heat of the fire and sprayed in that direction until the bottle was exhausted. I hoped that my effort would contain the fire long enough for me to escape its grasp. I crawled my way to the nose gear tires where I felt two sets of arms grab and lead me away. The three of us ran as fast as a blindman could to a truck that screeched to a halt near us. I was thrown in the back, and the truck sped away to the hospital while my two companions, whose voices I still did not recognize, comforted me.

As we raced to the hospital, I could see, in my mind's eye, the events of the past few moments replayed in a continuous loop. The adrenalin that propelled my actions earlier was now expended. An emotional flood bottle-necked at my throat as I heard the explosion—again and again. I put my soiled hands to my face, and without shame, began to cry.

3

My transition from a conventional, middle-aged and overweight Mid-westerner to a slim, trim and laid-back Californian has been a slow and painful process. The first illusion to go was that I should have purpose and direction in my life and that my actions should be tailored to those principles. I realize now that I am but a small part of an ongoing cosmic event, that my karma should flow naturally, allowing me truly to participate in that great chain of Being called Life. Now, I am not all that sure what all of that means, but my guru, Swami Watchamacallit, assures me that this is the true path.

Having tended to my psyche, that middle-aged overweight body of mine cried for attention. My response was to "get into" jogging, which is a sort of ritualized suicide complete with uniform, dogma, and no end of human sacrifice. With a bodyweight of 240 pounds and size 13 shoes, I kick up quite a dust cloud going around the track. Unfortunately, I am not yet fast enough to outrun that cloud, so my mile and a half is done under sand-storm conditions. Still, all that abrasive dust gives me a rosy complexion and serves as an incentive to run faster.

My attempts at coming to know the real me have not stood in the way of efforts to achieve the "California look." Accordingly, I invested in several tank-tops and tight, pre-faded, fifty-dollar jeans. My undoing was the attempt to match all that tight clothing with a pair of Famolare shoes. It has been some time since I have been to sea, so in trying to walk with a wavy soled shoe I lost my balance and fell over. My new, tight clothes not only prevented me from sitting up, but constricted the blood flow enough to cause periodic black-outs. I laid there at rigid attention, until a kindly street-sweeper came by and levered me up with his broom. The clothes and shoes are now in the closet until I get my karma together.

This transition period has not been a complete disaster. I have gone from Schlitz to Chablis, from Lawrence Welk to Dave Brubeck and, finally, from Lucky Strikes to Juicy Fruit. I have not given up on my dream. One day will find me in my Famolare shoes, a glass of Chablis in the left hand and a stick of burning incense in the right, gazing off into a beautiful, California, smog-red sunset.

EXERCISE 3.9

In the three longer narrative/descriptive examples on pages 72-75, which are pri-marily narration and which are primarily description?

EXERCISE 3.10

Which of the three examples identified in Exercise 3.9 use first person?

Now that you have studied examples that combine narrative and descriptive writing, think of some incidents in your own life that would make interesting reading. You might have had some experiences that were exciting or horrifying. Perhaps you have participated in some remarkable adventures. Select one of these experiences, an adventure, an accident, or a catastrophe; choose one that you feel has had an effect upon your life. Write a combined narrative and descriptive composition of 500-750 words on that event. (Remember what you learned in Chapters One and Two. Spelling, sentence variety, and word usage count.)

EXERCISE 3.12

Before you submit your narrative/descriptive composition, make certain that you can answer "yes" to each of the questions on the narrative/descriptive paragraph checklist that follows.

Narrative/Descriptive Paragraph Checklist

1. Will readers be able to recognize easily the purpose of your narrative?

2. Is your narrative paragraph limited to one main idea?

3. Is your narrative in chronological order?

4. Does your narrative/descriptive paragraph consistently stay in either first or third person?

5. Does your descriptive paragraph appeal to the senses (sight, touch, sound, smell, and taste)?

6. Does your narrative/descriptive paragraph tell a story as well as appeal to the senses?

7. Are each of your sentences complete?

8. Did you use a variety of sentence types (simple, compound and complex)?

9. Have you proofread for errors in punctuation and mechanics?

CHAPTER

4

Body Paragraph Structure

The body paragraphs of your essay will be located between the introductory paragraph and the concluding paragraph. (See the diagram on the next page.) In a 500-700 word essay you will probably need at least three and perhaps as many as five or six body paragraphs. There is no set number required. Write as many as you need to develop the point you are trying to make. In this chapter you will practice writing body paragraphs one part at a time. By concentrating on single paragraphs now, you will find it easier to write a whole essay later (see Chapter Eight).

The body paragraphs of your essay will show readers that you have a good understanding of your subject. Good body paragraphs explain and support your ideas. They show that you have facts and figures to support your argument; they also show that you know how to organize your discussion. After reading your body paragraphs, readers will be convinced that your paper makes sense.

People are persuaded by good explanations; that is primarily what well-written body paragraphs contain. Consequently, information—a great deal of it—must be communicated by you to your readers. If you do a good job of writing, readers will not have to ponder the meaning of generalized statements you have made. You will follow general statements with as many sentences as are needed to make the generalizations clear. And readers will not have to think of their own examples or facts and figures; you will provide all that they need.

Writing good paragraphs is hard work. It is not always easy to think of what to say. There will be times when your thoughts will flow onto the paper almost like magic. But those moments will be relatively rare. It is more usual for the writing process to take place much more slowly. You should remember that nothing is wrong when you have had to revise a body paragraph three or four times and it still does not seem right. Even professional writers revise again and again. Planning, gathering information, organizing, writing, evaluating, rewrit-

DIAGRAM OF A TYPICAL 500-WORD COMPOSITION (Chapter Eight)

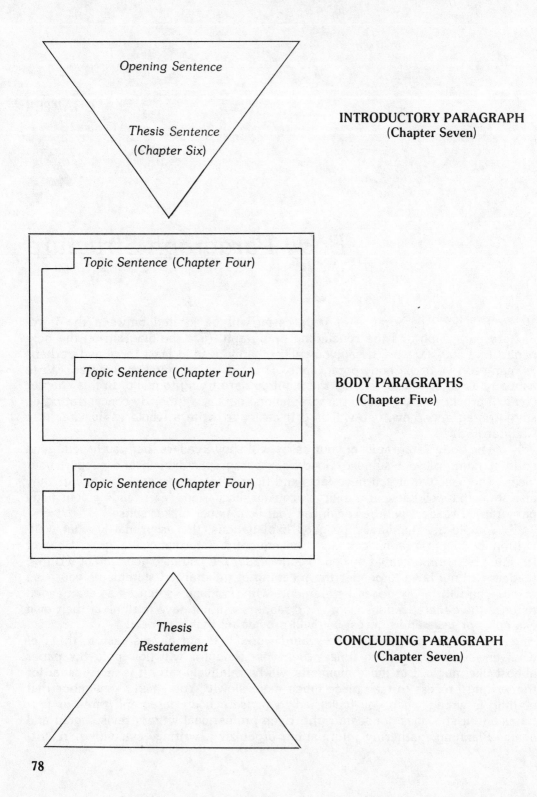

Opening Sentence

Thesis Sentence
(Chapter Six)

INTRODUCTORY PARAGRAPH
(Chapter Seven)

Topic Sentence (Chapter Four)

Topic Sentence (Chapter Four)

BODY PARAGRAPHS
(Chapter Five)

Topic Sentence (Chapter Four)

Thesis
Restatement

CONCLUDING PARAGRAPH
(Chapter Seven)

ing, editing, proofreading, correcting—good writing takes time. You can do it, though. When your thoughts begin to come together in a well-informed and interesting discussion, it will all seem worthwhile.

The basic guidelines for writing body paragraphs are quite simple. The advice can be summarized in a very short list. Memorize the advice because you will be using it for the rest of your life.

1) Write a topic sentence that announces the main idea of the paragraph.

2) Explain yourself in sufficient detail.

3) Include more than enough examples, facts, and figures.

4) Do not wander from the topic, and make certain each sentence leads smoothly into the next.

5) Keep rewriting until the paragraph is acceptable.

STUDY QUIZ

1. Where are the body paragraphs located?

2. Will you be writing a complete essay in this chapter?

3. Why do you write body paragraphs?

4. What persuades good readers?

5. Why is good writing hard work?

6. What are the guidelines for writing good body paragraphs?

LESSON ONE—Begin With a Topic Sentence

Begin each body paragraph with a **topic sentence**. Your readers should be able to read the first sentence and know where the paragraph is heading. Develop the habit of starting every body paragraph with a topic sentence.

This simple advice is not just for beginning writers. Most experienced writers employ this basic writing principle. They use the technique in research papers, lab reports, essay exams, speeches, business letters, Ph.D. dissertations, legal documents, corporation proposals, government position papers, and books—in fact, in almost everything they write.

The Topic Sentence Tells the Main Point of the Paragraph

Any reader should be able to answer the following question after reading one of your body paragraphs:

What is the main point of that paragraph?

Do not take chances. Make it practically impossible for your readers to misunderstand. You can expect readers to forget some of the details of the paragraph. After all, how often do you remember everything you read? But it is the writer's responsibility not to allow anyone to miss the main point. The best place to communicate the main point first is in the topic sentence.

Examples

This subtle form of discrimination must be stopped.

Alexander Hamilton and Thomas Jefferson were two of the most influential figures in the formation of the government under its new constitution.

Checking a crankshaft for cracks by the wet magnaflux method is a simple procedure.

Opponents of the space program use the old argument that money would be better spent in research and development of new food sources right here on earth.

Every Topic Sentence Should Be Limited

Do not try to cover too much in any one paragraph. If your topic sentence is too broad, the whole paragraph will be taken up with very general statements. As a result, there will not be room for interesting details. It is better to cover a small portion of your essay topic. You can set strict limits on a paragraph by carefully wording its topic sentence. With the limits set, you will have a chance to conduct the kind of in-depth discussion necessary for a top-quality paper.

The following examples of topic sentences were taken from students' essays. The student who wrote each sentence was told to revise the topic sentence because it was too broad. In each case, the rejected topic sentence would have required at least two or three pages of good explanations and supporting examples.

TOO BROAD

Science is an area where wonders will never cease.

The environment that we live in is damaged more and more because of air pollution, water contamination, and the never-ending building of houses.

Receiving a good education is very important for the individual, the employer, and the nation.

Music plays a big role in movies, people's attitudes, and the teenage drug scene.

If one of your topic sentences turns out to be too broad, do not hesitate to narrow it. Almost all writers encounter this problem, at least in the early stages of their writing. Often, a teacher, editor, or other observant reader can help point out where a writer has attempted to cover too much in the topic sentence.

Look back at the second example of a topic sentence that was "too broad." The student's writing teacher requested that the topic be limited. A second version was presented to the teacher, but it was still too general:

STILL TOO BROAD

The Sacramento environment is being hurt by air pollution.

This topic sentence was still so comprehensive that it would have taken an entire paper to develop it. Working together, the student and teacher wrote down four possible topic sentences that were further derived from the topic sentence above:

FOUR POSSIBILITIES

As the population of Sacramento has grown, the smog has increased.

For many years Sacramento-area farmers have burned their rice fields to destroy the straw after harvest, but now the urban residents want them to stop.

As new industries locate in the Sacramento Valley, they add to the air pollution.

By far the biggest cause of increased air pollution is automobile, truck, and bus traffic.

The student preferred the first topic sentence but decided to narrow it even more by making it more specific. This time the student wrote about "haze, smoke, and exhaust fumes" and the rapid population growth that "began in the early 1960's." The topic sentence and body paragraph developed from it follow. The topic sentence is italicized.

THE FINAL PARAGRAPH

Haze, smoke, and exhaust fumes have become more noticeable in the Sacramento air each year since the population boom began in the early 1960's. Long-time residents report that they used to see the snow-capped peaks of the Sierra Nevada and the dark outlines of the Coastal Range on sunny days. Now the mountains are only visible ten or twelve days a year when a strong north wind is blowing. Driving on Interstate 5, one can typically see a light brown haze dulling the downtown skyline. Sunny, cloudless days are normal from June until the end of October. Yet the skies are rarely blue as one would expect. Instead they are often a grayish, leaden color. During the fall and winter months, the cold and frequently foggy air traps smoke from the burning rice fields and residential fireplaces along with exhaust fumes from traffic and holds the polluted mass close to the ground. Each year the smog grows worse.

With the narrowed topic sentence the student was able to develop the paragraph successfully. Many specific details are included that the student would have had to leave out if one of the broader topic sentences had been used. When the topic sentence of the body paragraph is too general, the rest of the paragraph often ends up being too general as well.

Adjusting for Focus—Stating the Controlling Idea

A good topic sentence gives a body paragraph **focus**. You can achieve that focus by stating in your topic sentence precisely which part of the paper's subject you intend to write about. As you focus on a specific aspect of the subject, you are limiting what you can write about in the paragraph. In the last section you learned how to *narrow* the topic sentence. In this section your concern is how to *express* the limits you have decided upon. The words in the topic sentence that reveal the focus of the paragraph state the **controlling idea** of the paragraph. In the last section, for example, the topic sentence of the sample paragraph was changed to make the limits clear:

> (first version)   As the population has grown, the smog has increased.

> (final version)   Haze, smoke, and exhaust fumes have become more noticeable in the Sacramento air each year since the population boom began in the early 1960's.

With a clear statement of the controlling idea, both you and your readers know what is being emphasized in the paragraph. You could, of course, keep the content of your paragraph limited without specifically stating the controlling idea. Then the reader would discover the limits of the paragraph by reading it. But why make the readers' job more difficult than it need be? The writer's rule in this case is to help the reader whenever possible.

By reading your topic sentence with the *controlling idea* clearly stated, readers will immediately see the focus of the entire paragraph. Then the whole paragraph—all of the support sentences—will help the readers gain a deeper understanding of that controlling idea. As they absorb the details of the paragraph, they can turn back to the topic sentence for an instant reminder of what the controlling idea is. That is why it is better to make the controlling idea stand out clearly.

Examples

(vague)   Harold and Lugenia had *an experience* in Venice that they will never forget.

> In the example above the controlling idea (italicized) is not clearly stated. Harold and Lugenia probably had a number of experiences in Venice that they will never forget.

(clear)   Harold and Lugenia had *a frightening experience* in Venice that they will never forget.

> The controlling idea is clearer in the revised topic sentence. The couple probably had just one experience in Venice that was so frightening that they will never forget it.

(vague)   People use hospitals more than they need to.

(clear)   People are using emergency rooms at hospitals for treatments that could just as well be given by their family physicians.

> While the first example above relates the general idea about excessive use of hospital facilities, the second version is clearer because the controlling idea is much more limited. The focus of the paragraph will be on excessive emergency room use—the limits of the paragraph are made quite clear.

Specific detail is what makes the difference between mediocre writing and distinguished writing. Most beginning writers do not know this simple secret, but if you keep it in mind, training yourself to state an effective controlling idea should be easy. Do not generalize about the need to cut government costs. Write about the extra costs that occur when the Air Force is forced to design an all-purpose fighter instead of air-to-air combat planes and bomber interceptors. Do not write vaguely about the increasing problem of agricultural pests. Write instead about the catastrophe that could result if the Mediterranean Fruit Fly becomes established in California or about the multi-million dollar damage caused by nematodes.

Pay Attention to the Complete Subject and Complete Predicate

The controlling idea of the topic sentence can be made clearer by reworking the complete subject, the complete predicate, or both.

Examples

(subject general)   Computers / will revolutionize the household.

(subject expanded)   Incredibly compact multi-purpose computers / will revolutionize the household.

(predicate general)   Lake O'Brien / was dying.

(predicate expanded)   Lake O'Brien / was dying because of the chemical dumping by the plants at the mouth of the Tempest River.

83

Simple, Compound, or Complex Sentence?

As a careful writer, you should also think about the type of sentence that will work best for a particular topic sentence. A *simple sentence* may work fine, especially if the complete predicate has been expanded by adding phrases.

Example

SIMPLE SENTENCE

Lake O'Brien / was dying (because of the chemical dumping) (by the plants) (at the mouth) (of the Tempest River).

When you want to coordinate ideas in your topic sentence, use a *compound sentence*.

Example

COMPOUND SENTENCES

The technology for the revolutionary light rail system is available, *but* the Corridor Project would be too expensive.

In *Roots*, Haley points out, as many others have done, that slavery also existed in Africa, *but* Haley goes one step further and shows how totally different it was from American slavery.

You may need a complex sentence to state your topic sentence exactly. Remember that ideas are subordinated in dependent clauses.

Example

COMPLEX SENTENCE

Although the technology for the revolutionary light rail system is available, the Corridor Project would be too expensive.

STUDY QUIZ

1. With what kind of sentence—transitional, topic, thesis, or concluding—do most experienced writers begin a body paragraph?

2. Where is the best place first to tell the reader the main point of the paragraph?

3. What does it mean to say that every topic sentence should be limited?

4. How do you adjust the focus of a body paragraph?

5. How can you make the controlling idea of a topic sentence clearer by paying attention to the subject or the predicate?

6. How do you decide whether to use a simple, compound, or complex sentence?

On scratch paper write three topic sentences. Choose your own topics. Evaluate them using the following questions, and revise them as many times as is necessary. *Write only topic sentences: do not write whole paragraphs.* Neatly copy the final versions on notebook paper.

EVALUATION QUESTIONS

1. Does each topic sentence tell the main point of the body paragraph?

2. Is the topic sentence, as a whole, narrowed enough for a single body paragraph?

3. Is the complete subject specific enough?

4. Is the controlling idea accurately stated in the complete predicate?

5. Is the type of sentence—simple, compound, or complex—appropriate?

6. Is the topic sentence highly readable so readers can quickly review it to remember what the paragraph is all about?

LESSON TWO—Developing Body Paragraphs

Once you have stated your topic sentence at the beginning of a body paragraph, you must add sentences that develop the controlling idea of the topic sentence. The discussion begins in the topic sentence and continues in the sentences that follow it. The discussion ends with a concluding sentence that fits smoothly with the first sentence of the next paragraph. Whether the discussion is an explanation or an argument, it must be complete enough for every reader to understand what you are saying.

Primary and Secondary Support Sentences

PRIMARY SUPPORT SENTENCES

A **primary support sentence** is any sentence in a body paragraph that ties back directly to the topic sentence. A body paragraph is simply a sequence of sentences. Some of the sentences in the sequence are more important than others because they carry the main line of reasoning. These are the primary support sentences. After the topic sentence they are first or highest in rank of importance. The other, less important sentences are called *secondary support sentences*.

As you plan your paragraphs, keep in mind the following schematic. It shows a hypothetical sequence of primary and secondary support sentences. There could be any number of primary and secondary sentences, but the diagram shows how, in general, the sentences relate in the sequence.

TOPIC SENTENCE (Controlling Idea)

    I. Primary Support Sentence

        A. Secondary Support Sentence

        B. Secondary Support Sentence

    II. Primary Support Sentence

        A. Secondary Support Sentence

        B. Secondary Support Sentence

    III. Primary Support Sentence

        A. Secondary Support Sentence

        B. Secondary Support Sentence

    Concluding Sentence

A body paragraph may have just one primary support sentence or several, depending on how many are needed in a particular paragraph. The topic sentence plus the primary support sentences form the framework of the paragraph. These sentences outline the paragraph. By reading the topic and primary sentences of your body paragraphs, readers will understand the controlling idea of each paragraph and the sub-points connected with that idea.

At first glance the three examples that you are about to read look like full paragraphs, but they are not. The paragraphs are underdeveloped. They have not yet had secondary support sentences added to them. Notice, however, that the basic point of each paragraph is clear.

Examples

1

TS Although the whale has been slaughtered for a number of reasons, the major commercial interest has been its oil. PS A single whale can yield up to twenty tons of it. PS All whale oil is not alike. PS It is the "oil" of the sperm whale that is the most sought after.

2

TS Marvel comics are interesting because the characters and their situations change. PS New characters are added. PS Also, Marvel characters appear in each others' books as often as they do in their own. PS Bad guys and gals become good guys and gals, and vice versa. PS Furthermore, in Marvel comics the characters mature and age as time passes. PS Even death, the ultimate character change, is not uncommon in Marvel comics. PS What makes Marvel characters most realistic, though, are the inconsistencies in their make-ups and unexpected defeats they suffer.

3

TS Three hundred years ago in London during the plague, the city was not a very sanitary place to live. PS Londoners, both rich and poor, did not bathe very often. PS The city had no underground sewer system. PS Heaps of solid refuse were left in the open.

SECONDARY SUPPORT SENTENCES

Sentences added to clarify the meaning of a primary support sentence are called **secondary support sentences.** The main purpose of these sentences is to carry on the discussion begun in the primary support sentence. It is these secondary support sentences that you will probably have to train yourself to include. In these sentences you will furnish your readers with additional explanations, reasoning, facts, and statistics. In these sentences you will also—and this is most important—give your readers specific examples. Without these secondary support sentences a body paragraph is underdeveloped.

Ordinarily you will follow each primary support sentence with at least one or two secondary support sentences. Yet not every primary support sentence needs them. As is the case with primary support sentences, there is no set number required. Add secondary support sentences as they are needed to make your point. Do not add so many that the paragraphs become tedious.

Now read the same skeleton paragraphs you read a short while ago. They have been expanded by adding secondary support sentences. In other words, they have been "*developed.*"

1

TS Although the whale has been slaughtered for a number of reasons, the major commercial interest has been its oil. **PS** A single whale can yield up to twenty tons of it. **SS** *Fifty to eighty percent of the blubber, ten to seventy percent of the weight of the bones, and two to eight percent of the meat of the whale is oil.* **PS** All whale oil is not alike. **SS** *The oil of the baleen whale, for instance, can be found in all plants and animals and is identical to the fats found in the human body.* **SS** *But the oil of toothed whales, such as sperm whales and dolphins, is not an oil at all; it is a wax.* **PS** It is the "oil" of the sperm whale that is the most sought after. **SS** *It is far superior to baleen oil for making wax candles—the finest available.* **SS** *Since the nineteen thirties sperm whale oil has been used in pressing steel, dressing leather, sizing textiles, and making fine soap.* **SS** *When combined with sulphur, this oil produces an unequaled lubricant for extremely high-pressure applications.* **SS** *Until recently, sperm whale oil was a common ingredient in automatic transmission fluid.* **SS** *Sperm oil is considered so crucial to the national defense that a large stockpile is maintained for emergencies.*

2

TS Marvel comics are interesting because the characters and their situations change. **PS** New characters are added. **SS** *Saint Francis, for example, became a Marvel superhero in 1980.* **PS** Also, Marvel characters appear in each others' books as often as they do in their own. **SS** *For instance, in one issue The Angel and The Iceman appear with The Incredible Hulk, and in another Tigra becomes an ally of Spider-Man.* **PS** Bad guys and gals become good guys and gals, and vice versa. **SS** *Tigra, under the evil Kraven's command, tries to kill Spider-Man.* **SS** *But then Spider-Man saves her from death, and, released from Kraven's power, she becomes good and saves Spider-Man from being trampled by a stampeding herd of Kraven's trained jungle animals.* **PS** Furthermore, in Marvel comics the characters mature and age as time passes. **SS** *Spider-Man and The Human Torch both graduate from high school and attend college.* **SS** *Mr. Fantastic and The Invisible Girl are married and even have a baby.* **PS** Even death, the ultimate character change, is not uncommon in Marvel comics. **SS** *The Human Torch's father dies, and so does Sergeant Fury's girlfriend.*

3

TS Three hundred years ago in London during the plague, the city was not a very sanitary place to live. **PS** Londoners, both rich and poor, bathed infrequently. **SS** *Most families bought a limited amount of water daily from waterbearers, and there were no private baths.* **SS** *Samuel Pepys wrote in his secret diary that his wife actually dared to wash herself all over at a public hot-house and that a few days later he bathed also, an unusual event.* **PS** The city had no underground sewer system. **SS** *Instead of sewers, kennels (open gutters) were used for waste liquids from chamber pots and wash-up water.* **SS** *The evil-smelling liquid trickled along until it reached the River Thames.* **PS** Heaps of solid refuse were left in the open. **SS** *Solid human waste, garbage, and other refuse was heaped in the courtyard or dumped in the street to be carried away by the parish "raker."* **SS** *On* *irregular visits the raker collected the waste in his cart and took it to one of the laystalls (refuse dumps and dung heaps) at the outskirts of London near the riverbank.*

SUPPORT CLUSTERS

In the sample paragraphs above, primary and secondary support sentences work together in **support clusters**. A support cluster consists of a primary support sentence and any secondary support sentences that immediately follow it. Each cluster—usually two, three, or more sentences—helps readers comprehend the full meaning of the topic sentence.

To determine how many clusters there are in a body paragraph, simply count the primary support sentences. If, for example, a paragraph contains four primary support sentences, there are four clusters. When a primary support sentence has no secondary sentences following it, count the primary sentence as one cluster.

Think in terms of support clusters when you write or analyze a body paragraph. Seeing clusters rather than isolated sentences will remind you that it normally takes several sentences to develop a primary support idea.

Example

> **TS** During World War II the city of Coventry, in England, was devastated by a German bombing raid. **PS** What is not generally known is that the British high command knew long before the raids occurred that the Germans were planning to bomb the city. **SS** The British had cracked the German communications code weeks earlier. **PS** If, however, the British had mounted a defense of Coventry, the Germans would have realized their code was broken. **SS** The Germans would have then changed the code and, thus, would have prevented the Allies from obtaining intelligence vital to the success of the Normandy invasion.

The above example contains two support clusters. Although all four sentences join together to form a discussion, you can see that each secondary support sentence belongs with its primary support sentence. Since there are two primary sentences, there are two clusters.

STUDY QUIZ

1. What is a primary support sentence?

2. How many primary support sentences are needed in a body paragraph?

3. The topic sentence plus the primary support sentences form the _____ of the body paragraph.

4. What are secondary support sentences?

5. What is the main purpose of these sentences?

6. List five kinds of support that secondary support sentences give the reader. Which type is the most important?

7. How many secondary support sentences are needed in a body paragraph?

8. How do you "develop" a paragraph? What is wrong with a paragraph that is "underdeveloped"?

9. What is a support cluster?

10. How can you determine how many clusters are in a body paragraph? If no secondary support sentences accompany a primary support sentence, should the lone primary sentence be counted as a cluster?

EXERCISE 4.2

Count the support clusters in the example paragraphs on page 88.

1. How many clusters does paragraph 1 have?

2. How many clusters does paragraph 2 have?

3. How many clusters does paragraph 3 have?

EXERCISE 4.3

For the following paragraphs write **TS** for each topic sentence, **PS** for each primary support sentence, and **SS** for each secondary support sentence.

1

(1) No matter where Americans go, they are confronted with drugs. (2) Drug companies across the country advertise their products in magazines, on television, and on billboards. (3) Anacin is the aspirin "more doctors recommend"; Contact releases "hundreds of tiny time capsules"; "Use Sominex when you have trouble going to sleep." (4) Moreover, local pharmacies and supermarkets, regularly visited by every member of the family, advertise drugs in sale ads and in store displays. (5) Signs promise that Cope will help people through a tension-filled day. (6) Other display signs in the stores insist that the host or hostess who serves Smirnoff vodka will become the happiest, most popular person on the block. (7) If, however, people escape being influenced by the advertisements, they almost certainly will not escape social pressure. (8) When surrounded by people who drink alcoholic beverages, smoke tobacco, and drink coffee and tea with enthusiasm, one finds it difficult not to go along with the crowd. (9) Then, finally but inescapedly, there is the subculture of illegal drugs. (10) Chic hosts and hostesses tolerate marijuana and may even serve cocaine with silver spoons. (11) Some sixth graders have been reported selling "pot" and pills at recess.

2

(1) Making ink for calligraphy in China was a fairly simple, but time-consuming process. (2) Everyday materials were used. (3) The standard materials were lamp-black and glue mixed with preservative and aromatics. (4) Pinewood or vegetable oils were used to form the subject called lampblack. (5) The technique was then quite easy to master. (6) First, the lampblack was burned to form a rich, black soot. (7) The soot was then bound with glue. (8) The raw ink was cooked again, again, and again to refine it. (9) It needed to be just the right consistency for use in writing. (10) Finally, the refined ink was hardened and pounded over and over to form a carbon cake. (11) This ink cake, when dissolved in water, formed the ink used in calligraphy. (12) The ink was mixed for use in the calligrapher's personal inkwell, which was often made of silver.

PREPARING TO WRITE

Plan a body paragraph on a topic of your choice. You will have to narrow your topic considerably because you are to imagine that the paragraph is just one of several in the body of an essay.

1. Make a list of possible topics. Think of general topics; you can narrow them later.

   Sample Topics

   One of your pet gripes

   The effect of television viewing on student learning

   Is a college degree necessary?

   What do you do on your job?

   A crucial local, state, or national problem

   Living together before marriage

   The causes and effects of divorce

   Violence in sports

   Your favorite automobile

   Fashion fads at school

   Groups and cliques at school

2. How can you narrow the topic you have chosen?

   Sample Narrowed Topic

   Groups and Cliques at School (broad topic)

   The cowboy table during lunch hour (narrowed topic)

3. After you have narrowed your topic, decide upon the *controlling idea* for the topic sentence. Then rough out a topic sentence. (You will fine-tune this sentence later.)

4. Next, make a list of some things you could say to develop the topic sentence. (The best of these will become primary support sentences.)

5. List examples, explanations, facts, figures, related personal experiences, and any other kinds of details that would make your primary support sentences clearer or your paragraph more interesting. (From this list you will draw material for your secondary support sentences.)

6. Outline your paragraph as you imagine it at this point. (You may want to change some of your outline once you begin writing the paragraph.)

WRITING

Write the first draft of your body paragraph. Write rapidly, or slowly and carefully, whichever method works best for you.

EDITING

1. After the paragraph is written, label the topic sentence **TS**, each primary support sentence **PS**, and each secondary support sentence **SS**.

2. Edit the sentences to make their meaning as clear as possible, and revise them until they flow smoothly.

3. Correct any errors in grammar, spelling, punctuation, or capitalization.

4. Recopy the paragraph neatly; then doublecheck for any errors in the final copy. If necessary, recopy the paragraph again.

Concluding Sentences

A body paragraph may need a **concluding sentence** that will bring the paragraph to a close. Not every paragraph needs one. In some paragraphs the last secondary support sentence serves as a concluding sentence.

Strictly speaking, the concluding sentence is neither a primary nor a secondary support sentence. The concluding sentence brings the entire paragraph into final perspective. The concluding sentence often summarizes the content of the paragraph, but it also may make a final generalization based upon what was said in the paragraph. Often, too, the concluding sentence serves a transitional purpose, preparing the reader for the next paragraph.

None of the sample paragraphs on page 88 have concluding sentences. Although the paragraphs read fairly well without them, they are improved when concluding sentences are added. Here are examples of concluding sentences that might be added:

Examples

CONCLUDING SENTENCES

1

Thus, the key to saving the whales is finding high quality, economical substitutes for their oil.

2

Marvel comics, therefore, are more realistic than DC comics where the characters and plotlines are static and predictable.

3

In this germ-ridden environment, which most Londoners took for granted, the plague-bearing rats grew fat and multiplied.

STUDY QUIZ

   1. What is the function of the concluding sentence?

   2. Does every body paragraph need a concluding sentence? Is it possible that a body paragraph not needing a concluding sentence can be improved by the addition of one? Explain your answers.

   3. Why is a concluding sentence neither a primary nor a secondary support sentence? Explain your answer.

EXERCISE 4.5
_____

   Write a concluding sentence for the body paragraph that follows.

   Studies have shown that variation in body temperature has great bearing on mood, energy, and intellectual capabilities. Performance is usually best when temperature is high. Body temperature is lowest during the very early morning hours and gradually increases to normal, at which time a person awakens on his or her own. Studies of this phenomenon have discovered two distinct groups of people, referred to as "larks" and "owls." The larks' temperatures rise quickly in the morning, and they wake alert and ready for the day. The owls' temperatures rise more slowly in the morning, and they are slower starting the day's activities; however, they generally remain up later at night. They may be better off finding shift work in the evening, or at least scheduling their more important tasks for late in the afternoon. (Concluding sentence missing)

EXERCISE 4.6
_____

   Examine the body paragraph you wrote for Exercise 4.4. Does it have a concluding sentence? Does it need one? If the paragraph would be improved by adding a concluding sentence, write two or three that would work; then choose the best of the three. Copy the best version neatly, making any revisions or corrections that would improve its readability even more.

Alternate Modes of Paragraph Development

   At times you may find it difficult to label the sentences in a body paragraph. The paragraph may not seem to begin with a topic sentence, or the distinction between primary and secondary support sentences may not be clear. The problem can occur in a paragraph written by you or in one written by someone else. Each time you read the paragraph you may change your mind about how to label the sentences, yet the whole paragraph seems to hold together. It unfolds as an organized, detailed discussion that flows smoothly from beginning to end.

If you normally do a satisfactory job labeling sentences but suddenly cannot figure out a paragraph's layout, consider the possibility that you have encountered an **alternate mode of paragraph development**. In other words, your reading skills may not be at fault, and the paragraph may be well written. It is just that whoever wrote it, you or another author, did not build it in clusters of support sentences, and maybe not even with a topic sentence at the beginning. You are apt to write such paragraphs when you are "turned on" by your writing and roughing out your paragraphs so rapidly, one after another, that you do not have time to plan them carefully. You may want to write down your thoughts before you lose them. You must not think that the primary-secondary support method advocated in this book is the only correct way to build body paragraphs. You should be flexible and receptive to other composition techniques.

The three sample paragraphs that follow demonstrate alternate modes of development. In the first example *the topic sentence has been placed at the end of the body paragraph.* Although you will not use this technique very often, you should know that by placing the topic sentence at the end, a writer can lead readers to the main idea rather than confronting them with it first.

Example

TOPIC SENTENCE AT END

PS In January, 1968, the world's mightiest navy ignored the desperate pleas for assistance from a ship about to be captured. **SS** Unknown to the commander of this ship, highly classified documents were aboard this vessel, a vessel supposedly conducting oceanic research. **PS** For the next several months, two nations bombarded each other with accusations and diatribes while eighty-two men were brutalized behind prison walls, subjected to cruel and inhuman punishment, and treated like animals. **SS** Their release was only secured when the more powerful of the two countries bowed to the demands of the lesser and signed an apology nearly a year later. **PS** The subsequent court-martial of the commander of the ship was conducted for the violation of the famed "Military Code of Conduct." **SS** One of the prosecution's arguments was that the commander, who was responsible for saving the lives of his crew, should not have surrendered his ship. **SS** In the course of the proceedings, the defense revealed that vital information regarding the ship's mission was passed from bureau to bureau in the Department of the Navy and never reached those responsible. **SS** By the end of the trial, however, the Navy succeeded in "passing the buck" from the highest echelons down to one man. **TS** *The "Pueblo Incident" will go down in history as yet another outrageous example of the cold insensibility of the government and the ranking military regime for the ordinary fighting personnel.*

In the second sample there are no secondary support sentences. The paragraph is long enough, but the writer chose not to include the secondary sentences. It was left "underdeveloped" because all that was needed was a brief *step-by-step* explanation of the process used by the Chinese to make paper. This is just one body paragraph in an essay on the history of Chinese calligraphy; therefore, the concise description of the paper-making process is sufficient.

Example

NO SECONDARY SUPPORT SENTENCES

TS Making paper in ancient China was even more complicated than making ink. **PS** In papermaking the basic materials used were hemp, bamboo, and mulberry bark, all sized with alum. **PS** The first step was to soak the material thoroughly. **PS** The material was then pounded into a pulpy mass. **PS** It was then cooked, pounded again, and bleached. **PS** A sieve-like bamboo frame was then dipped into the newly made liquid pulp, which formed a thin mat on the frame's surface. **PS** These mats were pressed and stuck like billboards on heated walls where they dried. **CS** With these simple materials and a great deal of labor, the ancient Chinese formed paper.

The third sample paragraph summarizes in *chronological order* the sequence of events that took place in London when a house with plague victims was quarantined. The distinction between primary and secondary support sentences is not clear, but the paragraph is well written because in just eleven sentences readers are given a clear understanding of what happened. (Notice that each time you read the paragraph you change your mind about what should be labeled primary or secondary.)

Example

DISTINCTION BETWEEN PRIMARY AND SECONDARY NOT CLEAR

TS When plague came to a London house in 1665, it was sealed by the law. A watchman guarded the house to see that no one escaped. Both the sick and the well of the household were forced to stay inside during the forty days of quarantine. For the duration of that period, food and other necessities were delivered. A red cross was painted on the door of the household with the plague. A sign saying "Lord have mercy on us" was painted or nailed on the door of each house doomed with the malady. The quarantine was extended as members developed the disease. If no one else showed symptoms during the forty days, a white cross replaced the red one. The white cross remained for twenty days. Meanwhile, the home was thoroughly cleaned, filled with fumes of burning sulphur, and coated with lime before it was declared free of infection.

EXERCISE 4.7

PREPARING TO WRITE

1. The assignment is to write a body paragraph in which you use one of the alternate modes of paragraph development:

   1) Topic sentence at end

   2) Step by step, no secondary support sentences

   3) Chronological, difficult to tell which sentences are primary and which are secondary.

2. Look back at the previous sample paragraphs. Reread them until you can see how they are organized and how each differs from the other two.

3. Which type do you want to try? Which type would be the easiest to write? Which type would be the most interesting to write? Make your decision.

4. Choose an appropriate topic for your paragraph. The topic should be suited to the organization you want to demonstrate, and the topic should be narrowed sufficiently.

>   *Samples* (Must be narrowed further)
>
>>   A great injustice that people should know about (*Topic sentence at end*)
>>
>>   The procedure for making something, for instance, homemade pizza, a ceramic pot, a patio deck (*Step by step*)
>>
>>   The unfolding of events in a natural or human-made disaster, for example, a collision with a meteorite or the meltdown of a nuclear power plant (*Chronological*)

5. Formulate a topic sentence, an outline, and a list of details you could include.

WRITING

Write the paragraph—several times if necessary—until it clearly demonstrates one of the alternate modes of body paragraph development.

EDITING

Revise and proofread your paragraph; write a neat, presentable final copy.

PARAGRAPH CHECKLIST

1. Skip two lines after the end of your paragraph, and write answers to the following questions:

>   1) Which of the alternate modes have you used?
>
>   2) Can you label the sentences, TS, PS, and SS? If there are no secondary support sentences, would the paragraph be improved if you added them, or would it be too long?

2. Is the paragraph interesting, smoothly written, free of writing errors, and neat?

LESSON THREE—Write Full Paragraphs

A good body paragraph is a full paragraph. It is a thorough discussion very much like a miniature essay. You will fill each body paragraph two different ways. First, you will make it long enough by writing enough primary and secondary support sentences. Second, you will pack these sentences with specific details.

Paragraph Length

How long should a body paragraph be? Any body paragraph that does not contain **at least five sentences** should be filled out with more secondary support sentences or be expanded by adding one or more additional support clusters. One-, two-, three-, and four-sentence paragraphs might be found in newspapers and magazines, but not in academic compositions. Journalists write short paragraphs in part because the narrow printed columns in newspapers and magazines make just a few sentences look like a long paragraph. But you will write in ink or type your essays; therefore, five-to-twelve-sentence paragraphs will look good and be very readable.

Occasionally in a long composition you can use a very short paragraph for a bridge between two major sections. But you will not need any short transitional paragraphs in the essays you will be completing for this book.

In general, long paragraphs are better than short ones, but paragraphs can be too long. A paragraph that runs more than one or two pages will be difficult to read. When body paragraphs are too long, readers lose their places and the lines of reasoning they were attempting to follow. The *indentation* at the beginning of a new paragraph provides a place to pause, rest, and perhaps to reflect upon what has been said. For most compositions, body paragraphs that contain **five to twelve sentences** are the most readable.

Example

FIVE SENTENCES

Among both opponents and proponents of the death penalty there are those who would like to see televised executions. Those opposed to the death penalty think that if supporters of capital punishment were allowed to see an execution, they would realize the inhumanity of the act. By seeing a person electrocuted, hanged, gassed, shot, or drugged to death, the advocates of the death penalty might be moved to think again about the morality of their position and move to have capital punishment abolished. Advocates of the death penalty, however, hope that a public execution every now and then would act as an added deterrent to crime, that is, boosting the fear of punishment for those prone to commit murder, kidnapping, and hijacking. By showing executions live on television, the potential felon might experience a more realistic fear of the consequences.

The body paragraph that follows lacks sufficient development. Expand and fill out the paragraph by adding primary and secondary support sentences. Add explanations and specific examples—facts and figures. (You may make up the facts and figures, but make them reasonable.) The revised version should be between five and twelve sentences long. Proofread your final version, making sure it is neat and free from errors.

Inflation causes serious problems for the family. Prices keep rising. The prices of new homes, for example, have risen sharply. Because money buys less, people are forced to spend more to maintain a status-quo standard of living instead of saving money for better things.

The paragraph below is too long. Edit it, selecting the sentences that you want to keep, so that it will be no longer than twelve sentences but not shorter than five sentences. Remember that you will need both primary and secondary support sentences. Feel free to change the wording of some of the sentences to make them fit together smoothly. (Breaking the one long paragraph into two logically divided paragraphs is acceptable, too.)

If the old saying that people are what they eat is true, the students who eat in Thompson Hall at this university are in bad shape. The cafeteria should be the cleanest place on campus because of its importance to the health of all the students who eat there, but instead it seems to be the dirtiest place for a student to eat. The cafeteria, along with the roaches and bugs, has a foul odor that seems to linger in the air. The smell of the food and the garbage does not produce an appetizing atmosphere in which to dine. Most of the odor is created because the cafeteria's disposal system is not up to par. The workers are very slow at emptying the trays and plates. That is one of the reasons the cafeteria runs out of glasses and silverware during breakfast, lunch, and dinner. Most of the time the eating utensils are unclean, whether washed or not. Food is left on trays and silverware after washing, and detergent is left inside the glasses. Sometimes the dishwasher is broken, and at other times there is no detergent. If there is anything worse than the dirty dishes, it has to be the food. The food in Thompson Hall is more terrible: it is ridiculous! There is no telling what might be served, from spoiled food to insects. Most of the food is cold—the food that is supposed to be hot, that is. The food that is supposed to be cold is warm. The milk is sour, and the bread is stale. The food is not cooked properly; either it is overdone and hard, or it is undercooked and tough. The menu is never properly balanced; some days they serve too much starch and fat, and they never provide enough protein food. To pay $230.50 for a meal book each semester and not be able to get good balanced meals is absurd. This problem needs to be investigated as soon as possible.

The Importance of Details

More than anything else, every body paragraph needs **pertinent details**. Readers expect detailed discussion, not a series of unsupported generalizations. You may know what you mean when you make a generalization, but you cannot be certain your readers will know what you are thinking unless you explain your ideas thoroughly.

Of course, easy-to-follow organization helps. Begin each body paragraph with a topic sentence, and support the topic sentence with a clearly organized pattern of primary and secondary support sentences (support clusters). To write detailed paragraphs, you should make a special effort to include enough secondary support sentences. To do this, use *explanations, examples, quotations, statistics, anecdotes*, and other kinds of specifics. In this way you can increase the chances that readers will understand—and believe—what you are trying to say.

Support Your Generalizations with Specifics

In the following illustrations of *secondary support* sentences, the topic sentences and primary support sentences have been stripped away so you can see more easily how effective secondary support sentences are written. Notice that even though six types of secondary support sentences are offered, they all have one thing in common: they give detailed, specific information about the topic.

Use Factual Explanations

Instead of sewers, kennels (open gutters) were used for waste liquids from chamber pots and wash-up water. The evil-smelling liquid trickled along until it reached the River Thames.

Rising college costs are causing problems. This year a fresh group of parents and students must grapple with grim economic realities as admission notices arrive. Savings accounts are smaller, more inflation is almost certain, and competition for loans and scholarships is increasing.

Use Examples

For example, fewer students major in liberal arts programs to learn how to work with people. But more students enroll in business and science programs to gain vocational and professional know-how.

Then in 1950 Sidney Poitier starred as a medical intern in *No Way Out*. In the film the intern was charged with professional malpractice by a psychopath played by Richard Widmark. Poitier averted a race riot, protected himself from an assassin, and cleared himself of the charges.

Use Statistics and Figures

Johnson notes, for instance, that one of every three students filing for admission now asks for financial aid, compared with one of every four last year.

Both the University of California and the State University system predict twelve percent cost increases this coming academic year. At a public four-year campus, the report estimates, tuition and fees will average $647, transportation $226, personal expenditures $508, room and board $1425, and books and supplies $194.

Use Quotations

Elrod stated, ''A family must save almost $2,500 a year for nine years for each child planning to attend college.''

Speaking of this cover-up, Keyhoe stated, ''I believe that this censorship is dangerous. The thousands of UFO reports by veteran observers prove beyond a question that the saucers are machines from outer space. The Air Force's insistence that it has no answer only heightens the possibility of hysteria.''

Use Anecdotes

When I attended the University of Michigan, costs were much lower. Tuition, for example, was only $125 per semester. Yet we were always short of money and welcomed the summer vacations when we could replenish our empty bank accounts.

Use Description and Narration

On that cool, crisp morning, the sky was high and free from clouds. The silence was broken by a faint but clear honking of geese. Looking to the north along the highway, I could see large waves of geese flying in V formations. When the black specks grew clear enough that I could distinguish the long slender necks and huge wing spans, we began calling them toward us. ''Keronk-Keronk,'' went the goose calls. Then the geese turned toward our massive spread of decoys. All that the geese could see were what seemed to be several dozen geese feeding in a field. As the formation grew closer and closer, our calls guided them and finally we no longer called. The geese set their wings and were gliding toward us like 747's about to land— eighty, sixty, forty, thirty yards from us. Then the silence was broken by the roaring of our guns. The geese screamed at the sounds of the blasting guns and hurtled skywards like rockets shooting for the sun. When the guns stopped and the geese had fled, all that was left to remember that morning by were four dead geese lying among our decoys.

Note that when you quote, you must use the exact wording of your source. Furthermore, quotation marks must be placed at the beginning and end of the quoted passage (see pages 207, 210-211).

WHERE TO FIND THE SPECIFICS YOU NEED

Where do you find these specific details? You can find the information you need in books, magazines, pamphlets, lecture notes, on television, in movies, interviews, and discussions. However, the best source of supporting information is your own experience. You know more than you may realize you do. You have read. You have listened to others. You have lived and worked and played. Through all this experience you have been gathering ideas, opinions, and facts that you can use in your paragraphs. If you take the time to think, you can probably come up with most of the specifics you need to develop your ideas without consulting other sources.

WARNING: Do not copy your sources word for word unless you place the quoted material in quotation marks (see *Plagiarism,* page 212).

For each generalization that follows, add a secondary support sentence that contains the type of specific details requested. (Feel free to write two or three sentences.) For this exercise, you may invent the facts, figures, quotations, and other kinds of details you are asked to use—but try to make them believable. *Copy the primary support sentence and then add the secondary support sentences.*

1. (Factual Explanation) **PS** Many students attend school part time because they have jobs.

2. (Examples) **PS** Most students like to dress casually.

3. (Statistics and figures) **PS** Due to the high cost of new homes, the majority of newly married couples will soon live in apartments and other types of multiple-housing units.

4. (Quotation) **PS** Aging industrial plants threaten the nation's ability to fight a war.

5. (Anecdote) **PS** People seem to like standing in lines.

6. (Narration and Description) **PS** No one was prepared for what was about to happen.

EXERCISE 4.11

In the following paragraph the secondary support sentences have been omitted. Complete each cluster by adding one or more secondary support sentences.

TS When asked why they had fallen behind schedule with their English work, the students gave three major reasons. **PS** The biggest reason, they admitted, was that they did not do enough homework. **PS** They also complained that it was very difficult to get their thoughts down on paper. **PS** Almost half of the students who were behind thought that it was their own fault for not finishing their work on time. **CS** The researchers were very surprised to find that only two students thought that the teacher should have "run a tighter ship," setting strict deadlines and lowering grades for late work.

BE REASONABLE AND HAVE SOMETHING TO SAY

Think through what you want to say in a sentence or cluster of sentences before you write it—or at least before you finish revising it. If your thinking is empty or muddled, your writing will be, too. Try to be logical, and try not to overgeneralize. Do not tell readers what they are likely to know already. Tell them what they need to know or what they have not yet realized about what they think they know!

Do not write—

There are nothing but police dramas on television every day. (*Overgeneralized*)

Instead write—

> Evening television is glutted with police dramas. (*More reasonable but still forceful*)

Do not write—

> Millions of Americans watch television. (*Your readers know this.*)

Write instead—

> A growing minority of converted television addicts refuse to watch television except to see very special programs. (*Your readers may not know this.*)

> *or perhaps*

> I have not watched a single television program for three weeks. (*Your readers, both those who watch television regularly and those who do not, will be interested in this statement and read on to find out why.*)

Just sit and think a bit, or read a little; a visit to the library will produce ideas and information. With only a small effort you can use your knowledge of everyday experiences in such a way that the content of your paragraphs will become interesting and worthwhile for your readers.

EXERCISE 4.12

The statements below are overgeneralized, unreasonable, or merely say what everyone already knows. Rewrite them so they will be more effective.

1. Welfare recipients are all a bunch of cheaters.

2. Television programs and movies are full of violence.

3. Millions of Americans drive automobiles.

4. Because of the women's liberation movement, every woman hates being a housewife.

5. Only foods with "natural" on the label are good for you.

LESSON FOUR—Smoothly Connecting Sentences Within the Paragraph

After you have added all of the primary and secondary support sentences that the body paragraph needs, go over it to make sure that the sentences connect smoothly. The line of reasoning should flow easily from sentence to sentence, with the sentences placed in the most effective order, and none of them off the subject. Use a variety of simple, compound, and complex sentences. Revise your paragraph several times if necessary to increase its readability. After working hard to organize your discussion, you want to make your delivery as smooth as possible.

Transitions

After your body paragraph is written, you may have to add **transitional words and phrases.** They help readers make the logical connection between one sentence and another. (See the list on pages 12-13.)

Examples

BEFORE REVISION

A college education is very expensive. College graduates earn much more during their lifetimes than do high school graduates without college degrees.

TRANSITIONS ADDED

Of course, a college education is very expensive. *But* college graduates earn much more during their lifetimes than do high school graduates without college degrees.

NO TRANSITIONS

During World War II the city of Coventry in England was devastated by a German bombing raid. The British high command knew that the Germans were going to bomb the city long before the raids occurred. The British had cracked the German communications code weeks earlier. If the British had mounted a defense of Coventry, the Germans would have then changed the code and would have prevented the Allies from obtaining intelligence vital to the success of the Normandy invasion.

TRANSITIONS ADDED

During World War II the city of Coventry in England was devastated by a German bombing raid. *There is good reason to believe, however, that* the British high command knew the Germans were going to bomb the city long before the raids occurred. The British had cracked the German communications code weeks earlier. *Surely*, if the British had mounted a defense of Coventry, the Germans would have then changed the code, and *thus* would have prevented the Allies from obtaining intelligence vital to the success of the Normandy invasion.

Smooth transition can be achieved by **repeating key words** from previous sentences.

Example

> The District Attorney and the defendant's lawyer arranged *a deal*. *This deal* depended upon *several conditions*. The *first condition* was that the kidnapping charges would be dropped.

Parallel construction in sentences, especially introductory phrases and clauses, can be used to make transitions clear. (See pages 237-240.)

Examples

> *Winston's first act of rebellion is to purchase* a diary. . . . *Winston's second act of rebellion is to engage* in an affair with Julia.

> To my grandparents "the old days" were the 1930's and the Great Depression. To me the old days were the late 1960's and early 1970's. They mourn the nation's "loss of moral fiber." I celebrate the gain of freedom.

Sentence Order

As you edit your paragraph to improve the transitions, pay some attention to **sentence order**. Look for sentences that do not really belong or ones that should be moved to a different place in the paragraph.

In the sample paragraph below the writer has told a fairly complicated story in a single paragraph. To do this the writer had to eliminate any parts of the story that were not critical. Also, the sentences had to be arranged so they were in exactly the right order.

Example

> My high school physics teacher had an unusual way of teaching his students to have confidence in their calculations. One Monday this daring instructor showed the class a small, dangerous-looking guillotine. Each of the twenty-five students was told to figure the height from which the blade could be dropped without cutting off the teacher's fingers. A half-inch piece of dowel was neatly chopped in half to prove to us that the lethal machine worked. Then we elected a Calculations Committee. The committee figured and refigured for two class periods. Then on Friday our worried-looking teacher finally raised the blade 6¼ inches and let it fall. Not a single finger on his hand was scratched, though, because he had secretly replaced the razor-sharp blade with a very dull one. The rest of the students never knew what he had done (he confided in me years later when I saw him at a party). At the time of the demonstration, we had all assumed that we had been successful at making some extremely accurate calculations.

Sentence Variety

Sometimes simply adding some transitions and changing the order of a few sentences will not be enough to make your paragraph highly readable. **Sentence** variety is a must, and you may have to rewrite most of the sentences if it is lacking. Every paragraph should contain a mixture of simple, compound, and complex sentences that gives the paragraph energy and rhythm. Some sentences should begin with phrases and dependent clauses to break up the monotony of always beginning with the subject and following it with the predicate. Some sentences should be long, and some should be short. The rhythm of the sentences should be varied and pleasing.

In the original draft of the sample paragraph that follows, the writer did not think of creating a variety of sentence forms.

Example

LACKS SENTENCE VARIETY

Television police programs frequently show high speed chases. The cops plunk the flashing dome on top. They skid around corners. They fly over bumps and hills. They cause motorists to jam on their brakes. They like to go down alleys. They also like to smash fruitstands. They are often seen sailing off a bridge or flying into a pond. In real violent programs the bad guys blast at the cops with shotguns. Then the crooks get cornered or crash. Then they get arrested. But those chases are dangerous to innocent people. In real-life chases, four hundred people were killed. Five hundred people were injured.

Now study the revision of the previous paragraph. The revised version is smoother and clearer. The sentences no longer seem clumsy and choppy.

Example

GOOD SENTENCE VARIETY

Television police programs frequently show high speed chases, making them look exciting and ignoring the great danger they pose to the public. The detective plunks the flashing dome on top of the sedan; the siren wails, and the chase is on. The police and the pursued skid around corners; they fly over bumps and hills with sparks flying from the undercarriages of the cars as they bottom out. Squad cars join the chase, screeching around in u-turns. Zooming down alleys and turning corners on two wheels, they barely miss pedestrians and sometimes crash. In a city chase one car always seems to hit a fruitstand, sending everything flying in a juicy mess. In country chases, the state trooper or county sheriff often ends up sailing off a bridge or flying into a pond. In the more violent chases one of the bad guys leans out of his window and blasts away with a shotgun: baroom! Then the crooks are forced to a stop in a fender-crunching squeeze-play, or they are cremated in a spectacular flaming crash and explosion. But these chases, although exciting to watch, downplay the extreme danger of the real-life police chases. Last year in the United States, accidents during police pursuits killed four hundred people and injured five hundred. Television producers should cut back on chase scenes and emphasize their real dangers, not glorify and popularize them as they are doing now.

List the types of improvement you may need to make in order to make the sentences in a body paragraph connect smoothly.

EXERCISE 4.13

Rewrite the paragraph below so that the sentences will connect more smoothly. (Use no more than ten sentences.)

Scientific evidence is mounting. Too many Americans do not eat right. Today's diet apparently is the cause of numerous nutrition-related problems. Too many Americans eat too many calories. They do not burn up enough energy. Most Americans become overweight. They eat too much animal protein, saturated fat, and cholesterol. Too many people develop heart disease. They also eat too much refined sugar and starch. They do not eat enough complex carbohydrates. They do not eat whole grain cereal and bread. And they develop metabolic disorders. They develop diabetes. They do not eat enough crude fiber either, such as vegetables, and they develop many diseases, such as diverticulosis and cancer of the colon. Americans must reconsider their eating habits.

EXERCISE 4.14

PREPARING TO WRITE

1. In this assignment you will write a body paragraph on one of the suggested topics.

   Suggested Topics (You may narrow further)

   Relate the important facts about an important historical event. In the topic sentence make a statement about the importance of the event.

   Tell an interesting but true tale about your school days—narrate a significant episode or the actions of an interesting teacher or student. In your topic sentence make a statement about the significance of the event or the individual's actions.

   Describe a television commercial that you either like or dislike. Explain why. Make sure to state a controlling idea in the topic sentence.

2. After choosing and, if necessary, narrowing one of the above topics, think about what you will have to do to get the information you will need. Can you remember enough about your topic to write, or will you have to do some research first? For example, if you have chosen to write about a television commercial, will you need to see it again and take notes about it? Is the commercial still being shown? When will you have time to watch for it? Can a friend or relative help you remember some of the details?

3. Do any background research, reading, recollection, television viewing, or interviewing that will aid you in the development of your paragraph.

4. Make any notes you will need—ideas and details you want to include.

5. Plan the layout of your paragraph: rough out a topic sentence and brief outline of the support sentences.

6. Review Lesson Three and Lesson Four. Make a list of the writing skills that you will be expected to demonstrate in this paragraph. For example, your statements will be reasonable, and your paragraph will demonstrate sentence variety.

WRITING

By now you should be ready to write. You have probably developed some insight into the best way for you to compose a paragraph. Use your own favored method of drafting your paragraph.

EDITING

Refer to the list of writing skills you made for step 6 of PREPARING TO WRITE. Edit your paragraph until you feel confident that you have done your best to demonstrate your mastery of those skills.

PREPARING TO WRITE

The purpose of this exercise is to give you the opportunity to put into practice all of the basic paragraph-building techniques you have learned in this chapter.

Write a single *body paragraph,* choosing one of the topics suggested below.

Topic Suggestion One

On which one of the following do you think emphasis should be placed in the punishment of criminals? Explain your reasons.

- Revenge or compensation for the victim's suffering and losses
- Deterrence of similar crimes in the future
- Rehabilitation of the criminal
- Reduction of the costs of catching, convicting, and imprisoning criminals
- Maintenance of a safe community
- Some other principle not mentioned above

Choose only one of the above principles even if you think more than one of them plays a part in effective punishment. If possible, limit yourself to a specific type of crime, for example, armed robbery, burglary, car theft, rape, extortion, embezzlement, computer crime, treason, kidnapping, hijacking, drug dealing, or murder. If you do not limit yourself to one type of crime, be sure to specify the type you are thinking about each time you make a statement or give an example.

If you choose this topic, you must write in the *third person.* Instead of writing "I think" or "In my opinion," state your point directly, letting readers assume that what you are saying is your opinion.

Example

WRONG   It seems to me that revenge for the victim, friends, and loved ones should be the most important goal in sentencing a murderer.

RIGHT   Revenge for the victim, friends, and loved ones should be the most important goal in sentencing a murderer.

Topic Suggestion Two

Which do you believe has more influence on your life?

Luck, chance, fate, powerful people, and events beyond your control.

or

Your ability to shape your own future, to control people and events, and to make plans work out.

Describe *one* incident from your life that demonstrates how one or the other of the statements above is true for you. Word your topic sentence so readers will know which belief you support. Give a detailed account of the incident, but also explain how the incident demonstrates that the belief applies to you. For this topic you may use *first person,* as you would in any narrative-descriptive writing.

Scenario: Next Friday you plan to cook a dinner for four people, for example, your family, two couples, or yourself and three friends. You have $12.50 to spend for food and drinks—no more and no less. Write a paragraph on this after visiting a grocery store and taking notes. Explain what and how much you will need to purchase, for instance "two twelve-ounce jars of Italian Delight spaghetti sauce." Cite the cost for each item, and the total cost for all items.

Alternate Topic: Write a paragraph explaining how an extremely attractive and appetizing meal can be served for $12.50. Concentrate on the tricks involved in making the meal seem more expensive than it really is.

Use *third person* for either topic.

WRITING

As you write and rewrite your paragraph, make a conscious effort to write a paragraph that is well organized, full of details, and smoothly written. Try to make this paragraph fuller than the mandatory five sentences, perhaps up to twelve sentences.

EDITING

Refer to the following checklist as you revise and proofread your paragraph.

Paragraph Checklist

1. Is the topic narrowed sufficiently?

2. Does the paragraph begin with a topic sentence?

3. Is the controlling idea clearly stated?

4. Is the paragraph thoroughly developed (5 to 12 sentences) and full of details?

5. Does the paragraph need a concluding sentence?

6. Is first or third person used as directed?

7. Are your statements reasonable?

8. Do your sentences connect smoothly?

9. Does your paragraph have sentence variety?

10. Are your sentences free from errors in spelling, punctuation, capitalization, and grammar?

11. Is the final copy neatly written?

5

Paragraph Strategies

In this chapter you will continue your study of body paragraphs. In the last chapter you studied the basic structure of body paragraphs. You mastered topic, primary-support, secondary-support, and concluding sentences. You learned what it means to write "full" body paragraphs. And, finally, you practiced editing the sentences in body paragraphs to make the sentences tie together smoothly.

Now you need to be concerned with planning individual body paragraphs. As the word *planning* suggests, you must be deliberate. You should decide before you begin writing exactly what you want to achieve in each paragraph. Since your purpose for writing each paragraph will be different, you need to choose an organizational technique that fits the purpose for that particular paragraph. There are a number of techniques that you will learn to use. These are called **paragraph strategies**. Simply put, a paragraph strategy is the method you use to develop the paragraph.

The strategy you use will probably differ from paragraph to paragraph. If you were to write a 500-word paper with three body paragraphs, you might even need to use three different strategies—a different one for each paragraph. In other papers you may want to write body paragraphs that all use the same strategy, for instance, three paragraphs that rely primarily upon illustration. But it is just as common to need a mixture, perhaps one paragraph using illustration, another using comparison, and a third arguing con and pro.

As you learned in Chapter Four, effective body paragraphs begin with carefully written topic sentences. You saw how the controlling idea of the topic sentence gives the paragraph focus. Now it is necessary to observe how the topic sentence should fit the paragraph strategy you select. For example, a definition paragraph would begin differently than a contrast paragraph.

DIAGRAM OF A TYPICAL 500-WORD COMPOSITION

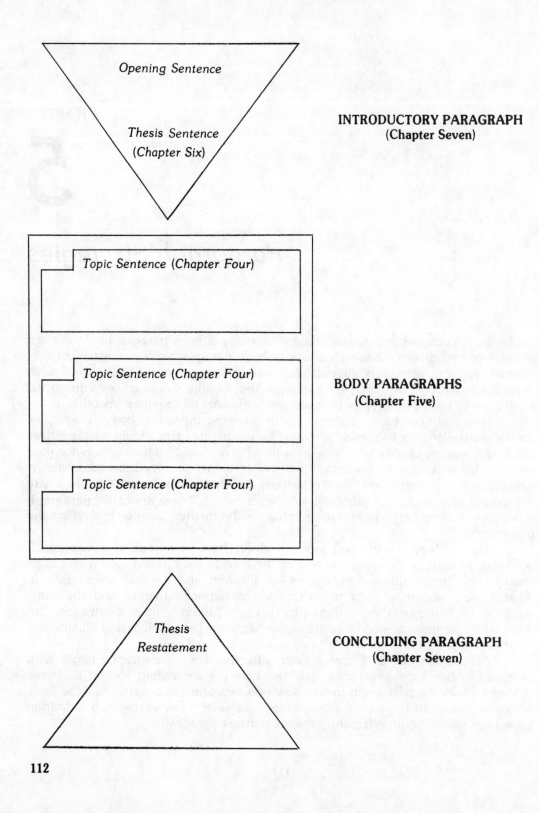

Opening Sentence

Thesis Sentence
(Chapter Six)

INTRODUCTORY PARAGRAPH
(Chapter Seven)

Topic Sentence (Chapter Four)

Topic Sentence (Chapter Four)

BODY PARAGRAPHS
(Chapter Five)

Topic Sentence (Chapter Four)

Thesis
Restatement

CONCLUDING PARAGRAPH
(Chapter Seven)

Examples

Definition: *Tight money* is a term used by bankers, realtors, builders, and buyers to describe a scarcity of loan funds.

Contrast: Although often considered as synonyms, *tight money* and *recession* describe two very different economic conditions.

The emphasis in the first topic sentence above is upon the meaning of the technical term *tight money*. On the other hand, the emphasis in the second topic sentence is on the difference between the terms *tight money* and *recession*. Thus, each topic sentence communicates more than just a controlling idea for a body paragraph. Each also gives a preview of the paragraph strategy that will be used. As a result, your reader is given a hint of the message of the paragraph from the outset.

LESSON ONE — The Strategy of Using Examples: Illustration

The **illustration** paragraph is one of the easiest types of paragraphs to write. This strategy allows writers to explain their ideas fully by giving information that illustrates the point made in the topic sentence. These illustrations may be examples, experiences, facts and figures, or anecdotes. What you use depends on the particular subject about which you are writing. Just remember to give sufficient secondary support for *every* primary support sentence. Generally, the more secondary support you give, the clearer your point will be. As you know, all paragraphs should have *at least five sentences*. Illustration paragraphs, however, will often be more convincing if you extend them to eight or ten sentences.

The following examples are illustration paragraphs developed from clearly stated topic sentences. The first paragraph uses three specific experiences to illustrate the point that "unique individuals will go to extremes to prove their theories." The individuals listed — Thor Heyerdahl, Dr. Sylvia Earle, and Jane Goodall — and their feats are given as examples.

Example

1

Although it often means risking their lives, unique individuals will go to extremes to prove their theories. Thor Heyerdahl, for example, has challenged the sea three times, once on *Kon-Tiki*, once on *Ra*, and once on *Tigress*. He wanted to prove that primitive people could have migrated across the ocean. In each case this brave man's boat was only a fragile craft that could easily have been destroyed by a storm. Exhibiting an equal amount of daring, Dr. Sylvia Earle walked on the bottom of the ocean under 1300 feet of water. By doing so, she demonstrated that humans could successfully function in the ocean environment in spite of the tremendous pressure. At the time of her dive, Earle's "Jim Suit" was relatively untried, and her dive could easily have been fatal. Another brave woman, Jane Goodall, has risked her life by living among the apes to prove her theories about them. The reactions of the apes and other animals to a human being could easily have cost Goodall her life. Each of these special people risked injury or death to help explain the world.

To decide on the contents of an illustration paragraph, read your topic sentence and ask "Who or what can be used to illustrate this point?" In the preceding paragraph, three individuals are used to illustrate the point being made. The following paragraph is similar. It uses examples to illustrate the qualities that make the "sheltie" an excellent choice for a pet.

Example

2

The Shetland sheep dog, commonly called a "sheltie," has many qualities that make it an excellent choice for a pet. The first reason many people give for selecting a sheltie is its keen intelligence. Being smart, the dog is easy to train. After an owner has made the dog aware of what is or is not acceptable behavior, it will always attempt to comply. A sheltie will almost never do something for which it has once been corrected. But this dog also makes a good pet because of its personality. Calm and even tempered, the sheltie rarely barks without good cause. Moreover, children are not likely to get bitten by the family's pet sheltie. Even if this dog is abused, it will not bite if it can escape and hide under a bed. To many owners, however, the most important reason for owning a sheltie is appearance. Looking like a small collie, the sheltie has a multi-colored coat that always appears neat and clean. These are but a few examples of the sheltie's good qualities.

EXERCISE 5.1

PREPARING TO WRITE

1. Examine the previous paragraph on the sheltie dogs. On a piece of paper numbered from 1-12, label each of the sentences as TS for topic sentence, PS for primary support, SS for secondary support, or CS for concluding sentence.
2. Examine the sample paragraphs in Chapter Four and decide which, if any, use the illustration strategy.
3. Go through a magazine and select three paragraphs that use illustration. Copy the one you think is the best. Skip a line and write the name of the magazine, its date, and the page on which you found the paragraph.

WRITING

4. Write an illustration paragraph using at least three short examples. Choose your own topic.

EDITING

Before you submit your paragraph for grading, use the Paragraph Checklist on the next page to be certain you have not forgotten something.

Factual Details

When you develop a paragraph using any kind of numerical or statistical information, the result is an illustration paragraph using **facts and figures**.

Example

> As more and more Californians turn to boating for a hobby, finding a place to moor a boat becomes a bigger problem. In Southern California 96% of the marinas have waiting lists so long that new boat owners must wait years to get a place to park their boats. For example, the next person to sign the waiting list at Dana Point Harbor can expect to "work up" to the top of the list in slightly more than two years. Close to Los Angeles, the wait becomes longer. Newport Beach marinas generally have waiting lists of five to seven years. Northern California has a similar problem. In Sausalito one marina operator no longer accepts names of people who want a berth. The waiting list once grew to the point that 300 names were on it, and he no longer felt justified in adding more names to the list.

The student who wrote the paragraph above used many facts and figures to show the extent of the problem facing boaters in California.

Anecdote

The **anecdote** paragraph strategy is unique. It is the only one of the strategies covered in this chapter which illustrates the point made in the topic sentence by narrating a story. Usually the writer tells about something that he or she saw firsthand. Almost everybody can think of a story to tell about something funny or embarrassing that he or she has experienced. And everyone enjoys reading about such incidents. Since an anecdote tells a story to illustrate a point, people often find anecdote paragraphs thought-provoking as well as interesting to read and write.

To write an anecdote paragraph, begin with a carefully written topic sentence, just like any other illustration paragraph. After the topic sentence, and possibly a second sentence to make your point perfectly clear, you can then begin telling the story that you are going to use as an illustration.

Example

Some drivers learn only through near tragedy to keep their eyes on the road. I am one of those people. I had just come off of the freeway on the way home from a party. There were two other people in my car. Steve was in the back and Christine was in the front. I was driving 35 MPH in a 30 MPH zone because the road was very clear. I turned for one second to talk to Steve, and as I turned back to the front, I noticed I was too close to a new white Chrysler stopped at a red light. In an instant I downshifted, probably faster than A. J. Foyt. I slowed about 5 MPH, but I still felt a chill come over me as I realized we were going to hit that stopped car. I locked the brakes at thirty yards and felt the total loss of steering. As we hit, I saw my front end crunch up like an accordian. Various pieces of my car went flying. Then the back of my car felt as if it lifted off the ground. When everything came to a stop, I jumped out of the car very rapidly. The horn was stuck, and that really embarrassed me. I opened the battered hood and ripped out the wire to the horn. I checked out my friends in the car. Luckily only Christine had an injury. She had a small cut on her arm. Suddenly, I saw the man whose car I had hit walking angrily toward me. I knew my troubles had just begun.

In the anecdote paragraph above the writer clearly describes a personal experience. Notice that the first sentence of the sample anecdote paragraph is in third person but that the remainder of it is in first person. Many of the anecdotes you will use when you write will be from personal experience and therefore in first person.

The first person (personal pronoun), words like *I, we,* and *our,* may be used whenever the example is a personal experience. First person should be avoided in writing papers for classes, except when illustrating a point with an anecdote. As you write anecdote paragraphs, be careful they do not become so wordy that your reader forgets the idea presented in the topic sentence.

PREPARING TO WRITE

1. Find a newspaper or magazine article that makes use of factual detail. Copy it, writing on every other line of your paper. Underline the facts and figures.
2. Find a newspaper or magazine article that makes use of an anecdote. Copy the article, writing on every other line of your paper. Underline the portion of the paragraph written in third person.

WRITING

3. Complete the following underdeveloped paragraph using factual detail. Include two support clusters.

> Money is always a serious problem for students; there is never enough of it. At school the food the students actually want to eat is very expensive. . .

4. Complete the following underdeveloped paragraph using an anecdote.

> Some days are a disaster from start to finish. The worst of these days begins poorly and grows worse as the day progresses. . . . .

5. Write one paragraph using factual detail. (Make certain that your paragraph is between five and twelve sentences in length.)
6. Write one paragraph using an anecdote. (Begin with two or three sentences in third person; you may then shift to first person in the anecdote. Make your paragraph five to twelve sentences in length.)

EDITING

Before you submit your paragraph for grading, use the Paragraph Checklist on page 115 to be certain you have not forgotten something.

LESSON TWO—The Definition Strategy

As you are writing a paper or report, you will occasionally need to define a term that might confuse your reader. If the term is easily defined, your definition might be only a word, a phrase, or a sentence.

Examples

>Bartering—trading—has become big business.
>
>Euthanasia, or mercy killing, has long been practiced by veterinarians.
>
>A conservative is one who desires to keep things from changing.

However, many terms or concepts you write about will not be this easy to explain. These more difficult terms will require a fully developed paragraph of **definition**. An effective definition paragraph begins with a three-part topic sentence. These parts are:

(1) the *term*,
(2) the *general category*, and
(3) the *separation* of that term from all other items in its general category.

Example

>A ketch is a two-masted sailboat that has the taller mast forward and the after mast ahead of the rudder.
>
>*Term:* ketch
>*Category:* a two-masted sailboat
>*Separation:* that has the taller mast forward and the after mast ahead of the rudder.

You must be able to divide every topic sentence you write for a definition paragraph into its three parts. Divide your topic sentence carefully to avoid making it too general and the paragraph too long. If your three-part topic sentence is carefully written, the rest of the paragraph will be easier to write.

Defining with Examples

Read the following paragraph closely. Notice the three-part topic sentence. You should be able to identify each of the three parts. Notice, also, how the writer defines "passive resistance" by giving examples from different time periods and from different geographical areas. Use multiple examples whenever you think they will increase the reader's understanding of what you are defining.

Example

>Passive resistance is a method of demonstrating one's opposition to a law, an action, or an idea, without the use of physical violence or force. It is not a new idea—examples of passive resistance can be found all through

human history. Early Christians permitted themselves to be fed to wild animals rather than renounce their religious beliefs. At no time, however, did they attempt to fight back with physical force against their tormentors. During the Nazi occupation of France in World War II, French workers used this same method to disrupt German construction of military projects. They allowed themselves to be led to work sites, but on arrival they merely sat quietly and refused to go to work. Even the threats of firing squads and food restrictions could not persuade these people to participate in a task they felt was immoral. In America, one can hardly fail to be impressed by reports of the 1960's which tell of students blocking military trains simply by placing their bodies across the tracks. The entire nation saw this expression of opposition to war demonstrated by its youth and became more concerned with the country's goals.

The preceding paragraph is effective for two reasons. First, the topic sentence is properly structured:

1) *the term* - passive resistance
2) *the general category* - a method of demonstrating one's opposition to a law, an action or an idea
3) *separation from other items in that category* - without the use of physical violence or force

Second, three examples are used to illustrate the definition of passive resistance: early Christians, French workers during World War II, and young Americans during the 1960's.

Defining through Comparison or Contrast

The paragraph above uses illustrations to define, just like those you studied and wrote earlier in this chapter. But writers also define by telling readers what the thing being defined is like or not like or how it is the same or different from other things in its category. The writer of the following paragraph defines the term *yawl* by contrasting it to the schooner and the ketch.

Example

A yawl is a two-masted sailboat on which the rear mast is normally only half as tall as the forward mast. As a result of the difference in mast height, the rear sail, called the mizzen, is dramatically smaller than the main sail. The yawl can be easily distinguished from the two-masted schooner because the schooner's larger mast is its rear mast. The yawl, however, is not easily distinguished from the ketch. Both the yawl and the ketch have the smaller mast at the back of the boat, but the ketch has a rear mast that is normally about three-quarters as tall as the forward mast. By looking for these simple visual differences, though, most people can distinguish the yawl from the other two-masted sailboats.

One Caution

To avoid confusing your reader, be careful not to use the term you are defining in the definition. This is especially troublesome when you are writing the topic sentence. You will occasionally think it is impossible to define a term without using it in the second or third part of the sentence, but you must not do so.

Examples

(Weak)   An *electric mixer* is a *mixer* that is electrically powered.

(Strong) An *electric mixer* is a kitchen appliance that is plugged into a wall outlet and used to stir or blend food.

(Weak)   *Freedom* is the concept of each individual being *free*.

(Strong) *Freedom* is the concept of each individual being able to decide upon the course of his or her own life.

When you use the word being defined in the definition, you are *defining in a circle*. Writing such a topic sentence not only confuses your reader but also makes it hard for you to develop the sentence into a paragraph. Furthermore, do not copy your definition from the dictionary—use your own words.

EXERCISE 5.3

PREPARING TO WRITE

1. Write a definition of a term, a thing, or a concept you know especially well from your hobby or school course.
2. Find a definition paragraph in a textbook or a magazine. Copy it onto a separate piece of paper. When you have done so, underline the part of the topic sentence which states the category and circle the portion which separates the term.
3. Look up one of the following terms in a dictionary. Copy the dictionary's definition—then put it into your own words.

liberal	will power
marital law	sexism

WRITING

4. Write an extended definition of one of the following terms. You may consult reference works, if you wish, but write the definition in your own words.

pacifist	socialist
stereotype	chauvinist
scapegoat	prejudice
patriot	conservative
feminist	

EDITING

Before you submit your paragraphs for grading, use the Paragraph Checklist on page 115 to be certain you have not forgotten something.

LESSON THREE—The Comparison or Contrast Strategy

Comparison paragraphs stress how two or more things are alike. **Contrast** paragraphs stress how two or more things are different. The effectiveness of these types of paragraphs depends upon how well they are organized. You must be certain, for example, that the point of comparison or contrast is made clear in the topic sentence and then developed in such a way that your reader can see how each element of the comparison or contrast has been covered. It is not enough simply to mention each way the items are alike or different. You must go into some detail to make sure the point is clearly understood. In other words, you must use an adequate amount of secondary support.

Examples

COMPARISON

Olympic sailboats and soaring planes are very much alike in many ways. The first similarity one would notice is the lack of comfort in rough weather. Stuffed in a cockpit barely large enough for a small child, the pilots of soaring planes bounce around the sky when the winds are strong. Sailors on small Olympic sailboats find the cockpit of their boats slightly larger but hardly more comfortable. When the winds increase, the boats literally bounce from one wave to the next, hesitating only long enough to throw a fresh bucketful of water on shivering sailors. But an even more surprising similarity is in their method of propulsion—suction—which causes each to move. The soaring plane's curved wing tops, not the flat wing bottoms, create a suction that holds the craft up in the sky. In the same manner, the sailboat is pulled through the water by the suction created when the wind rushes by the curved sails. The airfoil created by the curved wing on one and the curved sails on the other makes soaring and sailing very much alike.

CONTRAST

The differences in personality characteristics of siblings are often very noticeable. Debbie and Patti, my sisters, are different in many ways. Debbie, the oldest, is a very outgoing person. She has confidence in herself and is very artistic. Debbie has learned to be assertive, a necessary trait in our society. She is twenty-three years old and works for the state in a supervisory position. This is quite an accomplishment for someone of her age with only a high school education. By contrast, Patti, who is twenty-one years old, is quiet and keeps her thoughts and feelings to herself. Because she is quiet and non-assertive, employers, fellow employees, and friends sometimes take advantage of her. She has not learned to be assertive when out of her home situation. She lacks confidence in herself in the artistic field, except for sewing. Throughout her elementary school years, her teachers always compared her creativity to Debbie's, a very painful experience. Patti, also a high school graduate, works for a department store as a salesclerk in the stationery department. Her wages are small compared to her sister's, but she managed to save enough money to buy a specially ordered 1980 Firebird TRANS Am and pay for it with cash. When she reached this goal, her confidence level did elevate. And the differences, while no less than before, have not stopped my sisters from being close to one another.

You will often be asked to compare or contrast political figures, characters in novels, philosophical points, or social ideas. The evidence for support in comparison or contrast paragraphs can be arranged in several ways. You may deal with two ideas, for instance, by devoting the first four or five sentences to one idea and then the rest of the sentences to the other idea. With this method you deal with each idea in a *block of sentences*.

Example

BLOCK OF SENTENCES DEVELOPED

The young American who wants to learn a trade finds it more difficult and expensive than the young German. Americans have to attend a two-year college or trade school. Either way, they have to spend a considerable amount of money and valuable time to attend school to obtain the necessary knowledge and skill. It takes money to maintain a vehicle for transportation, money for gas, repairs, and car insurance. Also, their training cannot compete with on-the-job training. Upon graduation they still lack the necessary experience that would guarantee them jobs. Most employers in the United States want experienced workers, so jobs are not easily found by these college-trained young people. German youths, on the other hand, start their apprenticeships with a small salary, which increases from year to year. This raise is usually sufficient to cover all expenses, provided they live thriftily. By the time they become seventeen and have passed their *Meisterprüfung*, they are experts in their trades. They have no problems whatsoever in finding jobs. Usually they continue to work for the same employers for years because employers would rather have someone trained in their own companies.

Another method is to *alternate points* of comparison or contrast several times in the paragraph.

Example

ALTERNATE POINTS DEVELOPMENT

Although one could point out many similarities in our state's country and city school systems of the past, the instructional differences were the most apparent. The small school in the country had approximately forty-five first-through-eighth-grade students. All eight grades were taught by the same teacher in one large room. By contrast, the city school had approximately five hundred students. Each grade was taught by its own teacher in a separate room. In the country school the members of one grade would go to the front of the room to demonstrate their knowledge by individually reciting or writing their lessons on the blackboard. The other grades would quietly do their assignments at their desks. The teacher spent about twenty minutes with each grade, once in the morning and once in the afternoon. In the city school the teacher would do most of the demonstrations on the board, and the students were, in general, quite noisy unless they were singled out by questions from the teacher. Very few actual work assignments were completed in the school. All assignments were completed in the home at night. The class would spend forty-five minutes on each subject, covering five subjects a day.

A third method is to deal with the points of comparison or contrast in the *same sentence.*

Example

SAME SENTENCE DEVELOPMENT

Many people fail to recognize the tremendous differences between sharks and dolphins. Basically, the shark is a scavenger who will eat anything while the dolphin is extremely selective about what it eats. And as everyone knows who saw the movie *Jaws*, sharks will eat human beings; by contrast, dolphins will not attack humans even in self-defense. Undoubtedly, the most significant difference is that sharks are fish and dolphins are mammals. That is, sharks must stay underwater to survive while dolphins must surface regularly for a breath of air. In spite of these obvious contrasts, many people consider sharks and dolphins as almost identical fish.

Each of these techniques works equally well. You will find, though, that the first —sentence blocks—is usually the easiest to write. Practice them all because each will work to make you a better writer.

Analogy

The **analogy** paragraph is a very creative kind of comparison. You can write an analogy paragraph when you wish to introduce an idea with which your reader may be unfamiliar. To do this, you compare the unknown idea or object to a more familiar and understandable idea or object with similar characteristics. If you were to explain what a food processor is, for instance, you might compare it to a blender. You could point out similarities and differences in appearance and function. The reader who knew what a blender was would then have an idea what a food processor was. Consider the following analogy:

Example

ANALOGY

When it attempts to take off, the gooney bird is like a bull in a bull-fighting arena. Both blindly crash into anything and everything that happens to be in the path of their charge. The bird's attempt to take off is not at all unlike the bull's attempt to move fast enough to destroy his adversary. Like the bull that requires a considerable distance to achieve his speed, the bird must have an incredible amount of room to reach enough speed to get airborne. Further like the bull, the bird refuses to stop or alter course once the charge has begun. Granted, the gooney does not deliberately attempt to kill any human being in its path, but this is of little comfort to the person who is struck by five pounds of flying gooney. Moreover, like a charging bull, this beautiful bird has been known to crash into cars and trucks. Drivers have occasionally found it necessary to drive off the road to avoid a collision with a gooney that is attempting to lift off the ground. Although a gooney is very different in appearance from a bull, its actions when becoming airborne are not different at all from those of a charging bull.

All of the following paragraphs should be from five to twelve sentences long.

PREPARING TO WRITE

1. Find a comparison paragraph in a magazine or newspaper. Cut it out or copy it and submit it.
2. Find a contrast paragraph in a magazine or newspaper. Cut it out or copy it and submit it.
3. List the points you might use to compare or contrast something in a full-length paper. For example, to compare or contrast two schools, you might select the following points upon which to base your discussion: (1) size of school and number of students, (2) facilities, (3) curriculum, (4) teachers, (5) extra-curricular activities.

WRITING

4. Use the list developed for number 3 above to write a comparison or contrast paragraph. (Will you use *sentence-blocks*, *alternate-points*, or *same-sentence* technique?)
5. Write a comparison paragraph in which you tell how two television programs or two movies are alike.
6. Write a contrast paragraph in which you tell how two television programs or two movies are different.
7. Write a contrast paragraph in which you tell how two of your instructors are different.
8. Write an analogy paragraph in which you compare a little-known object or person to a well-known object or person.
9. Write a paragraph in which you use both comparison and contrast to explain how two types of housing or two brands of automobiles are alike and different.

EDITING

Before you submit your paragraph for grading, use the Paragraph Checklist on page 115 to be certain you have not forgotten something.

LESSON FOUR—The Analysis Strategy

When you wish to write about a complex subject in order to make it easier for the reader to understand, you might *divide it into various parts or classifications*. This process is called **analysis**. (Some instructors and texts refer to this as paragraph development by *division* or by *classification*.) Analysis divides the subject in some logical way, usually either by *process* or by *structure*. An analysis can consist of a single paragraph or a full-length composition.

Process Analysis (Time Order)

When you want to write out the process of how to make or how to do something, *natural time order* is used. Every effective analysis paragraph of this type must explain, step by step, how the procedure is accomplished beginning with the first step and ending with the last.

Example

How to Feed a Shark

In order to feed a shark its favorite meal, you need only to follow the following six steps. The first step is to buy the tastiest looking package of cup cakes at your local market. The flavor is not important; they should be small, however, so they can be eaten quickly. While the cup cakes are still fresh, you can drive to the ocean; this is the second step. This step is important since sharks live only in the ocean. The third step is to put on a brightly colored swim suit. Studies have proved conclusively that sharks are more likely to approach feeders who wear bright orange, yellow, or red suits. Carefully carrying the package of cup cakes between your teeth, you are ready for step four: the swim into deep water. Sharks feed most happily in water over six feet; some even prefer water at least ten feet deep. The fifth step is to open the package of cup cakes, splashing wildly as you tread water. You should try to make sounds like a frantic fish while you splash as this excites the sharks to a feeding frenzy. When you see a shark swimming your way, eat the cup cakes rapidly. By the time you have finished eating the cup cakes, the shark should have eaten you. If you have followed these six steps carefully, you can rest assured that you have made the shark very happy.

When writing a process analysis paragraph, you may use second person—*you*—as you tell your reader how to perform some action. Second person should be avoided in any other type of paragraph development. (This chapter is written in second person because it tells you how to write body paragraphs. Second person is often used in textbooks.)

Structural Analysis

When you wish to break down a subject into its parts, types, subtopics, or elements, you must use the strategy called **structural analysis**. This development could be used to analyze an atom, a paragraph, an automobile, a body, or, for that matter, anything that may be divided into parts.

Example:

> Four types of American tourists are very conspicuous in Europe in the summer. One kind is the "See America First Tourist." Only rarely do these tourists venture outside of America, and when they do they are always disappointed. They complain constantly that European scenery, historical sights, food, accommodations, and consumer products do not compare with those in America. They always wish they could "find a good hamburger." Then there are those tourists who try to be exactly like the natives. These travelers will go to almost any length to look like the natives. They don the same type of clothing, eat the same kind of food, and if they survive long enough, they even try to adopt the customs of the country. These travelers are snobby about anything not absolutely "authentic." The third kind are tourists who never go anywhere without taking their two cameras—one for still photos and the other for moving pictures—and many other photographic gadgets. They spend most of their time snapping away at famous landmarks and always include their family members in each picture. The fourth type are college students. They hitchhike or bicycle their way across Europe. They are characterized by happy faces, backpacks, and Daddy's American Express credit cards.

EXERCISE 5.5

PREPARING TO WRITE

1. Find a process analysis paragraph in a magazine or textbook. Copy the paragraph on notebook paper. Write 1, 2, 3, 4 in the margin to indicate each step in the procedure.
2. Find a structural analysis paragraph in a magazine or textbook. Copy the paragraph on notebook paper. Write in the margin to indicate each part of the object being examined.

WRITING

3. Write a process analysis paragraph in which you explain to your reader how to do something. Be sure you include every step in the process. (Make your paragraph five to fifteen sentences in length.)
4. Write a structural analysis paragraph in which you divide the subject into its parts.

   water pollutants
   types of students or teachers
   an historical event
   components of some mechanical device
   a topic of your choice

EDITING

Before you submit your paragraph for grading, use the Paragraph Checklist on page 115 to be certain you have not forgotten something.

LESSON FIVE—The Cause-and-Effect Analysis Strategy

When you want to write about what causes any event, you will use the **cause-and-effect analysis** development. For instance, if you were to discuss the rising alcoholism among American women, you could begin by writing a topic sentence that states the problem.

Example

> Researchers have discovered an alarming link between the changing role of American women and the rising alcoholism among them.

You could easily develop this topic sentence into a paragraph in either of two ways. By considering this sentence to be the cause you are writing about, you could present all of the effects of this problem. For example, you could talk about the suffering these women experience, their divorces, their loss of identity, or any of the many other problems resulting from their alcoholism. This would be a normal cause-and-effect paragraph.

But you could also reverse the procedure above and write about what has caused the alcoholism mentioned in your topic sentence. In essence, you would then be writing an effect-and-cause analysis paragraph. If you used this type of development, you would follow the sample topic sentence above with a discussion of the changing status of the housewife, the increasing independence of women, and any other causes of this increase in alcoholism. Either of these methods of development is equally correct. You must decide which is best each time you are going to write a cause-and-effect paragraph.

The following paragraph explains what resulted when a ship went aground. The topic sentence identifies the event, and the remainder of the paragraph gives the effects.

Example

CAUSE-AND-EFFECT ANALYSIS

When the *Argo Merchant* ran aground on Nantucket Shoals in December 1976, a series of events resulted. The most serious from the standpoint of the sea creatures was the 6.3 million gallons of oil which spewed into the sea. This caused the death of an untold number of clams, oysters, fish, and birds. Unfortunately, the oil which gushed from the broken hull of the ship also destroyed the eggs of future generations of sea life. For many resort owners along the nearby coastline, the grounding began weeks of constant worry of economic disaster. Had the oil washed ashore, every beach, boat, and dock would have been rendered useless by the thick oil. However, the most noteworthy and potentially best effect of the incident was the awakening of the public and the maritime authorities to the danger presented by poorly constructed and haphazardly operated giant tankers. Provided that sufficient public pressure is applied in the future to continue research on better ways to control the merchant fleet, it is possible that fewer tanker disasters will occur.

The preceding paragraph uses three support clusters to tell of the effects of the grounding of the ship. Each support cluster includes clearly stated primary and secondary sentences that explain the topic sentence. This method of paragraph development is commonly used to explain what happened as a result of some major historical event.

When you wish to explain what generally happens or what will happen, you use the same paragraph strategy. In the following paragraph, the writer uses the present rather than the past tense used by the writer of the previous paragraph.

Example

Ingesting refined sugar and caffeine adversely affects blood-sugar levels. When too much refined sugar is consumed, the blood-sugar level temporarily sky-rockets. But after an hour or so the level drops far lower than before the sugar was eaten. This condition is caused by the over-secretion of insulin by the pancreas. Caffeine also can cause low blood-sugar; thus, anyone who has only a strong cup of coffee with a heaping teaspoon of sugar in it for breakfast may feel hungry and fatigued an hour or two after drinking it. This rapid and continued fluctuating of blood-sugar levels affects a user's sense of physical and mental well-being.

EXERCISE 5.6

PREPARING TO WRITE

1. Find a cause-and-effect paragraph in a magazine or textbook. Copy it onto notebook paper. Label the support clusters by writing SC #1, SC #2, and so on in the margin beside each cluster.

WRITING

2. Develop one of the following topics into a paragraph of 100 to 150 words, using cause-and-effect development. Use past tense to explain something that happened.

> an auto accident
> a divorce
> a murder
> the election of a political figure
> why you were selected to do a job
> your choice

3. Write a cause-and-effect paragraph in present tense, explaining what causes one of the following:

inflation	school drop-outs	fashion change
divorce	war	your choice
child abuse	engine wear	

EDITING

Before you submit your paragraph for grading, use the Paragraph Checklist on page 115 to be certain you have not forgotten something.

128

6

The Thesis Statement

Every paper you write should have an interesting *beginning*, a clearly defined *middle*, and an effective *end*. Before writing a composition, you must be aware of these parts and how they fit together.

A short paper might consist of the five paragraphs in the diagram on the next page. The first paragraph is the *introduction*; its purpose is to prepare readers for what is to be explained or argued in the body of the paper. It does this by narrowing from a broad *opening sentence* to a specific *thesis statement*. Following this introduction are the *body paragraphs*. These paragraphs explain or support the thesis sentence, which is located at the end of the introductory paragraph. You have already written many body paragraphs, so you know how to develop the middle part of your paper. Finally, a concluding paragraph sums up the composition. The *conclusion* restates the thesis idea, then reviews the supporting discussion, and ends with a generalization.

This chapter presents the steps leading to the construction of an effective thesis statement. An entire chapter is devoted to this single sentence because the thesis often determines whether or not a paper will succeed. The thesis statement is the focal point of your introduction; mastery of it now will result in better papers in the coming years.

SPECIAL NOTE

A thesis statement *may* be placed at any point in the introduction. Some compositions even have only an implied thesis. However, in this book you will be expected to write a one-sentence thesis for every introduction you write. You may wish to experiment with other techniques and arrangements later, but first you need to master this technique. Just as improvisational jazz musicians have to learn the basic melodies and patterns before they develop variations, you must learn the basic techniques of effective written communication.

DIAGRAM OF A TYPICAL 500-WORD COMPOSITION (Chapter Eight)

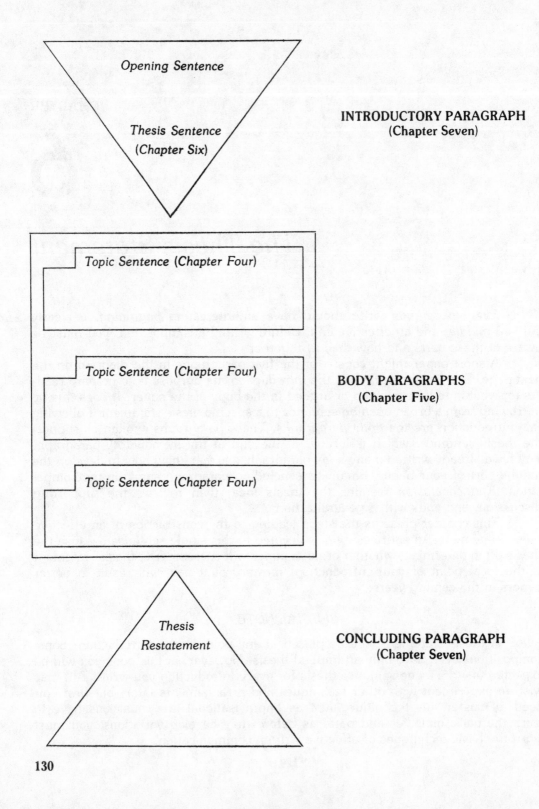

Opening Sentence

Thesis Sentence
(Chapter Six)

INTRODUCTORY PARAGRAPH
(Chapter Seven)

Topic Sentence (Chapter Four)

Topic Sentence (Chapter Four)

Topic Sentence (Chapter Four)

BODY PARAGRAPHS
(Chapter Five)

Thesis
Restatement

CONCLUDING PARAGRAPH
(Chapter Seven)

LESSON ONE—Choosing a Subject

Some people seem to have no trouble at all in picking subjects for their papers. They simply brim over with ideas and seem to have opinions about everything. Others seem to find **subject selection** to be a most difficult task. They agonize for hours trying to find something to write about. These worried students are overestimating the importance of choosing the ''right'' subject. In truth, almost any subject can be developed into a good composition. If you follow a logical, thoughtful procedure for choosing a subject, your compositions will be more interesting to read as well as easier to write.

Ask Yourself Some Questions About the Assignment

Whenever you are asked to write a paper that requires you to choose your own subject, answer the following essential questions about the assignment:

1. *What are the* **restrictions** *on the assignment?* Can you write about anything that you want, or are you required to confine your subject to some area such as history, science, sociology, or English? If you are restricted to the subject area of a particular class, can you write about anything related to that class, or has your teacher given specific instructions?

2. Within the assignment's restrictions, *what are your* **interests***?* What do you already know about, or what do you want to learn more about?

3. *What is the* **purpose** *of the assignment?* Are you to show that you know something particular about the subject, or are you to demonstrate that you can perform research in the subject area? Is the form or the content most important to this assignment?

4. *What is your* **approach** *to the subject?* Should you demonstrate what you already know about the subject, or should you go farther and try to convince readers to believe in a particular point-of-view? Is it necessary to write about broad aspects of your subject or only a part of it?

5. *What is the* **length** *of the assignment?* Are you assigned to write a ten to twenty-page research paper or a short 500-word composition?

For an example of how to use these *five steps*, assume that your social science teacher has asked for a short paper (500-1000 words) on a current problem in American society. You know that the concept of marriage is undergoing many controversial experiments and changes; suppose you are interested in examining some alternatives to marriage. The questions above might be answered for your paper on the subject of marriage as follows:

1. The **restriction** on the assignment is to write on a current American social problem.

2. Your **interest** is the future of the traditional American family.

3. The **purpose** of the assignment is to show that you can critically analyze and effectively present your analysis on paper.

4. For this assignment, your **approach** will be to convince the reader of the logic of your point of view.

5. In **length**, the composition is to be approximately one thousand words (four, double-spaced, typed pages); therefore, it will be necessary to narrow the subject to only that which can be effectively covered in a short paper.

Now that you have a subject and some guidelines, you are ready to narrow your subject. You cannot write effectively on a subject like crime, ecology, drugs, censorship, marriage, or equality. Those ideas are much too general. You need to be more specific—you need a *narrowed subject* about which to write. Your guidelines will give you a place to begin. Then simply list narrowed subject ideas as they come to you. For example, the general subject, *the future of the American family*, might be narrowed to:

1. The effects on the marriage when both partners work
2. Alternatives to marriage
3. Causes of the growing divorce rate in America
4. Living together
5. Children in the non-traditional family
6. Equality in relationships

Your list of possible narrowed subjects could be longer, but five or six should be enough from which to choose. You will probably notice that most narrowed subjects are still too broad for a short paper. Some might work well for a longer research paper, but most would be unmanageable in a paper of less than 1,000 words. You will need to select a topic from your narrowed subject, or save it for a longer writing project.

EXERCISE 6.1

Choose three different subjects and divide each into five narrowed subjects. Write them down in an outline form.

Example

SUBJECT — Equal Rights

NARROWED SUBJECTS — 1. Women's rights
2. Racial minorities' rights
3. Children's rights
4. Students' rights
5. Handicapped individuals' rights

LESSON TWO— Choosing a Topic

You have a subject that you want to write about and have restricted it to a list of narrowed subjects to explore. But most teachers would not want you to write a paper on a subject as general as "Women's rights" or "Students' rights." Therefore you now need to consider ways to focus your chosen narrowed subject further in order to write an effective paper—you need a **topic**. Without a topic, your paper will jump from point to point without purpose. A short paper on a broad subject cannot offer the kinds of examples that show readers what you are trying to communicate. By being thoughtful and by engaging in some creative planning, however, you can narrow your broad subject into a manageable topic.

How Can You Reduce a Narrowed Subject to a Topic?

Suppose that you have been given a writing assignment, and you have chosen a subject. Now you need to narrow it into a manageable topic. The first step in this process is to ask yourself some questions that will suggest ways to narrow and restrict it so that it interests you:

Is there something **controversial** *about the narrowed subject that will allow you to write either for or against it? If so, can you limit your subject to one side or the other of the controversy in such a way that you can write only about the advantages or only about the disadvantages of one particular point of view?*

Examples

SUBJECT	NARROWED SUBJECT	TOPIC
Censorship	Personal Freedom	How censorship of library books violates the constitutional right of free speech
The Family	Living Together	The problems of adjusting to living together in married life
Drugs	Marijuana	The harmful effects of becoming habituated to marijuana

Is there a way to choose a topic by **limiting the subject to a particular time or place?**

Examples

SUBJECT	NARROWED SUBJECT	TOPIC
Censorship	Censorship in other countries	The effects of Soviet censorship upon Russian artists in the 1960's
The Family	Equality in relationships	Switching sex roles between husbands and wives in Sweden
Drugs	Learning and drugs	How the use of drugs affects the study habits of students at State University

133

*Is it possible to discuss some **historical part** of the narrowed subject?*

Examples

SUBJECT	NARROWED SUBJECT	TOPIC
Censorship	Censorship in the media	Movie censorship in the 1920's
The Family	The traditional family	Marriage customs among the Hebrews during Christ's lifetime
Drugs	Drug culture	The hippies of San Francisco in the 1960's

*Is there some way to divide the narrowed subject into some **natural divisions**?*

Examples

SUBJECT	NARROWED SUBJECT	TOPIC
Censorship	Kinds of censorship	Military, press, pornography, political, school, books, movies, television, radio
The Family	Kinds of marriages	Traditional, group, trial, common law, platonic
Drugs	Kinds of drugs	Soft, hard, addictive, habituating, hallucinogenic, prescription

*Is there a way to **combine limitations** that will lead to a topic?*

Examples

SUBJECT	NARROWED SUBJECT	TOPIC
Censorship	Censorship in the media of other countries	Television censorship in American Samoa during the Nixon Administration
The Family	Equality in relationships in the Third World	The role of affection in marriage for lower-caste couples in India
Drugs	Drugs and the media	The censorship of the subject of drugs in movies made during the 1930's and 1940's

Some of these topics are still too broad for a short paper. Often these can be even further restricted, but you should now be able to narrow some subjects of your own.

EXERCISE 6.2
_____

Choose *three* subjects. For each of these subjects write *three* narrowed subjects using a different narrowing technique for each. Then write two topics for each narrowed subject. (You may use subjects from Exercise 6.1, page 132.)

Example

SUBJECT — EQUAL RIGHTS

NARROWED SUBJECTS	**TOPICS**
1. Women's rights	1a. The fight for the ERA
	1b. Women in the military
2. Student rights	2a. A public education free of religious interference
	2b. A free student press
3. Handicapped's rights	3a. The struggle for mobility in public places
	3b. Parking problems for the handicapped

LESSON THREE—Narrowing the Topic

Suppose that you have chosen a subject and have reduced it to some suitable topics. You probably have what you need to begin a long paper. If, however, your assignment is to write a short paper—500-1,000 words—you will need to **limit your topic**. Most teachers favor short papers that go into detail about several specific points related to the whole topic.

How Can the Topic Be Limited

Once you have chosen a topic on which to write, consider what you wish to write about the topic. Usually you will need to limit yourself to two or three points about the topic, or the paper will become too long. You can reduce the length of your paper by focusing on part of your topic—the part that you are interested in enough to write about. For example, suppose you have an assignment to write a paper dealing with some aspect of political persuasion (the subject). You have narrowed the subject to terrorism. You might choose your topic as follows:

> *SUBJECT* — Political Persuasion
>
> *NARROWED SUBJECT* — Terrorism
>
> TOPIC #1   Terrorism as a *political* technique
> TOPIC #2   Terrorism's effect upon its surviving victims
> TOPIC #3   The relationship between terrorism and religious fanaticism

Topic #2—*Terrorism's effect upon its surviving victims*—is still a broad topic, probably requiring several thousand words for full development. For a short paper, this topic must be narrowed in a way that indicates just what you want to write about. You might narrow the topic this way:

> *SUBJECT* — Political Persuasion
>
> *NARROWED SUBJECT* — Terrorism
>
> TOPIC #2   Terrorism's effect upon its surviving victims
>
> *NARROWED TOPIC #1*   Victims' attitudinal change from fear, to sympathy, to love for terrorist captors
>
> *NARROWED TOPIC #2*   Terrorist captors' attitudinal change from hate, to understanding, to sympathy for their victims.
>
> *NARROWED TOPIC #3*   Victims' physiological, sociological, psychological problems during captivity by terrorists

You should remember that your teachers can give you an assignment at any of these step levels. For example, your teacher might assign a paper that requires you to choose your own subject. Or the assignment might include the narrowed subject or even topic suggestions. Only occasionally will teachers actually supply a narrowed topic.

EXERCISE 6.3

For each of the topics listed below, identify those that would be suitable for a 500-1000 word paper and those that would be too broad.

1. Some of the contributions of John Lennon's music to the young people of the 1960's.

2. The victimization of the island people of the South Pacific by the colonial nations.

3. Some possible uses of solar power in the near future.

4. How seeing a play affects the viewer differently than a movie.

5. The main functions of each branch of the American government.

6. The contributions of Sigmund Freud to the field of psychology.

7. The role of the big corporations in setting foreign policy for the United States.

8. Why giving grades does not fairly measure achievement in your school.

EXERCISE 6.4

Choose any five of the topics you wrote for Exercise 6.2 and narrow them.

LESSON FOUR—The Thesis Statement

After you have *narrowed the subject* to a topic and *narrowed the topic* so that it may be developed into a short composition, you are ready to write the most important single sentence in your whole paper, the **thesis statement**.

The thesis statement tells the reader what your paper is all about. If the composition is argumentative, the thesis statement tells readers what you are trying to persuade them to believe; if it is an informative paper, it tells them, without elaboration, your main idea or ideas.

The thesis statements of long compositions may be two or three sentences in length. The thesis for a short paper—the type you will write for this book—should not be more than *one sentence*. Because students most commonly write short papers, many speak of the *thesis sentence* rather than the *thesis statement*. Either term is correct. Since the thesis is so important, however, it must be thoughtfully composed.

The thesis statement will be most easily written if you carefully follow the series of steps outlined in this chapter as you limit your topic. Suppose, for example, that you are asked to write a short composition on the subject of animal behavior for your psychology class. You might produce a thesis by following these five steps:

The Steps:

1. Choose a **subject** (this is often determined by your teacher).
   - *animal behavior*

2. Decide upon your **narrowed subject** (remember the guidelines!).
   - *the behavior of birds*

3. From your narrowed subject, select some possible **topics** that deal with the subject.
   - *snowy egrets*
   - *the gooney birds of the Midway Islands*
   - *the bald eagle*
   - *the Capistrano swallows*

4. Select one of the topics, and **narrow it** in such a way that you can write a short paper.
   - **the gooney birds of the Midway Islands**
     - *the mating dance of the gooneys*
     - *the humorous antics of gooneys taking off and landing*
     - *the war between the gooneys and the U.S. Navy*

5. Transform a narrowed topic into several possible **thesis sentences**.
   - **the war between the gooneys and the U.S. Navy**
     - *The continuing conflict between the United States Navy and the gooney birds of Midway Island illustrates the strength of the birds' determination to remain on the island of their birth.*
     - *The gooney birds' determination to remain on the islands of*

their origin has foiled every attempt by the U.S. Navy to drive them away.

Despite great expense, the U.S. Navy has been unable to drive the gooney birds from Midway Island.

After considering these three thesis sentences, suppose you choose to develop the first statement—**The continuing conflict between the United States Navy and the gooney birds of Midway Island illustrates the strength of the birds' determination to remain on the island of their birth**. If you did not already know about gooney birds, you would have to begin by reading up on the subject. After you had acquired enough information, you could begin writing by developing your thesis statement. Since the composition is to be short, the one-sentence thesis would be sufficient. It must, however, reflect exactly what you want to write without being too simple. For instance, a statement such as *"I am going to tell you about the gooney birds"* would never do because it is too broad for a short paper. Besides, it is not interesting.

A thesis statement places restrictions on the length of a composition. For example, you could write on the narrowed subject of the behavior of birds. If you wanted to write a book on that subject, you would *not* need to narrow it to the topic of gooney birds, as in Step Three. Versions of the topic of gooney birds might be developed into a twenty-to-thirty-page paper. It is especially important therefore, to narrow your thesis statement adequately. It is clear from the thesis above that the intention of the writer is to illustrate only the point about the birds' determination. Thus, both writer and reader know what is to be discussed and the direction the paper will take.

The chosen gooney bird thesis restricts the writer to a discussion of only *some* of the Navy's attempts to drive the gooneys away, and nothing else. Another topic under this thesis statement would be irrelevant and would be considered a serious writing flaw. Consequently, once the selection of the conflict between gooneys and the Navy has been made, the writer must omit anything about mating behavior or humorous antics, no matter how interesting they may be—those are topics for another composition.

By following the steps used in developing the gooney bird thesis, you should now be able to write a thesis statement that will keep your paper directly on the narrowed topic. By checking your thesis statement regularly, you will prevent your paper from wandering into irrelevant ideas. Checking back also helps you make certain that you discuss everything that you said in your thesis. You must cover everything you promised your reader, and little more.

EXERCISE 6.5

Number your paper 1-10. Then by writing Yes or No, identify those topics that are sufficiently narrowed to be suitable for a short paper.

1. The disadvantages of living together before marriage.
2. The effects of switching sex roles between husbands and wives.
3. The consequences of alcohol abuse by teenagers.
4. The three strategies used to persuade voters to support a candidate.
5. The executive, legislative, and judicial branches of government have a few basic similarities.
6. Freedom of choice is the goal that humanists, feminists, and libertarians share.
7. Telepathy and telekinesis have some basic similarities and one big contrast.
8. Organized sports have many dangers for the young player.

EXERCISE 6.6

Number your paper 1-5; write Yes or No to show which of the following thesis sentences are suitable for 500-1000 word compositions.

1. The purpose of this paper is to show you how the Indians were able to survive during times of severe drought.
2. In order to write well-developed compositions, a writer needs to understand the relationship of the thesis statement to the whole composition.
3. Photography as a hobby is rapidly growing.
4. The space program represents only a very small portion of the American budget.
5. Australian movies have been attracting an international audience during the past few years because they have been skillfully produced and tell entertaining stories.

EXERCISE 6.7

Write a thesis sentence for each of the narrowed *topics* you developed in Exercise 6.4.

LESSON FIVE—The Divided Thesis

A particularly good method of controlling your paper's length and scope is to **divide your thesis** into two or three parts. A divided thesis sentence may be more effective for a short paper because it can tell readers more precisely what is to be discussed.

The most effective type of sentence for a divided thesis is a *complex sentence* because it indicates to the reader what the most important point is by placing it in the *independent clause*. Your reasons for making this important point or any qualifications of this point can be summarized in the *dependent clause*. The dependent clause for thesis sentences should contain ideas that are important but not as important as the main idea found in the independent clause. If your thesis sentence is well divided, your paper will divide naturally into sections that make the whole composition easier for you to write and more logical and readable for your readers.

In each of the following examples the *undivided* thesis is satisfactory for a longer paper. For a short composition, however, the *divided* thesis would be more effective.

Example

(Undivided) Sailboat racing is a demanding sport.
(Divided) If sailors possess *skill, endurance,* and *determination*, they can win at sailboat racing.

The three conditions for winning are listed in the *dependent* clause. The main idea—that sailors can win—is emphasized by placing it in the *independent* clause. The reverse is true in the following example.

Example

(Divided) Sailboat racing requires *skill, endurance,* and *determination* if one expects to win.

In the above example, the conditions for winning are placed in the independent clause; consequently, the winning is subordinated, made less important, to the requirements for winning.

Another Example

(Undivided) The novel *Cane* by Jean Toomer seems very contemporary.
(Divided) Because of the author's effective use of *imagery, characterizations,* and *setting*, the novel *Cane* seems contemporary although it was written in 1923.

Here the reasons for *Cane's* wide appeal are subordinated to the fact that the novel seems contemporary.

To change the emphasis, reverse the clauses:

Example

(Divided) Although the book was written in 1923, the author's use of *imagery*, *characterizations*, and *setting* make *Cane* seem contemporary.

In this version the reasons for *Cane*'s contemporary appeal are emphasized by their placement in the independent clause.

By dividing the thesis, you not only let readers know just what to expect, but you make it easier on yourself to stick to the points mentioned in your thesis. Notice how well the *complex sentence* lends itself to division because the reader can immediately determine a composition's purpose and emphasis. In the divided thesis on *Cane* (above) for example, you can easily see that the writer is helped to stick to the point by the limits placed upon the paper. In this example, the discussion of anything but *imagery*, *characterizations*, and *setting* would be irrelevant. Each of the three divisions could become a body paragraph. By outlining them in the thesis, the writer makes it easier for the reader to follow.

EXERCISE 6.8

Number your paper 1-5. Write Yes if the thesis is divided or No if the thesis is not divided.

1. Skindiving can be dangerous.

2. The energy crisis is posing some problems.

3. Because it interferes with free speech and restricts the flow of ideas, censorship is harmful to a democracy.

4. The founders of the American system of government insisted upon the separation of church and state because they mistrusted organized religion and because they did not want religious leaders to influence political decisions.

5. A great many of the most profound political decisions, those that have severely altered the lives of huge numbers of people, were made only after consulting astrological forecasts.

EXERCISE 6.9

Develop the three thesis sentences you wrote in Exercise 6.7 (page 140) into divided thesis sentences. (While you could divide them into two, three, or four parts, for this exercise write each with *three* parts.)

The Order of Division

How you divide your thesis is important. When you use a divided thesis, you are telling your reader what will be discussed in the body paragraphs. But more than that, you are telling your reader the order in which you plan to present those ideas. That order must be deliberately chosen to avoid confusing your reader.

The three most common ordering techniques are *time, location,* and *importance.*

TIME ORDER

If you are describing something that happened, begin with the earler part and end with the most recent. This technique is often referred to as **chronological order**. The following thesis sentences are divided in such a way as to illustrate time order.

Examples

A comparison of the special effects used in films of the 1960's with those in movies made during the 1980's suggests that American movies are becoming too reliant on technology.

Because they are so dependent on their mothers at birth, so vulnerable at mating, and so useful at death, whales are an endangered species.

Because the 1964 tidal wave started in Alaska, killed twelve people in Crescent City, California, and alarmed islanders as far away as Samoa, a tidal wave early warning system should be established.

Each of these examples uses the time order technique, as each begins at an earlier time and progresses forward.

LOCATION ORDER

The second common technique of ordering what you write is **location order**. Whenever the points in your thesis division can be organized according to which is closest to and farthest from you, use location order. Because this ordering technique is concerned with the distance of objects or events, it is sometimes called *distance order*. Like time order, location order begins with whatever is farthest away and works toward the writer's position. Also, when you use location order to describe a tall object, you would normally begin at the top and work to the bottom. With a long item, you would normally start at the right and move to the left.

Examples

After the flood waters receded, the house's owners had to *repair the back wall, clean up the eight inches of mud on the carpet, and replace all of the doors and windows in the front wall.*

Because *Australia, Tahiti, and Hawaii* are the best sources of spare parts, the cruising sailor should plan to put into each when following the trade winds across the South Pacific Ocean.

Student loan aid must be preserved on the *federal, state, and local* level if America is to remain a democracy.

In the last example, the federal government is more distant from the individual than state government, and local is the closest. Consequently, student aid on the federal level should be discussed first, then the state level, and finally the local level.

IMPORTANCE

When developing an argument, you should save the most important point for the last. This is the **importance order** technique. Positioning the "best" reason last increases the chance that the reader will support the opinion that the paper presents. Consider the following thesis sentences:

Examples

Research into creating new life forms should be delayed because *it is too expensive and it may endanger people's health and safety.*

The 55 mph speed limit should be discontinued because *it has saved few, if any, lives, has not saved much fuel, and has not been obeyed.*

By presenting your most important point last, you will retain the reader's interest until the end of the composition. You can use your lesser arguments to build up interest in the topic and prepare readers for your main point. Also, readers remember best what they read last, so you will want to conclude with a strong finish —your most significant point.

Regardless of the kind of order you use when you divide a thesis, be certain to make your point strongly. In the student aid example, the thesis sentence would be far weaker if it simply read, *Student loan aid must be preserved on the federal, state, and local level.* Without the rest of the sentence, readers would not know why student loan aid must be preserved.

The order that you choose for your thesis is the same order that you will use in the rest of the paper. This organization allows readers to anticipate a paper's structure. The presentation of the ideas is clearer as a result.

EXERCISE 6.10

Identify the correctly divided thesis statements.

1. Freeways are a good investment for the motorist because they save time, nerves, and lives.

2. If people want to maintain their good health, they must have a well-balanced dinner, a nutritious breakfast, and a light, wholesome lunch.

3. Cigarette smoking should be severely restricted because it causes cancer, is noxious to others, and damages carpets and floors.

4. Whales should be protected because they are near extinction and because they are important to the ecological balance of the oceans.

5. Many people think that if a relationship progresses slowly from first date to engagement, and swiftly from engagement to marriage, the union will be more likely to last.

Some Thoughts on the Thesis Statement

In most student writing you can expect to see the thesis statement at the end of the introductory paragraph. You should not, however, expect to see a thesis statement at the end of every introductory paragraph in magazine or newspaper articles or in chapters of books. Some journalists prefer not to be straightforward, choosing, rather, to intrigue readers by keeping them guessing until near the end. Sometimes these writers only imply a thesis, leaving readers to puzzle out exact meanings on their own.

Regardless of these other styles, most of the writing you will be required to do in school or on the job will be enhanced by a well-developed thesis statement. And, of course, the thesis will assist your paper considerably with its focused target. It will add clarity and contribute to your readers' understanding. A correctly written thesis will prevent a paper from wandering from point to point.

The thesis statement is the primary tool for controlling the length of your paper. A short paper needs a highly specific thesis. The longer your paper, the less specific your thesis needs to be.

The best thesis sentences are either simple or complex—almost never compound or compound-complex. Thesis sentences can be very effective without being complicated. One of the most effective techniques to use when you wish to write a short paper, however, is division. By indicating to your readers in a complex thesis sentence exactly what ideas you plan to cover in your paper, you tell yourself what to include and what is irrelevant, and you do not send mixed or false signals to your readers.

By mastering the art of writing good thesis statements, you will not only become a better writer, but you will find writing much less difficult.

Chapter Six Review

PART ONE

In one of your classes you are assigned to write a short paper on one of your favorite musical groups or performers (this is the SUBJECT).

1. Choose three (3) NARROWED SUBJECTS for the paper.

2. For *each* of these narrowed subjects, select three (3) TOPICS suitable for a short paper (500-1000 words).

3. Select one of the nine topics that you wrote for number 2 above and write one paragraph in which you explain why you chose this topic and why it is a good one for this paper.

PART TWO

Listed below are six SUBJECTS for compositions. Write a TOPIC for each.

movies	music
economics	sports
education	your choice

PART THREE

Write a NARROWED TOPIC for each of the topics you wrote for Part Two (suitable for a 500-1000 word paper).

PART FOUR

Write a THESIS SENTENCE for each of the narrowed topics you wrote for Part Three.

PART FIVE

Write each of the following steps on a sheet of paper.

1. Choose a SUBJECT;

2. Choose a NARROWED SUBJECT from your subject;

3. Select several TOPICS from your narrowed subject;

4. NARROW one of these TOPICS;

5. Write *three* possible THESIS STATEMENTS from your narrowed topic.

PART SIX

Write two thesis sentences that are divided to show time order, two that show location, and two that show importance. (Write a total of six divided thesis sentences.)

PART SEVEN

Before submitting your thesis sentences, make certain that you can answer ''yes'' to each of the questions on the Thesis Sentence Checklist.

Thesis Sentence Checklist

1. Have you sufficiently limited your topic so that you could write a short paper?

2. Does your thesis statement tell readers what your paper is going to be about?

3. Did you carefully follow all of the steps for the construction of a thesis statement?

4. Is your thesis statement either a complex or a simple sentence?

5. If your thesis is for a short paper, is it divided?

6. Is your divided thesis ordered correctly?

7. Does your thesis statement focus your readers on the main point?

8. Does your thesis statement make its point strongly?

9. Have you proofread your thesis sentence for errors in punctuation and mechanics?

The Introductory and Concluding Paragraphs

The preceding chapters of this book have been concerned primarily with writing good sentences, various types of body paragraphs, and effective thesis statements. You now know, for instance, that topic sentences develop from good thesis statements and that primary and secondary support sentences further develop topic sentences. You also know that good paragraphs include enough support sentences and illustrative examples to allow readers easily to see what your point is.

In this chapter, you will learn to introduce your reader to the points that you want to discuss. In addition, you will learn to conclude your discussion in a way that clearly completes the ideas you have presented.

The **introduction** and the **conclusion** indicate both the direction and the scope of the body of your paper and hold it tightly to its subject. A strong introduction and a strong conclusion help a composition to become a unified whole. For this reason, you should master their construction well, for you will be expected to introduce and conclude all of your compositions effectively in the future.

LESSON ONE—How to Start It All

The **introduction** leads readers to the thesis statement. A properly written introduction will catch readers' interest and give them an idea of what the paper is about. The introduction, whether it is one or several paragraphs long, usually contains the thesis statement at its end. You should remember that *the thesis statement is the single most important sentence in the whole paper.*

The successful introduction accomplishes three objectives:

1. It attracts attention (the "hook").
2. It narrows the focus.
3. It establishes background.

Attracting Attention

The introduction should begin with an interesting, yet broad, **opening sentence**. The idea is to **hook** the reader's attention like an angler fishing for trout. Readers may not want to read beyond the first sentence or two unless the hook is well written. Each of the following opening sentences is designed to catch readers' attention and entice them into reading further.

Examples

- Play is the work of children.
- Strange objects have always been seen moving mysteriously across the sky.
- The small farm in America is a thing of the past.

Narrowing Focus

After arousing readers' curiousity, you need to narrow the scope progressively from the opening sentence to the last sentence in the paragraph: *the thesis statement*. This narrowing will establish the direction to be taken in the rest of the paper. For example, the writer of the following paragraph has something very particular in mind. Each succeeding sentence comes closer to the specific point being developed.

Example

Play is the work of children. It is the method by which they order their experiences and give meaning to their lives. Toys are the tools which facilitate learning. Most parents buy toys they hope will help their children grow emotionally and intellectually. But American toy manufacturers have distorted this natural selection process by manipulating children's tastes and intimidating parents' judgements through persuasive advertising. Millions of dollars have been spent to promote toys that are actually harmful to the developing values of children. The fashion dolls epitomize this corporate "rip-off" of American values. *Barbie and Dawn are two plastic young ladies who convey to children that superficial sexiness, consumer faddism, and competitiveness among females are positive values.*

In the paragraph above, the thesis statement tells readers that the paper will argue that Barbie and Dawn, two plastic dolls, are teaching children poor values. By contrast, the opening sentence begins with the very general statement *"Play is the work of children."* The second sentence narrows the discussion of children and playing by observing that children learn by playing. From that sentence on, the paragraph limits the concept of learning through playing until the thesis specifies the superficial values taught by Barbie and Dawn dolls.

150

By making the first sentence general and then using the next three or four sentences to lead to your thesis statement, you can persuade readers to see that your thesis is a logical outgrowth of your ideas.

Establishing Background

While you are narrowing the focus of the paper, you can give background information on the subject. Background information will give information that readers need to appreciate or understand fully the development of your thesis statement. In the example above of "Play is the work of children," the writer is giving some background information about toys and the attitude toward toys in America.

Background information is particularly important if a subject is likely to be unfamiliar to your readers. General knowledge about the subject should be shared before discussing a specific aspect of it. For example, few readers know about the struggle between the United States Navy and the gooney birds on Midway Island. Notice how the writer of the following paragraph gives a general background about gooney birds while gradually narrowing the focus to the thesis statement. In this way readers are told before they read the thesis why the Navy would want to rid the island of the birds and why the birds are reluctant to leave.

Example

> Two hundred fifty-thousand gooney birds have defeated the United States Navy for the past thirty years. The conflict began when the Navy decided the birds were endangering airplanes landing and taking-off from the airstrip on Midway Island. The birds have lived on the island for centuries and are unable to understand why they should no longer fly in the vicinity of the airfield. This leads to numerous mid-air collisions between gooneys and airplanes. To date there have been no airplane crashes as a result of these collisions, but the possibility of a tragic accident is ever present. Logically, the United States Navy decided to force the beautiful but clumsy birds to move to another island. Unfortunately for the Navy, the birds absolutely refuse to cooperate. Although the Navy has tried many frightening techniques, the birds still soar above the island. The continuing conflict between the United States Navy and the gooney birds of Midway Island illustrates the strength of the birds' determination to remain on the island of their birth.

Review

1. The opening sentence should attract readers' interest.
2. Middle sentences should lead readers toward the thesis.
3. The thesis should be a logical outgrowth of preceding sentences.

Note: Introductory paragraphs, like all others in a composition, should have at least *five* sentences.

EXERCISE 7.1

Find five introductory paragraphs with thesis statements at the end of each. Copy them and underline the thesis sentences.

EXERCISE 7.2

For each of the paragraphs that you found, write a different opening sentence. Make sure your new opening will catch your readers' attention.

EXERCISE 7.3

Write an *introductory paragraph* for a 500-to-1,000-word composition. After you have chosen a subject from the list of possibilities, narrow it down to a thesis statement. When you are satisfied with the thesis, write your paragraph. (Do not write the whole composition—just the introductory paragraph.)

Suggested General Subjects

Transportation

Advertising

Energy

Smoking

Sports

Your choice

LESSON TWO—Other Ways To Start

Now that you know how to write one kind of introductory paragraph, you should become familiar with others. There are a dozen or more ways to write that first paragraph, but a few introductory variations should be enough to cover most situations. Remember, an interesting beginning is important because that is where you attract your readers' attention and lay the foundation for your paper.

You might like to try some of these other techniques on some of your papers:

An Anecdote

An **anecdote** (a short narrative telling of an interesting or amusing incident) is a common way to gain attention at the beginning of a speech. It can be equally effective for a writer. Anecdotes are usually told to make or support a point. For instance, the example below tells a story and is interesting, but it also does something more. It suggests the writer's general idea. The thesis statement then points out the relevance of the anecdote and the main ideas that follow in the paper.

Example

When the young woman who had been hired to model was late for her session with the advanced art class, the teacher was irritated with the interruption to his instruction. After arriving a half hour late, she readily agreed to pose for the next class also rather than lose any money. The next class, however, was beginning art, and the students had painted only vases and bowls of fruit, not figures. Without warning to the beginning class, the model stood on the platform in the middle of the circled double art tables and shed her robe. Although the class members who were on time were surprised, the real shock could be viewed on the faces of the late arrivals. Each young woman who came through the door during the next ten minutes caught her breath, blushed, and walked briskly to an art table with another woman (quite unlike normal behavior). Each young man did a "double-take," quickly checked the room number to assure no mistake had been made, cast eyes to the floor, and did not again look up until art paper was in place and brush was in hand, all done with a pseudo air of sophistication. Although the sexual revolution has been widely touted by the press and television, this incident illustrates that most young people remain at heart quite conventional in their attitudes toward their peers, nudity, and human relationships.

A Statement of Fact

A **statement of fact** not directly related to the thesis can be used to inform readers as well as interest them. You must make sure, however, to demonstrate the relevance of the statement to your thesis. Statements of fact are most effective when the facts are striking or dramatic.

Nearly all major research into learning theory indicates that reward is far more effective than punishment. Experiments with both animals and humans reveal that punishment is simply not an effective way to change behavior: to learn. A parent or a teacher who uses rewards rather than punishment causes learning to be joyful and not fearful. The most obvious way to reward or punish in school is with the grading system. The grading systems used in most schools, however, do not emphasize learning through reward. In order to improve communications between students and teachers and to promote learning, the school grading policy should be changed to eliminate the negative, punishing "D" and "F" grades.

A Quotation

Sometimes the words of someone else may be so striking and pertinent that you may wish to include the **quotation** in your introductory paragraph. This works especially well if the quotation relevant to your subject is by a well-known person.

Example

Hammurabi wrote in 2100 B.C., "If a man destroy the eye of another man, they shall destroy his eye." Some 3847 years later Voltaire wrote, "It is better to risk saving a guilty person than to condemn an innocent one." The first statement means that the punishment should fit the crime, but the second statement admits the possibility of error. Under a jury system of criminal justice, mistakes in judgement may always be made. Consequently, capital punishment, a sentence from which no reprieve is possible once it has been carried out, must be eliminated from civilized society.

A Rhetorical Question

Although you should generally avoid asking questions in your papers, sometimes beginning with a **rhetorical question** can be effective. A rhetorical question is one for which no answer is expected (e.g., *How long will it take for Americans to realize the dangers of not voting?*). Even so, rhetorical questions force readers to respond in particular ways.

Example

How long are Americans willing to allow millions of dollars of their tax money to be spent to subsidize a product that is deadly to the health of everyone? This product also costs additional millions to treat its victims and relieve its untold grief and suffering. Still more millions are spent to clean up after its use and to bury its dead. Although sounding like an exaggeration and an over-statement, the facts are plain; smoking is a heinous crime against one's self and society. Stiff laws that are effective and enforceable should be passed immediately to encourage tobacco farmers to turn to useful crops, to end all promotion of tobacco for sale, and to prohibit tobacco use in any public gathering place.

EXERCISE 7.4

Read the introductory paragraphs on the student papers in Chapter Eight. Identify which type of introduction each one is. (Write down the page number on which each one appears to identify it.)

EXERCISE 7.5

Write two *introductory paragraphs* in which you use two of the four techniques discussed in this lesson. Choose subjects that interest you. They might be from your hobbies or from a favorite course. The choice is yours.

LESSON THREE—Revising Your Introduction

When you have completed your first draft, you are, of course, not yet finished. The first time through most writers make only a small effort to correct even the most obvious errors in mechanics or structure. They view the first draft as their opportunity to put their ideas into written form. Only later, after most of their thoughts are written, do they turn their attention to the form of their composition.

The process of **revision** requires that you reword or rewrite anything that can be even slightly improved. You need to check the *content*, the *structure*, and the *mechanics* of your writing as you proofread and edit.

Revising Your Opening Sentence

The **opening sentence** is so important that it should be edited first. Check it not only for interest but for its relationship to your thesis as well. Consider how you can best catch your readers' attention. Notice, for example, the opening sentence of the paragraph about the gooney birds (page 151). Because the conflict seems silly, the reader becomes involved in what is said about the defeat of the United States Navy by a flock of birds. Any of the following might also have served as a beginning sentence for that paragraph:

Who would believe that the United States Navy is being defeated by gooney birds?

or

The greatest navy in the world cannot defeat the gooney birds.

or

All the military might of the United States Navy is helpless against a comical but determined enemy: gooney birds.

or

"Don't fire until you see the yellow of their beaks," General Loathfeather said one October morning in 1981.

Although each of these opening sentences is different, each attracts interest. Each sentence is a "grabber," one that makes readers *want* to know more.

In addition to creating interest, these opening sentences hint at the content of the thesis. You should be careful that your beginning sentence does not lead readers' attention astray. If it does, your paper will have a weak beginning and may be unsuccessful from the start. If the opening sentence is not relevant, it will seem to promise something that the paper does not deliver.

Examples

(not related)   There are many beautiful birds in the middle of the Pacific Ocean.

(boring)   The Midway Islands are small islands in the middle of the Pacific Ocean.

(dull)	The Midway Islands are the home of the gooney birds.
(better)	The gooney birds and the United States Navy can be found on the Midway Islands.
(best)	Two hundred fifty-thousand gooney birds have defeated the United States Navy for the past thirty years.

Each of these sentences could be used as an opening sentence for an introductory paragraph about the conflict between the gooneys and the Navy. The last one, however, is the most effective because it is interesting and it introduces the subject of the composition. You should note, though, that opening sentences that are too close to the content of the thesis turn the thesis into little more than a summary statement. Weakening an introduction this way can cause readers to become confused.

EXERCISE 7.6

Write *opening sentences* for each of the following thesis sentences. Make sure you compose interesting sentences that are not too close or too far from the thesis. (Remember, for a complete introductory paragraph at least three additional sentences are needed between your opening sentence and your thesis.)

1. (*thesis*) Preventing crime is often possible if people would simply be alert for potentially dangerous situations created by apparently empty houses, deserted late night streets, and dark parking lots.

2. (*thesis*) The wearing of a motorcycle helmet when riding a motorcycle should be mandatory because the human head is so vulnerable, the cost of treating head injuries is so great, and the amount of suffering from head damage is so profound.

3. (*thesis*) While the actual number may be small, a hardy few have chosen to live aboard boats because their closeness with nature is intensified, their expenses are greatly reduced, and their lives are simpler.

4. (*thesis*) Although they should be respected and avoided if at all possible, sharks are not the evil creatures portrayed in story and film.

5. (*thesis*) The sharp rise in violent crime will continue until society revises the law to make punishment certain and begins to eliminate the root causes of antisocial behavior.

Perfecting the Transitional Bridge

In addition to the opening sentence, the *sentence just before the thesis* deserves special attention. Placed after the general background of the introduction, the second from the last sentence must move smoothly into the thesis by forming a **transitional bridge**. The ideas suggested in the introduction should conclude logically with the thesis sentence. If the second-from-last sentence does not form a smooth bridge into the thesis sentence, the introduction will seem to leap abruptly into the thesis. This leaves readers wondering just how they arrived at the thesis so suddenly.

The small farm in America is a thing of the past. The American ideal of being able to support one's family on a small plot of land began when the country was first settled. This ideal, however, has changed during the last fifty years. The profits from a small farm have not increased during this time but the expenses have. At one time in America, children could look forward to inheriting the family farm; however, very few children today inherit anything but the family debts. *The only way this sad trend can be avoided is through careful preparation*. Today farmers who do not have college educations, expensive machinery, and extensive land holdings will almost certainly fail to support their families without supplemental income.

Look back over some other introductions in this chapter and closely examine the transitional bridges.

"Grabbing" Readers

The best way to gain readers' interest and avoid potential problems with your introduction is to write confidently. A confident writing style will be more readily received than an introduction that sounds apologetic or weak. Do not discourage your readers before they have had a chance to read and evaluate what you wish to communicate. Readers need to be "grabbed" and have their attention held. The introduction should accomplish this by an opening sentence that interests, a transitional bridge that indicates how the introduction relates to the thesis, and a thesis that clearly states the central idea of your paper.

Compare the following examples. Note that the italicized phrases weaken the introduction. These phrases make the writer seem uncertain or seem to lack confidence about what position to take. Simply removing these phrases makes the writer sound more confident.

Examples

1

It would seem that moving from place to place has almost become a way of life for many American families. People sometimes feel compelled to relocate for several reasons. Besides sometimes unwelcome transfers, employees may want better working conditions, promotions, or healthier social environments for themselves or their children. Constantly relocating may have a psychological effect on children. Many people argue that children will become disoriented if they move too much. *I think that* this is a fallacy. Moving from place to place it not necessarily detrimental to a child's upbringing *in my opinion* because it can give the child a better perspective on human nature, broaden the child's thinking, and allow the child to experience a variety of places.

2

Moving from place to place has become a way of life for many American families. People often feel compelled to relocate for several good reasons. Besides sometimes unwelcome transfers, employees may desire improved working conditions, promotions, or healthier social environments for themselves and their children. Constantly relocating, however, is bound to have some psychological effects on children. Some argue that children become disoriented if they move too often; this is a fallacy. Moving from place to place it not necessarily detrimental to the rearing of children because relocating can give children a better perspective of human nature, it can broaden their thinking, and can allow them to experience a variety of places.

EXERCISE 7.7

Revise the paragraph below. Be certain to check the following points:

- relationship between opening sentence and thesis
- number of sentences
- sentence variety
- transitions
- irrelevant material
- the transitional bridge

I think that musical knowledge is an important aspect of learning in school for many people of all ages. We must not overlook the need for students to express himself creatively. Music is perfect for this. Money can be a problem but it can be solved. And at a much lower cost. The importance of music must not be overlooked if it is to remain a part of our culture. Today many musical groups play too loud and hurt their hearing. The playing and understanding of music can make your life worth living.

EXERCISE 7.8

Write an *introductory paragraph* on a subject of your choice. You may use a topic chosen in a previous exercise. For example, you could use a thesis you wrote in Chapter Six, or you could write an introductory paragraph to go with one of the body paragraphs you wrote in Chapter Four or Five.

Develop the introductory paragraph *carefully*, writing at least five sentences. Be certain that you consider all the elements of a good introduction.

Before you submit your introductory paragraph, make certain that you can answer "yes" to each of the questions on the "Introductory Paragraph Checklist" below.

Introductory Paragraph Checklist

1. Does the opening sentence in your introduction "hook" reader interest?

2. Does your introduction lead readers directly and logically to your thesis statement?

3. Did you include sufficient background information in your introduction?

4. Does a "bridge" sentence link the body of the introduction paragraph and the thesis statement?

5. Have you written your introduction confidently—is it a "grabber"?

LESSON FOUR—How To End It All

The **conclusion** wraps up all your ideas into one final section, usually only one paragraph long. It is your last chance to review and re-emphasize the main ideas in your paper. Since people remember best what they read last, your conclusion should leave them with an overall view of the composition. For some writers the second most difficult task in writing a paper is the conclusion. Starting is difficult, but after the words begin to flow, stopping them is often harder. The concluding paragraph, however, can be easily mastered. All it takes is familiarity with the process and some practice.

Visualize the shape of an hourglass. Notice that the top looks like the bottom.

Now, think of the structure of the introductory and concluding paragraphs as similar to an hourglass. The structure of the conclusion is opposite to the structure of the introduction. You need to remember, though, that the image of an hourglass omits the body of a composition. But the image can be helpful because an introduction begins with a general statement, proceeds through a series of sentences that become successively more specific, and finally ends with the thesis sentence. In the conclusion, just the opposite occurs. The conclusion begins with a specific sentence and ends with a general statement.

A concluding paragraph begins with a **restatement of the thesis** of the composition. This restatement is not word for word, however. The rephrasing of the thesis should restate the idea presented in the thesis, but it should avoid repetition. Next, add three or four sentences as a summary of the ideas developed in the composition. You want to leave your readers with an overall view of your paper. When you write your summary, keep in mind that the concluding paragraph is not the place to bring in new ideas, new evidence, or added appeals. Remind your readers only of your most important ideas; refresh their memories.

Finally, end your concluding paragraph with a relevant, decisive generalization. This last sentence after the summary sentences will reinforce your main ideas and fix them firmly in readers' minds. It is necessary in order to show the pertinence, universality, or applicability of your main idea. *Just as the opening sentence of the introduction must be both interesting and pertinent, the last sentence of the conclusion must communicate to readers that what you have written is of lasting significance and relevance.* The first and the last sentence of your composition help give your paper unity—a beginning and an end.

CONCLUDING PARAGRAPHS

1

The "organic way" refers to living in harmony with nature, reliance upon natural fertilizer, and dependence upon biological pest controls. Organic methods require coming to terms with nature and living cooperatively with the natural elements. Good nutrition comes from foods that have no growth hormones or other potentially harmful growth stimulants. Natural biological controls avoid the possibility of infecting humans with unhealthy substances. The organic way has the potential of bringing greater health and happiness to a society that is over-dependent upon the artificial.

2

The advertising industry has infiltrated the unconscious minds of consumers with subliminal techniques. Despite the general usefulness of advertising, this mental invasion has negative effects on society. Attacked by words, claims, and pictures, the inner mind is bombarded with attempts to convince people that they need products to validate their own existence. Those who are persuaded acquire what they cannot afford, do not need, and cannot use. Learning about these techniques and resisting their influences allows individuals to evaluate and judge for themselves what they really want and then to purchase accordingly. Knowledge is power, for it can make people free.

The concluding paragraph is your last chance to persuade readers. Remember, however, that "*I think* . . ." or "*In my opinion* . . ." are as ineffective in the conclusion as they would have been in the introduction. The content of the concluding paragraph is what readers take away with them, so take advantage of this last opportunity to demonstrate your assurance and conviction in what you have written.

Review

All compositions of 500 words or longer should devote a whole final paragraph to the conclusion of the paper. Be sure to keep the guidelines for a conclusion in mind:

1. Begin with a restatement of the thesis.
2. Restate the main points so that they are emphasized.
3. End with a generalization that shows the lasting significance of your composition.

Other Concluding Techniques

1. For *very short compositions*, less than *five hundred* words, it is usually not necessary to have a concluding paragraph. Sometimes the *final sentence of the last body paragraph* will be sufficient for an effective conclusion.

> When others are present in an emergency, any one bystander will usually assume that another observer is already taking action. Experiments have supported this theory. Every individual's reaction at the scene of an emergency is shaped by the action of others—and all too frequently by their inaction. A person can choose to realize the influence of a crowd, disregard it, and step forward to help. *The alternative is apathy and, often, guilt.*

The final point has impact; it can stand alone. As a result, this paragraph from a very short composition needs no concluding paragraph.

2. Sometimes, *two or three sentences at the end of a very short paper* that restate or summarize the main idea of the composition add an effective culmination.

Example

> Even if students feel threatened by exposure to new ideas, they should not be protected. Students need to have their ideas challenged. They gain in conviction and in self-confidence as a result. It is a concept called education.

3. Another effective technique is to conclude with a *quotation* that emphasizes the main ideas of the composition. (Make sure, however, that it is apt and to the point.)

Example

> The main function of the American system of government is to protect the populace from the righteous. The central democratic idea is that the majority of the people will save themselves. The only hope is that the majority can remain less righteous and more unsure of what is right. As the late Supreme Court Justice Learned Hand once said, "The spirit of liberty is a spirit which is not too sure it is right."

Be certain to *avoid writing conclusions that introduce new ideas*. Any new idea at the end of a composition will only leave readers dissatisfied. They will wonder why the writer chose to include it without development. In general, it detracts from the other ideas, the ones that were developed. The following paragraph contains a new idea that is not related to the topic of this concluding paragraph.

Example

> The brief career of the *Glomar Explorer* is but one example of a highly sophisticated and potent international intelligence gathering system. Granted, the surface publicity indicated that Project Jennifer was a failure, but an efficient information gathering network cannot publicly herald each new success. The raising of a Soviet submarine intact, complete with thermal-nuclear weapons, enabled American military scientists to ascertain the level of Russian technology. *After dismantling the Soviet Foxbat airplane, flown into Japan by a pilot wishing political asylum, American technicians learned that the plane, while an effective combat weapon, was not*

nearly as advanced as had been generally supposed. Putting this new knowledge to work for America may eventually save millions of lives. The future of the world necessitates an effective, well-trained, and adequately financed American intelligence community. No price can be too high for freedom.

One final word of caution when writing conclusions: be forceful. Weakness can only leave your readers wondering where you stand. For example, there will be doubt if the ending is inconclusive. Readers resist ideas that are tossed back to them for answers. They are reading for those answers. So ending with questions or statements that ask readers to investigate the problem further or to decide for themselves only leads to frustration. End with a statement that demonstrates the strength of your knowledge.

EXERCISE 7.9

Find five concluding paragraphs that restate the thesis at the beginning. Copy down both the thesis and the restatement of it in the conclusion.

EXERCISE 7.10

Write a concluding paragraph for the introduction that you wrote for Exercise 7.5 (page 155).

EXERCISE 7.11

Before you submit your concluding paragraph, make certain that you can answer "yes" to each of the questions on the "Concluding Paragraph Checklist."

Concluding Paragraph Checklist

1. Does your conclusion begin with a restatement of your thesis (in different words)?

2. Does your conclusion briefly restate all of your paper's main points?

3. Is the last sentence in your conclusion a relevant, decisive generalization?

4. Is your conclusion a whole paragraph (at least five sentences)?

164

8

The Complete Composition

Learning sentence structure and paragraph strategies is important because such skills are the foundation of effective compositions. At this point you should have mastered those skills and be ready to begin the development of your first complete composition. The skills that you learn here will help you in all your classes as well as throughout your life.

LESSON ONE—Reviewing the Parts of a Composition

Examine the diagram of the typical 500-word composition. As you do so, recall the highlights of the first seven chapters. One step at a time, you worked through many aspects of writing compositions. You began by composing simple sentences, then proceeded until you wrote the concluding paragraph. Your study and writing so far, however, have been concerned with the basic components of compositions. This chapter, by contrast, prepares you to write whole papers.

Read the following paper. It is about 850 words in length. After studying it carefully, work the exercise immediately following it. You will be identifying fifteen sentences in the sample composition as opening, thesis, topic, primary, secondary, or summary sentences. You may want to review parts of Chapters Three through Seven to complete the exercise.

KID'S LIB

(1) One of the most profound changes emerging from the twentieth century is the sexual revolution. (2) One result of this revolution is that people are becoming increasingly aware of the dangers of restricting the life choices of individuals to narrowly defined sex-roles. (3) The contemporary view is that individuals and ultimately society can reach highest fulfillment

DIAGRAM OF A TYPICAL 500-WORD COMPOSITION (Chapter Eight)

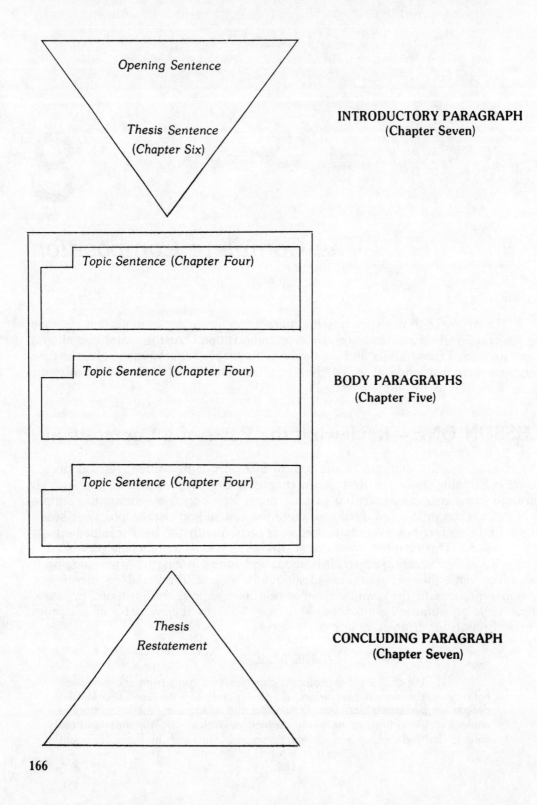

Opening Sentence

Thesis Sentence
(Chapter Six)

INTRODUCTORY PARAGRAPH
(Chapter Seven)

Topic Sentence (Chapter Four)

Topic Sentence (Chapter Four)

Topic Sentence (Chapter Four)

BODY PARAGRAPHS
(Chapter Five)

Thesis
Restatement

CONCLUDING PARAGRAPH
(Chapter Seven)

by encouraging the development of the unique talents and aptitudes of people rather than arbitrarily assigning traditional roles based on an individual's sex. (4) But what happens too often is that the institutions of society, through archaic practices, perpetuate these outmoded role models. (5) Public education is a prime offender, as demonstrated by the content of some of its textbooks. (6) The *Janet and Mark* series currently in use in many states as a reading primer is one example of the way archaic sex-role models are perpetuated. (7) The characterizations of the adults and children in the stories offer hopelessly narrow stereotypes bearing little relationship to beginning readers' life experiences because the *Janet and Mark* series offers an outdated view of how a good, decent family should live in middle America.

(8) Mother is a good, old-fashioned homebody. Her hair is short and plain in the 30's style, and she always wears drab house dresses of below-the-knee length. (9) She wears an apron to be sure to keep flour and sugar off her nice clean dress. (10) Her creative energies seem to reach fever pitch when she bakes and dusts. (11) Occasionally she is shown returning to the nest from her sole outside activity, grocery shopping. (12) Mother never seems to tire or become irritable even though most school children know from experience that shopping, cleaning, chauffering, and cooking are tiring jobs and that their own mothers become irritable and tired. (13) Janet and Mark's mother always looks calm, placid, and slightly amused.

(14) Other adults in the *Janet and Mark* series are hopelessly stereotyped, too. (15) Dad is a real "Nowhere Man" in appearance and action. (16) He has barbershop-trimmed hair and usually wears a white shirt and tie. (17) He is most often pictured arriving home from work in a grey suit and hat. (18) What he does all day is never explored, presumably because his activities are beyond the interest or mental capabilities of his children. (19) He expends his creative energies fixing toys, reading the newspaper, and smoking a pipe. (20) Dad is always calm and banally smiling, especially when he takes his leadership position as head of the family, assuming control of the car on the proverbial Sunday afternoon drives on that big family highlight, a trip to the farm to see Grandma and Grandpa. (21) The old folks are greyed, plump versions of Mother and Dad. (22) Their activities are similarly structured; Grandpa tends to the tractor and animals, and Grandma churns butter.

(23) "Normal" children's roles and activities are dramatized through the behavior of the protagonists, Janet and Mark. (24) Their activities are determined more on the basis of sex than personal inclination or interest. (25) Janet and her friends (all girls) wear dresses and hair ribbons. (26) In the one instance where a girl is shown in pants, she is playing in a field, so her transgression of the rule is forgivable. (27) Like Dad, Mark and his friends (all boys) have short, clean-cut looking hair and wear standard-Sears clothes, invariably neat and clean. (28) Mark and company are allowed more adventure in their activities than the girls. (29) A model relationship between the sexes is gently suggested when Mark climbs a tree to rescue Janet's kitten. (30) One of the few examples of cooperation between the boys and girls occurs when Janet agrees to teach Mark to roller skate if he will teach her to ride a bicycle. (31) But even their cooperation has a sexist bias. (32) The implication here is that boys ride bikes (symbolizing independence—a prototype of supposed male mechanical interest and aptitude)

sooner than girls. (33) But then the little lady has wheels of her own, even if smaller and more restrictive in function.

(34) One story in particular reveals the sexist bias of Janet and Mark. (35) Mark is given an astronaut costume complete with NASA-style blue jumpsuit and plastic bubble helmet. (36) He runs to show Janet his costume. (37) She responds by inviting him into her child-sized playhouse. (38) Inside she pours him pretend tea and shows him around the place. (39) Janet has a charming little bedroom and kitchen setup, complete with pretend baby (doll) in a cute little cradle. (40) She even has sweet miniature curtains on the little window. (41) They sit on the bed and talk about their playthings. (42) And so that leaves the couple happy—Mark literally equipped to "trip-out" to outer space, and Janet doing her best to keep him right there at home with her little seduction scene.

(43) The stilted vision of adult life in the Janet and Mark series adversely influences children's attitudes, especially as it is one of their earliest educational experiences. (44) Restricting options before children are even aware of the available choices discourages the development of mature adults. (45) If the goal of compulsory education is to produce aware, mature persons capable of making meaningful life choices and judgements, this stifling of human potential cannot be healthy for children or society as a whole. (46) Stimulating, imaginative textbooks will challenge children's creativity right from the start.

—Anne Bradley

EXERCISE 8.1

Number your paper from 1-15. From the list of terms on the right, select the letter of the term which describes each sentence designated on the left.

1. Sentence one
2. Sentence seven
3. Sentence eight
4. Sentence fourteen
5. Sentence fifteen
6. Sentence sixteen
7. Sentence seventeen
8. Sentence eighteen
9. Sentence nineteen
10. Sentence twenty
11. Sentence twenty-one
12. Sentence twenty-two
13. Sentence twenty-three
14. Sentence thirty-four
15. Sentence forty-three

a. thesis sentence
b. secondary support sentence
c. opening sentence
d. topic sentence
e. primary support sentence
f. summary sentence

LESSON TWO—Writing the Expository Composition

Writing that explains is called **expository writing**. An expository paper is a composition that explains in depth a concept, an event, a movement, or a process. Writing this kind of paper requires you to know a great deal about the topic. Most of the papers you write in school will be expository. Although your assignment will vary from teacher to teacher and class to class, the basic structure and purpose of all this kind of writing is essentially the same.

Your main purpose in expository writing is to *explain* what you know about your subject. Since your paper reflects this, you should make every effort to express yourself as clearly and completely as possible. Researching, reading, discussing, and reviewing your notes will help you write a better expository paper.

With experience you will gain a better understanding of how to organize your papers more effectively. You will find, for instance, that all papers are similar: collections of paragraphs which support a central idea or thesis. As you come to understand the organizational structure of compositions, you will realize that writing is not difficult; all you need are some basic skills, some imaginative ideas, and lots of facts.

In this lesson you will develop a five-paragraph expository paper. You will write an introductory paragraph, three body paragraphs, and a concluding paragraph. As you write the body paragraphs, you will use the strategies learned in Chapter Five.

Paragraph Strategies

1. Example
2. Definition
3. Comparison/Contrast
4. Analysis
   a. Process
   b. Structural
   c. Cause-and-effect

You have already written one or more paragraphs using each strategy, but they were always by themselves. You will now use them joined together. For instance, as you write an expository paper, your first body paragraph may use the definition strategy, your second may use the illustration strategy, and your third may use the structural analysis strategy. You will choose the best strategy after you decide what you want your paragraph to accomplish.

EXERCISE 8.2

Number your paper from 1-5. As you read the following composition, identify each paragraph as introduction, body, or conclusion. Then, write the name of the strategy used beside the number of each body paragraph.

THE PERFORMING GUITARIST

1

Successful guitarists must be more than instrumentalists; they must be performing musicians in every sense of the word. The music industry has become a very competitive field. Guitarists (because they are so numerous) cannot enter the field of music blindly or half prepared and expect to succeed. Talent alone will not guarantee much in today's music field; talent plus training is required. To become a success today, the performing guitarist must be a total musician—trained, equipped, and creatively sensitive.

2

Although not required at one time, training is the first step that must be taken by the aspiring guitarist. Guitarists of the past, the early 1960's in particular, could slide by without becoming proficient musicians. Rather than developing skill with the guitar, they developed exaggerated body movements. When these performers went on stage, the guitar became a stage prop. Musical training was less important to them than developing an image. Image and body movements are still studied by today's guitarists, but the skills are more important. Training for the guitarist now means studying under a private instructor, working on all areas of performing ability, from scales and theory all the way to stage presence and facial expressions. Preparation also involves playing as often as possible, sharing ideas, and learning to work several instruments into a unified expression.

3

The equipped guitarist is ready with the right tools at the right time, fully knowledgeable of their function and playing application. It is not enough to have a fine instrument. The successful guitarist must have experience with a guitar amplifier, speaker system, microphone, and pick-up. Sound devices, such as echo, reverb, fuzztone, and distortion are all good and fine, but they cannot be effectively employed at random. Proper knowledge and personal experimenting are necessary in order to produce the desired effects. These are older and standard-effects helps; however, advanced electronic inventions are being turned out almost daily. Thus, the guitar player should have a knowledge of new developments, too. Phase-shifters and flangers are popular effect units which can help produce desirable sounds when properly employed.

4

Despite these obvious needs for proper training and equipping knowledge, the factor that really distinguishes and establishes true artistic ability in a guitar player is the creative and sensitive touch given to a work. This is part of the reason people have favorite artists. Sensitivity requires of the musician attentiveness and understanding of the musical subject. This is where the musician has to gain emotional impetus and project personal interpretation and feeling in order to make a passage or sometimes even a single note communicate and live. This trademark of an artist, unfortunately, is difficult to teach, probably making this characteristic one that might be labeled as the mark of genius.

5

Thus, training, equipping, and creating sensitivity culminate in a perfect package, enabling professional guitarists to perform effectively and tastefully in any playing situation. So, whether it is pop, country, jazz, or the classics, successful guitarists must have the training and knowledge to know what to play and when. Furthermore, these guitarists will have a working knowledge of their tools, employing them to their best advantage. Using these skills and this knowledge, performing guitarists may then employ creative touches to enhance any presentation.

—*Randy Hendricks*

From Assignment to Final Draft

Every composition begins with an assignment, whether made by a teacher or initiated by you. How easily you progress from assignment to completed paper depends on how well prepared you are, how difficult the assignment is, and how you go about developing that paper. Of those three variables, the one you have the most control over is how you proceed with your paper's development. If you begin in an orderly, deliberate fashion, the final paper will be easier to produce. It will also be a better composition. Every paper you write should develop through an *eight-step process* between assignment and the final product.

Eight Steps To A Good Paper

1. Choose a general subject.
2. Narrow to a specific subject.
3. Divide your specific subject into possible topics.
4. Narrow the topic you have chosen.
5. Develop the topic into a thesis.
6. Outline the paper.
7. Write a first copy and revise, one or more times.
8. Prepare a final copy and proofread it.

Although it might be possible after you are an experienced writer to develop a paper without following each of these steps, you should not try it yet. This approach will give you the confidence of knowing that the paper you turn in is done correctly.

In the rest of this lesson, you will develop a 500-1,000-word paper, following each of the eight steps previously listed. You will be given a model upon which to base your first six steps. To save time, you may select a subject you wrote on in Chapters Four, Five, Six, or Seven. Even though the paragraphs you have already developed will require some revision, you can revise much faster than you can create entirely new paragraphs. Moreover, because you have already given considerable thought to those subjects as you wrote those paragraphs, you are probably better prepared to write on them than on others.

THE EIGHT STEPS TO BETTER COMPOSITIONS

Step #8—Preparing the final copy

Step #7—Writing the first copy

Step #6—Outlining the paper

Step #5—Developing the thesis

Step #4—Narrowing the topic of your choice

Step #3—Dividing the subject into topics

Step #2—Narrowing to a specific subject

Step #1—Choosing a general subject

Step #1 — Choosing a General Subject

Deciding upon a general subject can be easy or hard, depending on circumstances. If your teacher assigns a paper and the subject, Step #1 is done for you. Usually, though, a teacher will assign a paper and give you a choice of general subjects. One major consideration should always guide your choice of subject. What do you know the most about? You will, of course, spend less time doing research if you select something you already know about.

Sample Assignment

Write a 500-1,000-word paper on *one* of the following:

1. Computer crime
2. Endangered species
3. Unequal taxation

Choosing a *best* subject should not be a drawn-out process. Decide in a few minutes which is best and then stay with your choice. Do *not* switch back and forth. When you decide upon a particular subject, write it down. Do not just "keep it in your mind." To illustrate how a paper should be developed, the general subject of *endangered species* has been followed from Step #1 through Step #6; you will be asked to develop a subject of your own through the same steps.

Example

Step #1 — Endangered species

EXERCISE 8.3

Choose a general subject and write it on a piece of notebook paper. You may select your subject from those you wrote on in Chapters Four, Five, Six, or Seven. (Place your answers to Exercises 8.3, 8.4, 8.5, 8.6, and 8.7 on the same piece of notebook paper.)

Step #2 — Narrowing to a Specific Subject

Just as the general subject should be selected quickly, there is no reason to spend more than a few minutes considering specific subject possibilities. If the subject is familiar to you already, simply write down a list of three or more possible specific subjects under the general subject you chose in Step #1. If you do not know very much about the assigned subject, research the subject briefly.

The following is a list of possible specific subjects related to the general subject of *endangered species*.

Example

      Step #1—Endangered species

      Step #2—Specific subjects

          1. seal   4. wolf

          2. dolphin   5. polar bear

          3. whale   6 condor

EXERCISE 8.4

Below the words Exercise 8.4 on your notebook paper, write at least three specific subjects dealing with the subject you identified in Exercise 8.3.

Step #3—Dividing the Subject Into Topics

    After the subjects are listed, you can study them briefly. Consider which one you feel the most strongly about; that is often the specific subject you should write about. The next step is to divide your specific subject into possible topics. That is done by making a list of topics that your specific subject could be broken into. The following list is only a few of the total number of topics that could be identified by someone writing about seals.

Example

      Step #1—Endangered species

      Step #2—Specific subjects

          1. seal   4. wolf

          2. dolphin   5. polar bear

          3. whale   6. condor

      Step #3—Seal

          1. threats to the Harp seal by fur hunters

          2. dangers facing fur seals on the Pribilof Islands

          3. effects of the shortage of fish on seal populations

EXERCISE 8.5

Below the words Exercise 8.5 on your notebook paper, write at least *three* possible topics for your specific subject.

Step #4—Narrowing the Topic of Your Choice

You will begin this step by deciding which of the possible topics identified in Exercise 8.5 you will write on. Because your topic in Step #3 will invariably be general, you must consciously narrow it until it deals only with the aspect or aspects of the topic upon which you intend to write.

Example

Step #1—Endangered species

Step #2—Specific subjects

1. seal   4. wolf
2. dolphin   5. polar bear
3. whale   6. condor

Step #3—Seal

1. threats to the Harp seal by fur hunters
2. dangers facing fur seals on the Pribilof Islands
3. effects of the shortage of fish on seal populations

Step #4—The brutal slaughter of baby Harp seals

EXERCISE 8.6

Below the words Exercise 8.6 on your notebook paper, write your narrowed topic.

Step #5—Developing the Limited Topic into a Thesis

Writing a **thesis** is undoubtedly the most important step in writing a paper; if your thesis does not work, your paper will never succeed. Reread the section on the development of an effective thesis statement in Unit Six if you are not sure about thesis development. You may find it most convenient to divide the thesis for the paper you will write at the end of this lesson, but it is not necessary to do so.

Example

Divided thesis—

Because baby Harp seals are being slaughtered without restraint, the mating patterns of the flocks are being altered, the size of the flocks is shrinking, and the species is in danger of extinction.

Undivided thesis—

The unrestrained slaughter of the baby Harp seals will cause traumatic changes in the species unless immediate steps are taken.

Which thesis will produce the best composition depends on you. For one paper you write, the divided thesis may be best because it outlines the entire paper. For the next paper, the undivided thesis may be better because it provides freedom to be more spontaneous. You should be guided by whether or not you feel the need of the structure offered by the divided thesis.

EXERCISE 8.7

Below the words Exercise 8.7 on your notebook paper, write your thesis.

Step #6—Outlining the Paper

A **thesis-topic sentence outline** is composed of an opening sentence, a thesis statement which gives direction to the whole paper, a topic sentence for each body paragraph, and a summary statement for the concluding paragraph. Begin developing your outline by writing the thesis statement; it will give the rest of your outline the proper direction. Next, develop a topic sentence for each body paragraph. Remember that each topic sentence must support the thesis precisely. Make the relationship very clear so the final paper will be effective. The length of your paper will dictate the number of topic sentences in your outline. If the assignment is to write a five-hundred-word paper, you will probably need three body paragraphs and, therefore, three topic sentences. If, however, you are assigned a one-thousand-word paper, you will need about six topic sentences. Plan ahead before writing an outline to avoid trouble later. Assume that a good paragraph will have 100-150 words in it (at least *five* sentences), and construct your outline accordingly.

When you are certain you have written your topic sentences as carefully as you possibly can, write a summary or restatement sentence for the beginning of your concluding paragraph. The concluding paragraph should summarize every one of the major ideas you have covered in the body of the paper. Finally, if you have not already done so, write an opening sentence that will attract your reader's attention at the same time that it introduces the subject about which you intend to write.

Sample Outline

Opening Sentence: Babies are being killed in the most brutal ways imaginable.

Thesis sentence: Because baby Harp seals are being slaughtered without restraint, the mating patterns of the flocks are being altered, the size of the flocks is shrinking, and the species is in danger of extinction.

Topic sentence #1: Scientists have noticed that as the size of the flocks shrinks, the female seals are pressured into mating at a younger age.

Topic sentence #2: Although the Harp seals are still numerous in some areas, the total population of these beautiful creatures is merely a fraction of what it once was.

Topic sentence #3: As incredible as it sounds, the rapidly decreasing size of the flocks and the mechanization of their slaughter make the extinction of the species almost certain.

Summary sentence: Because the valuable pelts of these beautiful baby Harp seals are so highly prized, hunters and governments have furiously defended the slaughter as they continue their bloody business.

The thesis-topic sentence outline above would probably be adequate for a 500-750-word paper. As you work the following exercise, develop an obvious relationship between your thesis and topic sentences. (Use the thesis sentence you developed in Exercise 8.7.)

EXERCISE 8.8

On a piece of notebook paper, develop a thesis-topic sentence outline for a 500-1,000-word paper.

Step #7—Writing the First Copy of Your Paper

EXPANDING THE OUTLINE: TWO METHODS

The process a person uses to write a composition differs from writer to writer. There are, however, two primary approaches to writing a paper.

1) The most common technique for developing a paper is to *begin with the opening sentence in the outline and proceed as rapidly as possible with the writing until the last paragraph has been completed.* If you choose this technique, do not become bogged down with the introductory paragraph. If your first paragraph appears awkward and you cannot decide how to make any more progress, simply go on to the next paragraph.

2) The second approach to writing a paper is to *begin with the first body paragraph and write each following paragraph as rapidly as possible.* When all body paragraphs and the conclusion have been completed, you then go back and write the introductory paragraph. You should try both of these approaches before deciding which is best for you.

WRITING CONDITIONS

Write your paper under carefully controlled conditions. First, set aside a large block of time for your writing so you can write the entire first copy without interruption. One continuous writing period will produce a paper that has a pleasing smoothness to it. If you do some of the writing one day, more of it on a second day, and complete it on a third day, a rough and uneven paper may result. The second condition upon which you should insist is a quiet atmosphere in which to write. If you do not have such a place at home, plan to go to some isolated corner of the library during the quiet afternoon hours. No distractions should be permitted. Above all, though, the writing of the paper should be done rapidly. Write without too much concern for proper punctuation, spelling, sentence structure, and other mechanics. In the first copy you should only be concerned with putting your ideas on paper in the order they appear on your outline.

When writing your first copy:

1. set aside a single block of time for writing
2. create an undistracting environment
3. write rapidly

REVISING THE FIRST COPY—SECOND COPY

Once you have completed the first copy, you are ready to *revise*. Surprisingly, this second copy normally takes about the same length of time as the writing of the first copy. If you spend two hours producing the first copy, you will probably need at least two hours to revise it. Begin by going through your paper carefully, looking intently for spelling and mechanical errors.

After you have gone through your first copy one sentence at a time, you are ready for what might be the most important phase of the revision: the paragraph revision. Every paragraph should have at least five sentences in it; also, good sentence variety should be used. In addition, you must be certain that you have used transitions, interrupters, and conjunctive adverbs to smooth out the paragraphs.

SMOOTH TRANSITIONS

The most comfortable transitions for you to use at this point are those you learned in previous chapters. Words such as *however, therefore, moreover, consequently,* and *nevertheless* are common transitions you should have mastered. When you properly use one of them in the beginning sentence of a paragraph, two paragraphs join smoothly almost every time. To be even more effective, you might use a technique called "repetition of key word." In doing this, you repeat an important word or phrase from the end of one paragraph in the first sentence of the following paragraph. Read the following paragraphs and observe how skillfully the writer has tied her ideas together. Note, for example, how effectively the repetition of "seven methods" is used. The connecting transition, which ties paragraph one with paragraph two, is in bold face. Later, bold face identifies the repeated key word which connects paragraphs two and three. (This is only a portion of a much longer paper.)

In 1964, a Canadian film team, Artek Films of Montreal, happened to be on the ice while the annual sea hunt was taking place. Unknowing, the hunters produced for the film team quite a display of their handy-work. The white, silky-furred baby seals called "whitecoats" were the objects of the hunt, but because of the close proximity of the seals, slaughter is a better description. Boasting of "**seven different methods**" of killing the seals, the hunters quickly went about their task. Time was valuable because after the first week the pups moult, developing a coarser, shorter coat of less market value. In their haste, many hunters began to skin the pups before they were dead; several of their "**seven methods**" only injured instead of killed. (In 1966 the Canadian Government reacted and forbade the killing of the animals by any method other than clubbing with a specified hardwood bat.) The small baby seals were often killed in front of their mothers, and their bodies left on the ice since they have no market value as meat. Forlorn-looking mother seals mourned for days over the frozen carcasses of their babies. Subsequent pictures and disclosures by the film team shocked the world.

    Consequently, the Canadian Federation of Humane Societies asked Mr. Brian Davies to attend the **hunt** as an SPCA observer. During the next five years, accompanied by a veterinarian, photographers, and various newspaper and magazine reporters. Davies substantiated in great detail the sequence of events portrayed in the Artek film. The evidence of the savage brutality to the seals is overwhelming, yet the slaughter of the baby seals is allowed to continue. The divisions are strictly drawn between officials concerned over local economy, fishermen who want to preserve their industry, furriers who insist on the right to harvest a valuable marine product, and wildlife, environmentalist, and humane organizations who demand a permanent end to the **hunt**.

    Seal **hunting** has been a factor in local culture for many years. In a lengthy *National Geographic* article in July, 1929, Captain Robert A. Bartlett recreates the excitement and danger of that year's **hunt**. He compares the open day to opening of deer season in the United States. Captain Bartlett was a fifth generation seal **hunter** and boastfully tells of the year 700,000 seals were caught. In 1934 another Newfoundland sealing captain, Abram Kean, earned the Order of the British Empire by bringing in his millionth seal. Disregarding the commercial **huntsmen**, such as Captain Bartlett and Captain Kean, the annual returns for the local landsmen through the years have been very low. Most **hunters** are only casually employed during the winter, and the **hunt** represents a change from winter boredom. In recent years, their **hunting** profits have been as low as $39 and as high as $102 compared to the 1929 figure of an average $60 per year.

—Sonja Gorman

EXERCISE 8.9

Read *The Performing Guitarist* again on page 170. What five key words from the thesis are used in the body paragraphs? Also, count the number of times each word (or derivative of the word) is used; write that number after each word listed.

EXERCISE 8.10

Write your first copy of a 500-1,000-word paper. Do your work on notebook paper. Write on one side only and on every other line.

EXERCISE 8.11

Review the first copy of your paper. The success of your paper will depend on how well it achieves the following:

Composition Checklist

1. Does your paper have a strong, effective thesis sentence?

2. Are all topic sentences clearly stated?

3. Are there five or more sentences in every paragraph?

4. Have you used secondary support (details, facts, figures, and examples)?

5. Is the first word of every paragraph indented?

6. Does your paper have an interesting opening sentence?

7. Is the summary sentence precise and the conclusion effective?

8. Does your paragraph have adequate sentence variety and smooth transitions?

9. Have you used third person throughout, except in anecdotes?

10. Is your paper free of awkward or grammatically incorrect sentences?

11. Have you checked for fragments and comma faults?

12. Have you used correct spelling, punctuation, and capitalization?

Step #8—Preparing the Final Copy

Your final copy should be especially neat and carefully prepared, but it should also be easy to write. Once you have finished editing and proofreading, you will need only to recopy your work. However, you should always be willing to revise a paragraph—or your entire paper—if you find problems when making that final copy.

FORMAT FOR FINAL DRAFT

1. Write in ink, skipping every other line, or type, double spacing.
2. In an upper corner of page one, write your name, the class, the meeting time, your teacher's name, and the date the paper is submitted.
3. Write or type only on one side of each page.
4. Center the title of your paper two inches from the top. If you are writing in ink, capitalize the first letter of each word, except prepositions, articles, and conjunctions that are not the first word of the title. If you are typing, capitalize all letters in the title for appearance.
5. Indent at the beginning of each new paragraph; do *not* leave an extra-wide space between paragraphs.
6. Leave ample but not excessive margins—left, right, and bottom.
7. Beginning with page two, number each page in the upper right-hand corner.
8. Last-minute corrections can be made by neatly drawing a single line through the portion to be revised or corrected and printing the correction above the crossed-out portion. Additions should be inserted above a caret mark (∧).
9. Proofread your composition carefully just before you turn it in. If many corrections or extensive revisions are made, rewrite or retype the page or the entire paper.

EXERCISE 8.12

Prepare and submit your final copy (typed or in ink) of the expository paper you revised in Exercise 8.11.

LESSON THREE—Writing the Argumentative Composition

The previous lesson explained the expository composition in depth. You should now be able to write one with confidence. The expository composition is the one most often required in school assignments. However, two other types of compositions will occasionally be required of you—**argumentative** and **autobiographical.**

In this lesson you will learn how to recognize and write *argumentative compositions*. The argumentative paper is usually written differently than the expository paper. In the body of an expository composition, you explain why your thesis should be believed; in the body of an argumentative composition, you argue back and forth. First you admit that arguments against your case do exist. Then you give evidence that proves your position is correct. The order in which you present arguments for the opposing side and your side is important. Always acknowledge your opponent's position before you reason against it. In other words, always end up arguing for your position after stating the opposing position.

Preparing to write an argumentative composition is the same as preparing to write an expository composition. The first four steps you followed in Lesson Two are also used to develop an argumentative topic. Step #5, developing a thesis sentence, is somewhat different, however.

Thesis

When you write an argument, your thesis becomes especially important. Ideally, the thesis of an argument should be a precise sentence that outlines or foreshadows the rest of the paper. Furthermore, the thesis sentence must take a position and be debatable. The following are argumentative thesis sentences written by students (these are not necessarily true statements, but rather assertions that each writer attempted to argue):

Example

1. Even though many people consider them cruel killers, a close analysis reveals that hunters help deer more than do most environmentalists.

2. In spite of its beauty and insightfulness, *Children of Dune* is not as prophetic a book as *Dune*, the author's first book about the people of Arrakis.

3. People who have strict expectations of parenthood's rewards should not have children.

Writing an Outline of an Argumentative Composition

Before you can write the argumentative outline—Step #6—you must decide how you wish to structure your paper. The most common approach is to have the first body paragraph admit or summarize arguments against the position taken in the thesis. The second body paragraph would then present the author's arguments against the first body paragraph. Examine the following outline:

Example

Thesis: Even though many people consider them cruel killers, a close analysis reveals that hunters help deer more than do most environmentalists.

TS #1: People who are against deer hunting say it is cruel to shoot such beautiful animals.

TS #2: Although much of what they say is factually true, opponents conveniently forget that in the wild, many deer suffer starvation, the cruelest killer, if they are not hunted.

In the part of an outline above, the second topic sentence argues against the first. In doing so it supports the thesis.

Any sentence or paragraph that argues against the thesis is a "con" statement (*con-* is a prefix derived from the Latin *contra*, meaning against). The first of the two topic sentences above would be considered a "con" statement because it presents a position that is against the position presented in the thesis. The second topic sentence would be called a "pro" statement (*pro-* is a Latin prefix meaning for). It supports the thesis.

As you write argumentative compositions, you may write *con* paragraphs followed by *pro* paragraphs. You may also write paragraphs that are one-half *con* followed by one-half *pro*. Whatever you do, though, you must make it clear which side of the argument you are on at all times. One of the clearest ways to do this is to *make certain that your* **con** *statements always come before your* **pro** *statements*.

Transitions for Arguments

To write clearly structured arguments, you must make ample use of **transitional words and phrases**. You can think of these as road signs signaling the direction the argument is to take. You should use these transitions properly to avoid misleading your reader. For example, *But* placed at the beginning of a sentence is a traditional signal that a writer is turning from the *con* side to the *pro* side of the argument. If you use *But* to introduce a *con* point, you might send a false signal to your reader. Try to memorize this short list of transitional words and phrases, or at least consult the list repeatedly until you become experienced at writing arguments:

CON	PRO	CONCLUSION
of course	but	therefore
no doubt	however	thus
doubtless	yet	so
to be sure	on the contrary	and
granted	not at all	hence
granted that	surely	consequently

CON	PRO	CONCLUSION
certainly	no	finally
perhaps	still	on the whole
conceivably	nevertheless	all in all
although	notwithstanding	in other words
though	furthermore	in short
whereas	indeed	

Switching from Con to Pro Between the Paragraphs

The following composition demonstrates how easily a con-pro argument can be structured. While reading *Not Everyone Should Become a Parent*, notice how carefully the paper is organized and how effortlessly the writer moves from one idea to the next. From beginning to end the composition is very persuasive. Observe how the *con* statement is answered with two *pro* paragraphs that support the thesis.

NOT EVERYONE SHOULD BECOME A PARENT

Less than a generation ago mothers often told their daughters, "You are selfish and misguided if you do not want to have children." So, in order to avoid being branded "selfish and misguided" (among other things), young women would marry and have children. Of course, in those days and today, it does not matter why people have children, but how happy they are as parents. After raising their children, happy parents reflect on their parental experience with a sense of satisfaction and reward. However, not everyone can achieve happiness in the parental role. For instance, people who expect their offspring to be cheerleaders, football stars, or corporate presidents may be disappointed and unhappy if their children become something else. Therefore, for a variety of reasons, people who have strict expectations of parenthood's rewards should not have children.

Opponents of this idea will argue that parents can still achieve happiness even though they may not have received the rewards they originally sought out of parenthood. To be sure, children are responsible for much of the joy in their parents' lives. For example, parents can receive much happiness when their children graduate at the top of the class or are awarded professional recognition. Then, too, a vacation or outing, which sometimes becomes boring when shared by just a wife and husband, can be an exciting and unforgettable experience when children are along. Also, in the parents' declining years, a feeling of security can be obtained from having children close by. No doubt, in situations like these, children are often creators of their parents' happiness.

Nevertheless, parents with rigid ideas of parental rewards—for example, those who expect their children to become important people and good company for aged parents—are more likely to become disappointed and unhappy. What parents sometimes neglect to admit is that children are human beings, and as human beings have individual likes and dislikes. The archaic idea of raising children to enter certain professions or achieve certain honors is a sure source of disappointment to parents whose children's accomplishments do not fill a predetermined plan. In addition, children's tastes in leisure activities such as music, sports, literature, and travel often differ from their parents', thereby providing yet another source of disappointment for parents who expect to enjoy the same activities with their children.

Oftentimes, parents who want their children to be around to care for them in their old age end up lonely and unhappy. Today seven out of ten adult offspring live in different cities than do their parents, making a quick trip to do chores for Mom and Dad impossible. Not recalling the time consumed by the family and job, elderly parents often cannot understand why their children will not make themselves more available to lessen the burden of everyday life. Problems arise even when they can no longer take care of themselves. The very presence of grandparents or in-laws can produce conflict and tension. This situation can be very disappointing to the parent who expected to be showered with love, attention, and respect.

Raising children is a tremendous responsibility, full of many disappointments, and should be avoided by people expecting children to fulfill specific needs. All parents have preconceived ideas of what their children might be as adults, but happy parents are able to avoid the disappointment that traps parents with unrealistic hopes. Before having children, prospective parents should decide if their expectations of parenthood are reasonable. If their reasons for having children are in any way selfish, they should not allow themselves to be pushed into it by family or society.

— Virginia Fleming

The student paper you have just read clearly illustrates one way *con-pro* development can be used in an argumentative paper. Argumentative compositions such as this are interesting to write and read because they often take uncommon views on an everyday subject.

The second commonly used method of developing an argumentative composition is the alternating paragraph pattern. As you read the following paper, notice that the author answered each *con* paragraph with a *pro* paragraph.

DOPE IN SPORTS

Your favorite sports hero is a ''junkie.'' This is shocking but very possible. Many players who should know claim that athletes use more drugs than the average junkie. Various drugs are used by these athletes, but the most attractive to them are anabolic steroids. Because there are short-term positive effect and long-term negative effects, people are taking sides regarding the use of these drugs. Although many athletes use anabolic steroids, a consideration of the benefits and dangers clearly shows that any athlete caught using or dealing in such drugs should be permanently banned from competitive sports.

Granted, steroids seem to have three positive effects on athletes using them in proper doses. One good thing about steroids is the improvement of protein assimilation. Some gains in strength have been as high as 40 and 50 percent. In addition, steroids promote calcium retention. This extra calcium develops skeletal structure, thereby increasing height even in adults. Also, cell growth is aided, which in turn increases body and muscle growth. Some athletes have gained 40 pounds or more in a few months.

But the positive effects of steroids are overshadowed by the many negative effects associated with the use of this drug. Even in normal quantities anabolic steroids have been known to cause liver damage (chemical hepatitis), prostatic hypertrophy (enlarged prostate gland), testicular atrophy (shrunken testicles), and premature closure of the growing plates in the long bones of the growing, younger athletes. On top of that, they can aggravate and stimulate the growth of any pre-existing cancers or hormone-sensitive tumors, and can result in decreased libido and infertility. When these drugs are taken in excessive doses, physical complications become more likely and often more serious. Death can result in extreme cases.

Many athletes argue that the practice of using steroids is now so widespread that the younger groups who are just starting out have no choice if they want to get to the top. A survey of thirty-eight track and field athletes and weight lifters at one major university revealed that over half of them had taken or were taking one or more steroids. Many of these athletes stated that steroids were taken for granted as a normal part of training. Easy accessibility is one reason that steroids are so widely used. Also, the fact that they are legal makes them twice as tempting. According to some athletes, if something is known to improve performance, and is legal, there is no reason not to make it available to an athlete when the need arises.

Nevertheless, sportsmanship and fair play are on the verge of becoming obsolete as a result of steroids. Athletes have become automatons, simply reacting to whatever chemical compounds are given to them. It is becoming difficult today to find any successful athlete who does not take drugs of some sort. This practice is unfair to the athletes who refuse to risk their well-being in order to compete against others who are willing to put their health on the line to become winners. This problem seems hopeless. The only chance for fairness to prevail is in the young athletes who have not yet been ruined. The hope for the future lies in their outlook on life, self-image, and the respect given to their parents and coaches.

The honest athlete must refuse to use drugs that alter the mind or body. Anabolic steroids are not only dangerous but unsportsmanlike. Each individual must learn that hard work, fairness, and 110% devotion are the true traits of competition. The one chemical that can produce *honorable* results is the perspiration which is the product of a sound program of physical conditioning and skills practice.

—*Robert Hill*

EXERCISE 8.13

Write out Steps #1-6 for the preceding paper as if you were the paper's author.

EXERCISE 8.14

Argumentative papers are prepared exactly like expository papers: one step at a time. Develop the *outline* for a 500-750-word argumentative composition, from subject to outline, on a piece of notebook paper.

EXERCISE 8.15

Following the outline in Exercise 8.14, write the first copy of a 500-750-word composition.

EXERCISE 8.16

Develop a second copy from Exercise 8.15 and submit the final copy.

AUTUMN

Autumn was beautiful, gentle, and delicate. I met Autumn about one year ago, the first day I start work as a Play Therapist. She was then two years old; she was also unbelievably tiny and frail. I fell in love with her instantly as I walked into her hospital room. I wondered how anyone could have given her up for adoption at birth. Her mother must have felt her daughter would have a better life with someone else; little did she know Autumn would develop leukemia. When I met that adorable child, she had no one to love her; she had been abandoned again.

As a Play Therapist, or Play Lady as I was later called, my job was to deal with the psychological needs of hospitalized children. I would go into Autumn's room and spend hours playing with her. She needed so much love and attention that I was often overwhelmed. That beautiful child could not understand why she was so sick, why everyone hurt her with needles. But not the Play Lady; she only came to play with Autumn. In the year she spent in the hospital, we became very close friends.

As the end came closer, I could see Autumn becoming worse by the day. I had left word to call me at any hour if she worsened more. When the telephone awakened me that last night. I knew the end was here. While I got dressed, I knew my Autumn's pain would soon be gone. As I entered her room, I smelled death around me. I held her in my arms and tried to comfort her. As she gazed at me, I felt her body go limp. I knew in a moment it was over. No more hurt, no more tears, no more Autumn.

Although I felt a sense of loss, I also felt a warm feeling. I had been able to give this darling child a little of myself to love. She had not died without someone loving her. Autumn died knowing someone truly cared. This incident taught me how wonderful it can be to love another human being.

—Julia Duran

The composition that follows demonstrates many of the qualities that are expected in a well-written autobiographical paper. The author has limited the events to one small episode. Her thesis idea, that the exaggerated fears of childhood are easily calmed by an understanding parent, is clear, although the thesis is only implied and not explicitly stated. Her narrative framework makes the time sequence exact, and her use of descriptive detail is superb. She has chosen words carefully and edited and re-edited her sentences to make them unusually effective. Finally, her use of dialogue enhances the readability and the believability of the story. Although she had to write many drafts before getting the version that seemed right, her hard work paid off, because the paper is as good as one written by a professional writer.

THE VAMPIRE

We had no swimming pools in the small resort town of Chester, California, where I grew up. As a result, we spent our afternoons in the hot summer swimming in an icy creek, and we never missed having a pool, for creeks and culverts had their advantages—except for one particular afternoon when I was eight years old.

I lay down on my back, holding my head just above the frigid creek water and let the current carry me, feet first toward the drainage culvert under the asphalt road. My feet, knees, and hips disappeared into the circle of semi-darkness, and then it swept over my head. I felt a split second of panic, as I always did upon entering the culvert, for it was dim, tight, and inescapable if anything suddenly loomed up in that darkness. The hole of light showed beyond my feet, and with a yelp of relief I was swept out into the safety of hot, glaring sunlight. Around me in the creek were the wet, shiny hair-plastered faces of my brother, sister, and four or five friends. On the green, grass-clumped banks were the thick trunks of oaks, and above them the leaves made blinking patterns against the hot, blue sky.

"Safe!" I thought, leaping to my feet, throwing up my arms to sling water in all directions. I splashed happily through the water and clambered up the slippery grass to the top of the bank.

"Hey Pat!" my brother yelled from the far side of the creek. "What's that on your leg?"

I glanced down and froze. On the outside of my leg just above the ankle bone was a black lump about an inch in diameter. Against the cold white of my skin a narrow rivulet of bright blood ran from the glob down my ankle to my foot. While I stood there too afraid to move, my brother waded across the creek and scrambled up beside me, inspecting my leg curiously.

"Pull it off," he said.

I glanced at his wet face, at his expression of impatient encouragement toward his younger sister. Slowly I lowered my arm, my fingers hovering over the black lump, muscles stiff, my teeth clamped together in anticipation of pain. My fingers closed, touched, and I snatched them away with a feeling of sick revulsion. The thing was a wet, slick, and mushy glob of liver-like blackness.

I screamed, jumping up and down. "Pull it off! Pull it off!" I yelled at my brother. It was terrible, and it was bleeding, and I wanted it off, but I couldn't touch it. By now the other kids were out of the water and had gathered around, wide-eyed.

"It's a bloodsucker!" one of the boys said in an awed whisper: a whisper that sent a cold shock of horror through me. It was drinking my blood!

"Stand still!" my brother ordered. His fingers closed over the livery glob, and he yanked. I felt a pinprick of pain, but it didn't come loose.

"It won't come off," he said unnecessarily.

"It's gotta!" I cried, tears coming to my eyes. "Get it off!"

Before my brother could try again or answer me, I spun around and flung myself pell-mell through the grass toward the road. "Mom!" I had to get home to Mom!

I ran with all my strength, forcing my legs to their full stride in terror of the black thing on my leg, the horrible shiny thing that was drinking my blood like a vampire! I was going to die when my blood was gone, die and be buried in the dark, like the darkness inside the culvert! I was dying even while I was running!

Tears spilled out of my eyes, down my cheeks, blurring the great green oaks and the black asphalt road into blobs of color and twisting it into a Transylvanian forest of darkness and death. Stones bruised my feet, but I didn't feel them, or care.

I swung into the driveway, never slowing my pace, took the porch steps in one leap, flung open the door so that it banged against the wall, and fled into the kitchen. Mom turned, eyes wide, her mouth forming a rebuke as I came to a teetering, breathless halt beside her.

"Get it off!" I sobbed, pointing helplessly at the slimy, slick thing attached to my leg.

Mom bent down to look for a moment, then straightened to take a container from the cupboard, and led me calmly out into the hot sunlight of the backyard. Leaning over my leg, she sprinkled salt on the black glob. Almost immediately it fell off, an inky circle in the greenness of the grass.

I leaped away and hunched down to look at my leeched leg. Mom crouched down beside me to look too. The hole was barely visible.

"It was drinking my blood," I said, my fear subsiding. "I could'a died!"

"It could only drink a little," Mon said patiently. "It couldn't hurt you unless it was there for a long, long time."

"It couldn't?" I said surprised.

"No, there really wasn't anything to be afraid of."

And she was right. There wasn't.

—Pat Gerber

EXERCISE 8.17

Develop an outline for a 500-750-word autobiographical composition. Use natural time order like that in the example on page 191.

EXERCISE 8.18

Following the outline you developed in Exercise 8.17, write a 500-750-word autobiographical paper.

EXERCISE 8.19

Revise your first draft from Exercise 8.18 and submit the final draft.

9

The Library Research Paper

Before beginning a research paper, you should pause to consider why you are writing one. Teachers usually assign research papers to encourage you to read more than just the course textbook. The paper you submit as part of your research project should demonstrate how much you have learned through that extra reading.

Your research paper will be graded on how thoroughly you have searched for information on your subject. For instance, most teachers will expect you to read not only books but also magazines, newspapers, encyclopedias, and pamphlets. In the process of doing that reading, you will become familiar with many aspects of the library. Your goal should be to develop the skills necessary to use the library to find information and then to convert it into a neat, readable paper. By following the suggestions contained in this chapter, you can make certain that your efforts will result in the best possible paper.

As you work through this chapter, you will be asked to select a topic, research it, and write a paper that demonstrates your ability and knowledge. Your topic must be one you can find enough material on in your library; that is, it must be "researchable." Also, do not pick a topic that is too challenging. Rather, you should pick a topic that interests you.

LESSON ONE—Library Areas

The main purpose of any library is to serve as an information bank. Your library is made up of a number of areas, each specializing in certain types of materials and services. The larger the library, the more areas it will have. When you write a research paper, you will use the library extensively. You should, therefore, become familiar with its areas and services.

To make efficient use of the library, you should become familiar with each area. As a rule, libraries have at least six areas:

1. *Card Catalog*—The card catalog lists the library's total collection of books. The card catalog is a card system used to find the call number of books in a library's collection. (In some libraries, the catalog may be be on microfilm rather than on cards.)

2. *Stacks*—Books are kept on shelves called stacks. After you find the call number of a book which you would like to examine, go to the stacks to find the volume. If your library has "closed" stacks, simply ask a librarian to get the volume for you.

3. *Check-out Counter*—Information, reserve books, and check-out services are available at this counter.

4. *Reference*—Encyclopedias, almanacs, maps, biographical indexes, and dictionaries are kept in the reference area or room.

5. *Serials*—Often referred to as the periodicals area, the serials area contains all of the magazines and professional journals in the library.

6. *Vertical File*—The vertical file is normally found in or near the reference area. It contains pamphlets, newspaper clippings, government bulletins, and reprints on most current topics.

Library Services

If you use a large library, you will sometimes need help to locate something. The librarian who specializes in the area where you have trouble will be your best source of information.

INTERLIBRARY LOAN

You will often find that your local library does not have a particular book which you must have. **Interlibrary loan** may be able to borrow the book from another library for you. (Do not wait until the last minute—this procedure takes time.)

Similarly, libraries usually keep lists of the serials (magazines and journals) located in other libraries. If your library does not have the magazine you need, ask your librarian for the magazine lists from other libraries in your area.

COPY MACHINES

Modern libraries also have extensive equipment which can help you with your research. When you find longer articles that appear to be helpful, you can easily make copies on convenient machines. These copies can then be read carefully when you return home. Whether the article you want is in a magazine or book, you can use the **photocopy machine** for a small fee. Most larger libraries also have copiers that will produce copies of articles on microfilm and microfiche.

Answer the following questions in one or two *complete* sentences.

1. What is found in the vertical file?
2. What is found in the serials area of your library?
3. How can you get a book if your library does not have a copy?
4. Why do libraries have photocopy machines?
5. Why do teachers assign research papers?
6. In what area of your library would you be most likely to find the encyclopedias?
7. How would you find the call number of a book?

Finding and Narrowing a Topic

Writing a research paper actually begins with finding and narrowing a topic. In a few rare instances, you will be given a topic that is already focused, but you usually will not be so lucky. As a rule, you will be given a very general subject to research; the narrowing will be your responsibility. You might, for example, be investigating the general subject of "threats to ecology in California." But this is a subject on which you could write dozens of books. If you read about all of the different threats to ecology in California, you would spend years researching the subject. Using the narrowing technique learned in Chapter Six, you could, however, begin by deciding to research birds. You could continue by limiting your subject to "threats to the brown pelican" or "threats to the California condor." This step is important. Remember, if you do not restrict the scope of your subject enough, your paper will be too general.

Another basic consideration is time. How much time do you have for the project? If you had only three weeks to complete your paper, you might be wiser to choose a less ambitious topic.

If possible, select three or four potential topics before beginning research procedures. Carefully and thoughtfully, write down the topics so you can study them. Look back at Chapter Six if you need help. The following topics could be considered by someone wanting to research ecological threats to birds in California:

1. threats to the California condor
2. threats to the brown pelican in San Francisco Bay
3. threats to the bird population on the Farallone Islands

Any of these topics could be worthy of research, but for various reasons one might be best for you. For example, neither topic two nor three could be researched in most school libraries and would, therefore, be eliminated at this point if your research was to be done only in your school's library.

The following list of topics may contain one that interests you. If not, feel free to suggest one of your own to your teacher.

water pollution
air pollution
land pollution
wolves
grizzly bears
eagles
dolphins
whales
manatees
fights between students

drugs on campus
teenage alcoholism
the need for a school sports program
how divorce affects children
a hobby
child abuse
sex before marriage
police brutality
Sudden Infant Death Syndrome (SIDS)
women's equality in sports

NARROWED TOPIC

After you have selected a topic, write a narrowed topic by asking yourself a research question. This question can be informal and may vary from two sentences to one-half page in length; however, it should be written down to help you focus on what you want to say. The key feature of any research question is what you want to answer through your research. Consider the following research question.

> According to what I have read, the bird population on the Farallone Islands has decreased dramatically during the last hundred years. I would like to explore the subject in depth to find out *why the decrease occurred and if the birds are doomed to extinction within the next hundred years.*

When you have completed the proposal and considered its implications, begin your research.

EXERCISE 9.2

1. Write *three* potential topics on notebook paper and think about each. Which is the most interesting? Is one topic a better one for the library you will be using? Which one is best suited for the amount of time available for the project? Underline the topic you like best.

2. Write a research question on the potential topic you underlined in the item above.

Using the Library Effectively

Once you have written a research question, you are ready to begin working in the library. But receiving the most from the library is more involved than merely knowing how to check a book out. Indeed, you should go to the library ready to follow the series of steps described in the next few pages.

WORKING BIBLIOGRAPHY

A **working bibliography** is a list of available articles and books that might give you information about your topic. Some researchers list the references for their working bibliography one after another on notebook paper. But most prefer to use 3-by-5-inch index cards (or slips of paper), each one containing the information needed to locate and identify a potential source of information. If you decide to use 3-by-5-inch index cards (or slips of paper), use a separate card for each reference to be tracked down. The following is a sample working bibliography card for a book.

> Lopez, Barry Holstun. *Of Wolves and Men*. New York: Charles Scribner's Sons, 1978.
>
> An explanation of the myths surrounding wolves, and an examination of their slaughter by misinformed Americans.
>
> 599.74442
> L864
>
> City Library

In your working bibliography, list a variety of sources, beginning with the most obvious kind, such as books, magazine articles, and encyclopedias. Then you can list the more difficult-to-locate sources, like professional periodicals, government publications, newspapers, pamphlets, and unfamiliar reference materials.

Find two or three times as many sources as you think you will need. (Most writers begin with a minimum of twenty-five potential sources.) You will not be able to locate some of the materials, and others are certain to prove useless. A paper based upon two books will never appear as thoughtfully done as one based upon two books, a newspaper article, an encyclopedia entry, a reference book, and a few magazine articles. Although the list above might sound overly long at first, it is a practical list for a serious research paper. Consider only those materials that are housed in the library you are using or can obtain through Interlibrary Loan, unless you plan to travel to other libraries.

Prepare your working bibliography so that it is neat enough for you to read a year from now. Most important, be certain each entry contains all of the pertinent information needed to locate the sources. Your working bibliography will be used later to help you write your note cards, your footnotes, and your final bibliography.

SOURCES OF INFORMATION

As you do your research, check every possible source of information in the library. The more carefully you search through the various sources, the more convincing your final paper will sound. Also, do not overlook books and magazines that you have at home or that you can borrow. The library is the best but not the only source of information.

Card Catalog

In the **card catalog drawers** you will find three kinds of 3-by-5-inch cards. Each card appears similar to the others; however, each has a different piece of information at the top.

1. *The Subject Card*—These cards are filed alphabetically according to the subject listed at the top. (In some libraries the catalog is divided into two parts: subject cards in one section, title and author cards in another. In most libraries, however, subject, title, and author cards are filed together.) The following is a typical subject card:

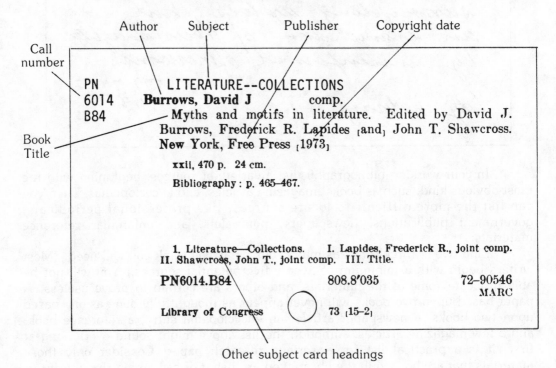

Unless you already have particular authors or titles in mind, you will be using subject cards initially. Simply look up the topic alphabetically, and read the short description of the contents. If the book looks promising, copy down all helpful information on your bibliography card. When you are researching an historical subject dealing with a particular country, you will find it listed under the country and then chronologically by historical period (e.g., United States—revolution, 1775-1783).

2. *The Author Card*—If you are looking for a book by a certain author, you will be looking at the author cards. The author card below is for the same book as the subject card above:

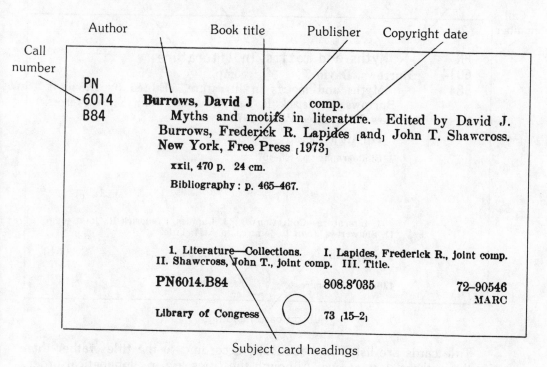

These cards are filed alphabetically according to the last name of the author listed at the top of the card.

3. *The Title Card*—When you are trying to locate a book and you know the title, you will be looking at the title cards. The following sample card illustrates the slight difference between the title card and the two previous cards:

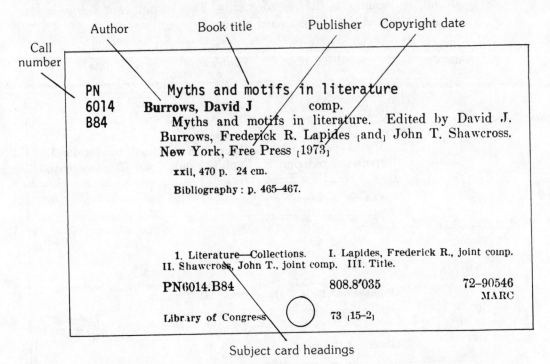

Author   Book title   Publisher   Copyright date

Call number

PN
6014
B84

Myths and motifs in literature

Burrows, David J   comp.
    Myths and motifs in literature. Edited by David J. Burrows, Frederick R. Lapides [and] John T. Shawcross. New York, Free Press [1973]

    xxii, 470 p. 24 cm.

    Bibliography : p. 465–467.

    1. Literature—Collections.   I. Lapides, Frederick R., joint comp. II. Shawcross, John T., joint comp. III. Title.

PN6014.B84   808.8′035   72–90546
                                                     MARC

Library of Congress   73 [15–2]

Subject card headings

Title cards are listed alphabetically according to the titles rather than the authors' last names. Although the titles are in alphabetical order, certain library rules for alphabetizing must be known. Articles at the beginning of titles, such as *A, An, The,* and *Les* (French) are ignored. Furthermore, abbreviations in titles are treated as if they were spelled out. Thus, *Mr.* would be considered *Mister,* and *St.* would be considered *Saint.* Also, titles beginning with numbers are filed as if the numbers were spelled out. George Orwell's book *1984,* for example, is listed under *N,* for nineteen.

Periodical Indexes

When you are researching a current topic, recent information is required. You need, therefore, to be able to find the most recently written articles in the hundreds of magazines and journals published regularly. To avoid searching through thousands of magazines, carefully consult appropriate indexes. An index or a bibliography is a listing of articles published during a given time period. Some indexes list only articles found in popular magazines. Others list only those articles found in professional publications.

The Reader's Guide to Periodical Literature, the most commonly used index, lists every article published in the 166 most commonly read magazines in the United States. Articles which appear in *Time, Newsweek, MotorBoating and Sailing*, and other such popular magazines are all listed in *The Reader's Guide* by subject and author. To use this or any other index, look in the alphabetically arranged listings for the subject or author you need. When you encounter abbreviations you do not recognize, consult the *key* at the beginning of the book.

In addition to *The Reader's Guide*, your library will probably have other indexes. In deciding which indexes to use, select ones that relate to your topic. For instance, for a paper on the funding of parochial schools, you would be wise to begin your research with *The Reader's Guide*. However, you would be likely to find other important articles listed in the *Education Index*.

Reference Books

The reference area of your library contains numerous sets of encyclopedias. As long as you use these books only for background, they can be very helpful as you search for information. Encyclopedias such as the **Americana, Britannica**, or **World Book** can offer basic information on most topics you might research.

More specific information on almost every topic can be found in the reference area. For instance, if you need information on a living individual, look in a *Who's Who in America* (or any other *Who's Who*). More in-depth information on personalities can be found in *Current Biography*.

Specific statistical information can also be located in the reference area. If you need facts or figures, you can begin with any of the many almanacs and progress to more specific publications. Two typical almanacs are the *Information Please Almanac* and *The World Almanac and Book of Facts*. Your librarian will be glad to suggest where you might find other reference material you need. If no librarian is available, you can begin by checking in the *Statistical Abstract of the United States*.

Newspapers

The most current source of information is the newspaper. Most libraries subscribe to a wide range of newspapers to provide full information on current events. But that variety creates a problem for you as you do your research for a paper. Most libraries have indexes for only a few newspapers. You could waste hours and days searching for information about something that occurred months or years earlier if you had to read through back issues. To prevent this wasted time, you need an index which lists all the articles in back issues. Small school or community libraries may not have any newspaper indexes. Larger libraries, however, normally have an index for the *New York Times, The Wall Street Journal*, and the *Christian Science Monitor*. Some libraries have indexes for even more newspapers.

Because of the number of newspapers most libraries subscribe to, it is common practice to discard all issues more than one month old. To enable you to read articles which appeared in discarded issues, many libraries attempt to purchase microfilm copies of those newspapers for which they can obtain indexes.

The Vertical File (Pamphlet File)

Although its size and location varies greatly from library to library, a **vertical file** can be found in almost every library. The vertical file, usually just some file cabinets located in an out-of-the-way place, contains newspaper clippings, pamphlets, and bulletins. In most libraries, the newspapers that are regularly discarded are cut up before being recycled. All articles with current appeal or social significance are cut out, pasted on 8½-by-11-inch paper, dated and identified (dates and page numbers are missing), and filed in the vertical file. This treatment is reserved for newspapers that are not indexed. For instance, local newspapers usually have no indexes, so your only opportunity to find articles which appeared in back issues would be in the vertical file.

In addition, the librarian in charge of the vertical file will place all relevant pamphlets in the file. Often you will not have time to request pamphlets from publishers when researching your topic. Therefore, your only hope of finding these valuable sources of information will be the vertical file. The same is true of bulletins from government and private agencies. To use the vertical file, you merely search for your subject alphabetically.

Microfilm and Microfiche

To conserve space, many libraries buy **microfilm or microfiche** copies of newspapers and magazines. To use microfilm or microfiche, however, you must have an index. You cannot browse through five hundred feet of microfilm and expect to find the needed information. You can use the *Reader's Guide* for an index to magazine articles. Those magazines which your library has discarded because of space limitations may be on microfilm. If they are, you can take the location information and easily find the correct reel of microfilm or microfiche card.

See your librarian for explanations about using microfilm or microfiche reader machines.

EXERCISE 9.3

Write the answers to the following questions, using one or two *complete* sentences for each.

1. How can you tell a subject card from an author card in the card catalog?

2. How do indexes save researchers time and effort?

3. What is the most frequently used index for magazine articles?

4. Besides the usual encyclopedias, what books are commonly found in the reference room?

5. What are the three most commonly found newspaper indexes?

6. Why is the vertical file a particularly important place to search for information?

7. Why do libraries buy microfilm or microfiche copies of magazines and newspapers?

In the library, perform the following tasks, using 3-by-5-inch cards or separate pieces of paper cut that size.

1. Make *five* working bibliography cards for articles you find listed in the most recent volume of the *Reader's Guide*. Use the topic you wrote a topic proposal on in Exercise 9.2.

2. Make *three* working bibliography cards for articles you find listed in the most recent volume of the *New York Times Index*. Use the topic you wrote a topic proposal on in Exercise 9.2.

3. Make *four* working bibliography cards for books you find listed in the card catalog. Use the topic you wrote a topic proposal on in Exercise 9.2.

4. Make *three* working bibliography cards for books you find in the reference area. Use your topic from Exercise 9.2.

5. Make *five* working bibliography cards for pamphlets or clippings you find in the vertical file. Use your topic from Exercise 9.2.

LESSON TWO—Writing Your Research Paper

Taking Notes

Reading books and articles while preparing to write a research paper is only part of the job. Taking notes effectively is just as important. Unless you can remember what you read and where you read it, your research effort will be wasted. You must take notes rapidly and orderly on everything you read. (Most researchers now use both notes and photocopies.)

To begin with, obtain a stack of 4-by-6-inch cards, or 5-by-8-inch cards, and a thick rubber band to hold them together. (Although you can use notebook paper for notetaking, it is not recommended because it is far easier to use cards when you are writing your paper.) Then, as you read the sources listed on the working bibliography cards, fill out note cards for every one determined worthy of a careful reading. A typical note card follows:

SUMMARY NOTE CARD

Nicholas Rosa, "All About Ooze,"
Oceans, Vol. 12, No. 6
(November-December 1979), pp. 30-33.

Describes the various types of ooze on the deep-ocean floor: red clay, globigerina, diatom, radiolarian, and pteropod.

ONE POINT PER CARD

Write only one point from an article or book on each note card. This procedure will help you organize your ideas as you begin writing. Of course, this will also mean that you often have several cards for a source. Separating the points on different cards is to your advantage, however, because later you will be able to arrange your cards in the order they will be used in your paper. Most likely, each note will be used in a different part of the paper anyway.

LABEL YOUR CARDS

If possible make a rough outline of the sections you think you will include in your paper, for instance, INTRODUCTION or BACKGROUND or ARGU-

MENTS AGAINST. Then label each note card according to the section where it belongs. Or, break up your big research question into smaller questions and label your note cards accordingly. The objective of this procedure is twofold: 1) to organize your notes and 2) to avoid having to take notes on everything you read.

QUOTING, PARAPHRASING, AND SUMMARIZING

As you take notes on what you read, you will need to use three types of note-taking methods. These are the quotation, the paraphrase, and the summary.

1. **Quotation**—When you copy a phrase, sentence, or more from your source, you are quoting. Because quoting takes an excessive amount of time, you should use this technique only when the writer's comments are particularly important. Be sure to put quotation marks at the beginning and end of the quotation, and carefully note the exact page or pages on which the quotation appears. When quoting, you must copy word for word, exactly as the passage is written.

   All punctuation marks at the end of quoted material are placed inside the quotation marks, *except for semicolons or colons*, which are placed outside the final quotation marks (e.g., ,″ .″ but ″;).

QUOTATION NOTE CARD

Ira J. Tanner, Loneliness: The Fear of Love, New York: Perennial Library, 1973.

"It is not always understood that the opposite of love is not hate but indifference," p. 21.

2. *Paraphrase*—A paraphrase rewords what you read and is frequently longer than the quotation itself. The advantage of a paraphrase is that it rewords the specific sentence that is important and the context in which it appears. The note card for the paraphrase also includes the page number on which the material was found. Do not use quotation marks.

T. George Harris, "The B. F. Skinner
Manifesto: All The World's a
Box, An Introduction," *Psychology
Today*, Vol. 5, No. 3 (August 1971),
pp. 33-35, 83, 87

Skinner argues that with less haughty
pride man might not become
extinct, even becoming as well
adapted an organism as the rat,
the pigeon — or the radish.

3. *Summary*—When you wish to make a general note of what is said by a source, you can summarize. One summary card might cover an entire magazine article, a chapter in a book, or several paragraphs. This kind of card explains the major point made by a source in general terms and is always shorter than the original. Include the page or page numbers of the source. Again, do not use quotation marks. See the sample Summary Note Card on page 206.

Making note cards is time consuming. However, the more note cards you have and the more accurately you have written them, the better your paper will be.

EXERCISE 9.5

1. Write *one* quotation note card for each of the following entries in your working bibliography (Note: Do not use the same articles or books in every item in this exercise):
    a. magazine article
    b. book listed in the card catalog
    c. newspaper article

2. Write *one* paraphrase note card for each of the following entries in your working bibliography:
    a. magazine article
    b. book listed in the card catalog
    c. newspaper article

3. Write *one* summary note card for each of the following entries in your working bibliography:
    a. magazine article   c. newspaper article
    b. reference book   d. book listed in the card catalog

Planning the Paper

When you have completed taking notes, you are ready to begin planning your paper. The first step in writing a research paper, as in writing almost anything, is to develop a thesis statement. A thesis is important because it states the point of the paper in the most direct terms. It tells your reader the conclusion you have come to as a result of your research. The thesis is also important because it forces you to bring your topic into focus before writing the first paragraph. Once your thesis is in written form, use it to guide you through the remainder of the paper. (Review Chapter Six for the development of the thesis statement.)

When you have developed the thesis, the next step is to develop a thesis-topic sentence outline. This outline consists of the already developed thesis and a sequential list of topic sentences for the body paragraphs supporting it. It should look exactly like those you developed for your papers in Chapter 8.

Example

THESIS-TOPIC SENTENCE OUTLINE FOR A SHORT RESEARCH PAPER

Thesis: In order to enjoy the music of the Baroque Era, modern listeners must have a fine ear, a rare musical taste, and a wild imagination.

Topic Sentence #1: Having a fine ear is necessary to hear all of the instruments of Baroque; without this, listeners receive little from it.

Topic Sentence #2: To most people, Baroque is very harsh sounding music; appreciating this music requires a very rare musical taste.

Topic Sentence #3: In order to get the full effect of this type of music, people must have wild imaginations so they can dream up the many things the music might be suggesting.

When your topic sentences are written, make sure that the relationship between the thesis and the body paragraphs is clear. (Do not hesitate to alter your outline as you write; your paper may improve if you do.)

EXERCISE 9.6

1. Working with the same topic you researched and wrote on in Exercise 9.5, write a thesis sentence for a 500-750-word composition.

2. Write three or four topic sentences for the thesis sentence you developed above.

Writing the Paper

After developing your thesis-topic sentence outline, you can begin the first draft of your paper. Where you begin depends on your own preference. Some writers prefer to begin with the opening sentence, others with the first body paragraph. There is no one correct way. Whatever works best for you is the best way to proceed. This is the point at which you should review your note cards and, using your outline as a guide, arrange them in the order that you plan to use them.

Once you begin writing the rough draft, write as rapidly as possible, leaving the corrections of spelling, punctuation, and sentence structure for the revision. As you write, support your ideas with facts, statistics, and quotations from your sources. However, you must remember to give credit when you borrow from one of these sources.

FOOTNOTES (ENDNOTES)

As you write your first draft, make temporary notations wherever you place borrowed words, facts, or ideas: for instance, (Rosa, p. 31). In your final draft these temporary notations will be replaced by *footnote numbers*. You use footnotes to give credit when you borrow from one of your sources. In other words, when you place a footnote after a sentence, you are telling your reader who said it and where the source can be found. You thus avoid presenting another person's thoughts as your own.

WHAT TO FOOTNOTE

If you wish to write a good research paper, you should incorporate the words and ideas of others into your writing. Placing a footnote number at the end of every sentence you write, however, will not produce a smooth paper. Generally, the following rules will guide you through footnoting.

1. Footnote all quoted or closely paraphrased material.

2. Footnote little-known facts, statistics that someone might want to check, and the unique ideas of others.

3. Do *not* footnote generally known information, especially if you find the same information in a number of sources. (Note that teachers' opinions differ as to what is "generally known," so check with your teacher in case you are in doubt.)

TYPES OF FOOTNOTED MATERIAL

Writers of research papers use quotations, paraphrases, and summaries as they write; each requires the use of a footnote.

Footnoting Quoted Material. Quoted material may be handled differently, depending on length. Short quotations are incomplete sentences, usually words or phrases placed within the flow of the writer's sentences. For instance, a writer doing a research paper on Richard Wright's *Native Son* might write the following:

> Bigger thought he needed the gun as he went into white society because it would "give him a sense of completeness." [1]

or

> Bigger, because "he did not have a wider choice of action," decided to take the job at Dalton's. [2]

Medium-length quotations are usually a sentence or two long. As you incorporate such quotations into your writing, be sure to lead into them smoothly.

        Jack London's separation from his first wife, Bess, accidentally became a great help to him in an unexpected way. As Andrew Sinclair points
out, "It was one of the first cases in the American market of scandal being
used to push the sales of a book." [3]

For long quotations, five lines or more in length, a special **blocked**
technique is used. While most quotations are double-spaced like the remainder of
the text, blocked quotations are single-spaced. And where other quotations are
extended to the normal left margin of the paper, a blocked quotation is indented
five spaces. Likewise, a blocked quotation is also indented five spaces from the
normal right margin.

Example

        Captain James Cook was an outstanding navigator; of that there can
be no doubt. He was, however, like Henry Hudson before him, frustrated
by the futile search for a passage between the Atlantic and Pacific Oceans.
He spent years fighting the elements in the cold North Pacific as he
searched for that dreamed-of route. But the search took its toll.

        By the time he returned from that cold forbidding northland
whose ice-walls had shattered his plans, and with his consort-ship
Discovery had anchored off Hawaii, James Cook was growing weary.
He was near fifty-one; he had held a world-encircling sea captaincy,
with all its burdens and cares, for nine long years without respite;
and now his fine and feeling mind was being overwhelmed by a
voyage which seemed to be stretching to infinity. [4]

Because the quotation here is more than five lines long, it is indented. Note that
quotation marks are not used to set off the quotation. It is identified by the
footnote number at the end.

Ellipsis Points

        To avoid making a paper unnecessarily long, keep all quoted passages as
short as possible. You should use long quotations only rarely in research papers.
When long quotations are used, they frequently contain ellipsis points to indicate
where some parts of the passage have been omitted. Ellipsis points, a series of
three periods separated by spaces, are the writer's method of identifying the
point at which part of the original passage was deleted. If a complete sentence or
more is deleted, use four spaced periods. In the following passage, eight sentences have been omitted because they were not needed to communicate the ideas
presented.

        Though he had killed by accident, not once did he feel the need to
tell himself that it had been an accident. . . . There was in him a kind of
terrified pride in feeling and thinking that some day he would be able to
say publicly that he had done it. [5]

In the above quotation, a period appears immediately after the word *accident*
because that is the end of the sentence. The three periods of the ellipsis follow

that period, making a total of four spaced periods. If the ellipsis appears within a sentence, however, only three periods are used.

"Polyandry . . . is very rare in birds, but it occurs in the phalarope."[6]

PARAPHRASED AND SUMMARIZED MATERIAL

When paraphrasing or summarizing your source material, do not use quotation marks, and be selective about footnoting. If you have read the same information in many sources, you can generally consider it common knowledge. In such an instance, you would not footnote. As a general rule, avoid excessive footnoting because your paper will become everyone else's paper rather than yours. Try not to use more than three footnotes per page. But if you must use more to avoid unnecessary vagueness or plagiarism, do so.

PLAGIARISM

Plagiarism is a unique form of theft. If you copy the words, ideas, or thoughts of someone else and pretend that you thought of them all by yourself, you are plagiarizing. If you are caught engaging in this form of theft, you will usually receive a failing grade for your paper. Be fair enough, and cautious enough, to give credit to your sources by the proper use of footnotes and a bibliography. Furthermore, merely changing a word or two of your sources' ideas will not exempt you from the charge of plagiarism. You must completely rewrite your sources' ideas and you must use a footnote to show where you obtained the information.

WHERE TO PLACE FOOTNOTES

The footnote number is placed after the quoted, paraphrased, or summarized material. Whenever possible, place the number at the end of the sentence it documents, after the punctuation. The note number is always placed slightly above the line of type that it references. The following quotation is typical:

As Hal Roth points out, "Cape Horn gales blow primarily from the west."[6]

You should also use a *lead-in* to a quote to make your paper flow smoothly. Observe the lead-in to the quote above.

In the past the footnotes were always placed at the bottom of the page, hence the name *footnote*. Today, however, the notes are commonly placed at the end of the paper. If you place your notes at the end of the paper, you can call them *Footnotes, Endnotes,* or simply *Notes.* To be safe, you should check with your teacher to determine which heading is preferred.

FOOTNOTE PROCEDURE

Begin numbering your footnotes with number one and continue numbering them sequentially until you reach the end of the paper. Do *not* start with number one again on the second page. If you use thirty-one footnotes in a ten-page paper, the last one would be number thirty-one.

When you use quoted materials, be certain to use exactly the same words and punctuation your source uses. Do not change anything in your quotation. In fact, if the person you are quoting misspelled a word or used faulty punctuation, you must copy it. In such a case you indicate that you recognized the mistake by placing (sic) immediately after the error. This prevents your readers from thinking that it is either your mistake or that you failed to recognize it.

"The man who invented blood plasma died because he did not recieve (sic) its benefits."[13]

SAMPLE FOOTNOTES

The following samples illustrate a variety of footnotes you might have occasion to write. The note in parentheses explains the situation.

(Book with single author)

[1]Richard Wright, Native Son (New York: Harper & Row, 1940), p. 44.

(Book with two or more authors)

[2]Joy Gould Boyum and Adriene Scott, Film as Film: Critical Responses to Film Art (Boston: Allyn and Bacon, 1971), p. 5.

(An anonymous book)

[3]Baja California (Los Angeles: Automobile Club of Southern California, 1978), p. 47.

(A work in several volumes or parts)

[4]J. M. Synge, The Shadow of the Glen, in Collected Works, 4 vols. (London: Oxford University Press, 1968), III, p. 37.

(A work in a collection by different authors)

[5]Sean O'Casey, "Purple Dust," in The Genius of the Irish Theater, ed. Sylvan Barnet, Morton Berman, and William Burto (New York: Mentor Books, 1960), p. 273.

(Articles in reference works)

[6]"Shanghai," Encyclopedia Britannica, 1980 ed.

(A work that has been translated)

[7]Albert Camus, Caligula and Three Other Plays, Trans. Stuart Gilbert (New York: Vintage Books, 1958), p. 46.

(A pamphlet)

[8]The Basic Guide to Spa/Hot Tub Maintenance (New York: FMC Corporation, 1980), p. 24.

(A play)

[9]Samuel Beckett, Waiting for Godot (New York: Grove Press, no date), p. 24.

(A poem)

10Al Young, "For Poets," in <u>Dices or Black Bones,</u> ed. Adam David Miller (Boston: Houghton Mifflin, 1970), p. 17.

(An article in a journal)

11John Rouse, "The Politics of Composition," <u>College English,</u> 41 (Sept. 1979), 3.

(An article from a magazine or newspaper; no author listed)

12"Opera's Golden Tenor," <u>Time,</u> 24 Sept. 1979, p. 60.

Note: If an article has no author listed, the entry will appear like entry 12 above. If the article has an author listed, present the author's name first.

A SUBSEQUENT REFERENCE

When you want to refer to the same source more than once in a paper, you will write a **subsequent reference**. Rather than to repeat all the information again in your second footnote, you can use an abbreviated format. References for footnotes 11 and 12 would look like the following:

13Rouse, p. 4.
14"Opera's Golden Tenor," p. 61.

EXERCISE 9.7

Answer the following questions in one or two *complete* sentences.

1. What is plagiarism?

2. How can you avoid plagiarism?

3. Where should you place the identifying number of a footnote?

4. What should you footnote in a research paper?

5. What is a blocked quotation?

6. What are ellipsis points used for?

7. Is a paraphrase or summary of your source material footnoted?

8. When would footnotes be called *Endnotes* or *Notes*?

9. What should you do if the author you are quoting misspelled a word?

EXERCISE 9.8

1. Write a footnote entry for each summary note card you wrote in Exercise 9.5.

2. Write a footnote entry for each quotation note card you wrote in Exercise 9.5.

3. Write a footnote entry for each paraphrase note card you wrote in Exercise 9.5.

4. Write a "subsequent reference" for item #2 above.

Writing the Bibliography

The bibliography is essential because it tells the reader where to find every source used in your paper. If you list every source you read while researching the paper, it is properly titled *"Bibliography of Sources Consulted"* or *"Reading Bibliography."* Such a bibliography is rarely used. More commonly, you will prepare a *"Bibliography of Sources Cited"* (normally, this is called simply *"Bibliography"*), which is a listing of those sources used in the footnotes.

Bibliographic entries differ significantly from footnote entries. Consider the footnote and the bibliography entries which follow:

Example

Footnote

10Dick Harrison, "Beyond the Slide Show," Skin Diver, Oct. 1979, p. 23.

Bibliography

Harrison, Dick, "Beyond the Slide Show." Skin Diver, Oct. 1979, pp. 22-24.

You should be able to distinguish many differences at a glance.

1. Footnotes are ordered by number; bibliography entries are ordered alphabetically, never numbered.

2. Footnotes are listed with the author's first name first; bibliography entries are listed last name first.

3. Footnotes have commas separating the items; bibliography entries have periods in some places.

4. Footnotes generally refer to a specific page. Bibliography entries refer to the total pages of the article in a magazine or an essay in an edited book of essays by different authors (no page numbers if a book is by one author).

5. Footnotes have information about the publisher in parentheses; bibliography entries do not use parentheses.

6. The first line of a footnote is indented five spaces and subsequent lines are brought back to the left margin; the opposite is true for bibliography entries.

SAMPLE BIBLIOGRAPHY

BIBLIOGRAPHY

Baja California. Los Angeles: Automobile Club of Southern California, 1978.

The Basic Guide to Spa/Hot Tub Maintenance. New York: FMC Corporation, 1980.

Beckett, Samuel. Waiting for Godot. New York: Grove Press, n.d.

Boyum, Joy Gould, and Adrienne Scott. Film as Film: Critical Responses to Film Art. Boston: Allyn and Bacon, 1971.

Camus, Albert. Caligula and Three Other Plays. Trans. Stuart Gilbert. New York: Vintage Press, 1958.

O'Casey, Sean. "Purple Dust." In The Genius of the Irish Theater. Ed. Sylvan Barnet, Morton Berman, and William Burto. New York: Mentor Books, 1960, pp. 262-340.

"Opera's Golden Tenor." Time, 24 Sept. 1979, pp. 60-67.

Rouse, John. "The Politics of Composition." College English, 41, Sept. 1979, 1-12.

"Shanghai." Encyclopedia Britannica. 1980 ed.

Synge, John M. The Shadow of the Glen. In Vol. III of Collected Works. Ed. Ann Saddlemyer. London: Oxford University Press, 1968, pp. 29-59.

Wright, Richard. Native Son. New York: Harper & Row, 1940.

Young, Al. "For Poets." In Dices or Black Bones. Ed. Adam David Miller. Boston: Houghton Mifflin, 1970, p. 17.

FURTHER EXPLANATIONS ON BIBLIOGRAPHY

1. If a source does not have an author listed, alphabetize it by its title, ignoring *A, An, The, Le,* or *La* when used as the first word.

2. Page numbers are not needed when listing a book by a single author unless the book is a collection of poems, plays, essays, or short stories. In such a case, list the total pages covered by the work being referred to (e.g. *pp. 30-36, p. 53, pp. 567-72*).

3. Spacing is also important. Begin the bibliography four lines below the title; then double-space everything else.

EXERCISE 9.9

Answer the following questions in one or two *complete* sentences.

1. What is the difference between a "*Bibliography of Sources Cited*" and a "*Bibliography of Sources Consulted*"?

2. What is the difference between the ordering of footnote and bibliography entries?

3. What is the difference between the indenting of footnote and bibliography entries?

4. What is the difference between page numbers given in footnote and bibliography entries?

EXERCISE 9.10

1. Write a bibliography entry for each footnote you wrote in Exercise 9.8, #1.

2. Write a bibliography entry for each footnote you wrote in Exercise 9.8, #2.

3. Write a bibliography entry for each footnote you wrote in Exercise 9.8, #3.

Writing the Final Copy

Once you have completed the writing of your first draft, you are ready to revise. The revision process is simple; you check everything you are unsure of. Check the punctuation and sentence structure carefully. Also, examine the structure of the paper. Be sure your paper says what you want it to say. When you are satisfied with the revision, you can write the final copy and submit your paper. As you write the final copy, follow the specifications in the Checklist.

Checklist for Research Papers

1. Paper has a title page with title, author, course, instructor, and date (repeat title at the top of page one)

2. Paper includes an outline page (if required)

3. Paper is written in ink or typed neatly

4. Paper has pages numbered in upper right corner; no number on page one

5. Paper is punctuated correctly

6. All words are spelled correctly

7. Paper is double-spaced

8. Margins are 1½ inches at the top and the left and 1 inch at the right and the bottom

9. Footnotes are numbered consecutively in the paper

10. Bibliography is on the last page of the paper

EXERCISE 9.11

1. Using the topic you have written on and researched in the exercises in this chapter, write a 1,000-word research paper. Use the "Checklist for Research Papers" to be sure you have included everything.

2. Select a topic not written on in this chapter. Research that topic and write a research paper on it. Use the "Checklist" to be sure you have included everything.

Sample Research Paper

The following research paper was written by a student. Read the paper to see how to use quoted material, footnotes, and bibliography.

THE CALIFORNIA DRUNK DRIVER

by

Mary E. Willoughby

ENGLISH

Mr. Mehaffy

November 25, 1980

Alcohol has become one of the most widely used and abused drugs in America.[1] It is used by some to soothe emotional turmoil. For these users it can become a crutch, never solving their problems but becoming addictive. These users can become chronic abusers--problem drinkers. Alcohol is also used as a social ritual. In many communities this social drinking is readily tolerated and at times promoted. This type of socially acceptable behavior may encourage the social drinker to abuse alcohol.

Nearly two million individuals are arrested for drunkenness in this country every year.[2] Hidden in this figure is an enormous number of arrests for drunk driving. In California alone, 283,797 individuals were arrested in 1979 for drunk driving.[3] But this statistic shows only the "tip of the iceberg." The actual number of drunk drivers may well be many times the number of those who are arrested. One estimate is that a drunk driver has only one chance in two thousand of being arrested.[4] Thus despite the large number of arrests, the odds definitely favor the drunk driver. Since these drunk drivers are involved in a frightening number of accidents, authorities are becoming increasingly concerned.[5] Especially in California, drunk driving has become a frustrating social problem, seemingly one without an easy solution.

Even when arrested, the California drunk driver is not always convicted. Of the total arrests for 1979, only 206,259 were actually convicted.[6] This low conviction rate occurred in part because the courts are usually lenient with first offenders. Also, the court system allows many drunk drivers to plead guilty to lesser charges. This plea bargaining has sometimes led to the striking of previous convictions to allow drivers to keep their licenses.[7] Consequently, more than 70,000 of those actually arrested and convicted in 1979 for drunk driving were literally absolved of their offense.

California law requires license suspension if a driver is convicted of

219

drunk driving for a second time within five years. The license is then revoked if a driver is convicted three times within seven years. In 1979, 20,009 licenses were suspended and over 16,000 were revoked.[8] But this type of punishment is not keeping the drunk driver off the road. Recent studies by the California Department of Motor Vehicles show that sixty-five percent of those who had their licenses suspended or revoked drive anyway.[9] It is apparent that no matter how many times drunk drivers have their licenses suspended or revoked, they continue to drive.

On the national level, Joseph A. Califano, former Secretary of the Department of Health, Education and Welfare, cited excessive drinking as the cause of 100,000 deaths a year.[10] In California alone, leniency with drunk drivers has cost the lives of over 2,000 people and resulted in injuries to over 73,000.[11] In addition, the financial costs are soaring, and these costs must eventually be paid for by all drivers through the increased cost of automobile insurance. Unfortunately, there is no way to measure the loss to the friends and relatives of the victims of drunk drivers. It would seem that drunk drivers affect everyone. Like a stone dropped into a pond, drunk drivers generate radiating circles of death and destruction.

Several methods of dealing with this problem have been advocated. The group known as Mothers Against Drunk Drivers (MADD), a grass-roots organization, is seeking a forty-eight hour jail sentence for first offenders, and stricter penalties for repeat offenders.[12] The American Council on Alcohol Problems (ACAP), an organization based in Washington, D.C., would go to the root of the drunk driving problem, alcohol. They advocate control and regulation of alcohol through higher alcohol taxation, stricter regulations on advertising, and stronger controls over marketing of alcohol.[13] But whether dealing with this problem at the cause, alcohol, or at the level of the drunk driver, a solution is desperately needed.

An educational program could be one means of reaching the potential drunk driver. A program aimed at youth should be made readily available to all youth-oriented organizations such as the Boy Scouts, Girl Scouts, religious clubs, and junior high and high schools. This program should be keyed to making every new driver acutely aware of the legal and moral consequences of drinking and driving. In fact, an awareness of the effects of drinking and driving should be part of every high school driver education course. In addition, an educational program should be made available to adult organizations, clubs, and senior citizen groups. This program should make adults aware of their individual responsibility to keep the drunk driver off the road. At social functions and private parties the drinking of alcoholic beverages should be kept to a minimum. Those who overindulge should not be allowed to drive.

At the community level, establishments that serve alcohol can be made to accept greater responsibility for their patrons who drink and drive. Greater community involvement could encourage these establishments to develop a program which would eventually benefit everyone in the community. Perhaps they could hire individuals who would do nothing but keep an eye on the drinkers and send home, by taxi or relative, those who overindulge. Surely the cost of these "bouncer" type individuals would not come near the present cost in lives and financial loss due to drunk drivers.

The following statement of the Reverend Donald W. Wells, Pastor of the Faith United Methodist Church, brings the problem to each individual's conscience.

> If by scientific, objective study we discovered that drinking alcohol was a wholesome way to develop an attractive personality, that it made all workers more reliable and more efficient, that it lessened crime and promoted good citizenship, that it reduced accidents and disease and in general improved our health--if, all these things considered, alcohol belonged on the asset side of our social balance sheet--then each of us would be honor-bound to encourage everybody to form the drink habit.
> But if we found the opposite to be true . . . then it is fair to say that we would be honor-bound to bend every effort to discourage its use.[14]

Penalties for those who are actually caught drunk driving have not prevented drunk driving, and proposed stricter penalties probably will not solve the problem either. Control over alcohol did not work during the days of prohibition, and the proposed partial controls, if instituted, may cause a greater problem. A more plausible solution to the problem would be to encourage greater community involvement and advance programs of education. Perhaps with more people educated as to the effects of drinking and driving, fewer will have the tendancy to drink and drive. But after all, the solution to the problem of drinking and driving is quite simple: Don't drink and drive.

NOTES

[1] Joel Fort, M.D., Alcohol: Our Biggest Drug Problem (New York: McGraw-Hill, 1973), p. 24.

[2] California Alcohol Data, State of California Health and Welfare Agency: 1973, p. 13.

[3] Lynn Ferrin, "Drunk Driving in California--How Bad Is It?" Motorland, 101, No. 6 (Nov/Dec 1980), 32.

[4] Ferrin, p. 33.

[5] "Alcoholism," Encyclopedia Americana, 1979 edition.

[6] Ferrin, p. 32.

[7] Ferrin, p. 33.

[8] Ferrin, p. 33.

[9] Ferrin, p. 33.

[10] "Califano Plans a Drive Against 'Problem Drinking,'" The New York Times, 2 May 1979, Sec. A, p. 19.

[11] Ferrin, p. 32.

[12] Ferrin, p. 33.

[13] Clayton M. Wallace, "Control and Regulate Alcohol," American Council on Alcohol Problems, Summer 1976, p. 2.

[14] "Alcohol Addiction No. 1 Public Health Problem," The Sacramento Union, 9 November 1980, Sec. C, n. pag.

BIBLIOGRAPHY OF SOURCES CITED

"Alcoholism." Encyclopedia Americana, 1976 ed.

"Califano Plans a Drive Against 'Problem Drinking.'" The New York Times, 2 May
    1979, Sec. A, p. 19.

California Alcohol Data. State of California Health and Welfare Agency, 1973.

Ferrin, Lynn. "Drunk Driving in California--How Bad is it?" Motorland, 101, No.
    6 (Nov/Dec 1980), 32-33.

Fort, Joel, M.D. Alcohol: Our Biggest Drug Problem. New York: McGraw-Hill,
    1973.

Wallace, Clayton M. "Control and Regulate Alcohol." American Council on Alcohol
    Problems, Summer, 1976.

Wells, the Reverend Donald W. "Alcohol Addiction No. 1 Public Health Problem."
    The Sacramento Union, 9 November 1980. Sec. C, n. pag.

A Handbook for Writers

Agreement—Subject-Verb

Agr

In a clause the *subject* and *verb* must **agree in number.** A subject and verb agree in number when a *singular subject* is used with a *singular verb* or when a *plural subject* is used with a *plural verb*. A word is **singular** when it refers to **one** of something—one place, one thing, one action, or one condition. A word is **plural** when it refers to **more than one** of something, for example, more than one person or more than one action.

Examples

SINGULAR		PLURAL	
Subject	**Predicate**	**Subject**	**Predicate**
child	is	children	are
city	grows	cities	grow
this	was	these	were

Singular

> A child sometimes **is** frightened when the *city* **grows** dark.

Plural

> *Children* sometimes **are** frightened when *cities* **grow** dark.

THERE IS

The phrase **there is** creates a subject-verb agreement problem for many writers. The phrase may be mistakenly used with *plural* subjects instead of using **there are.** Because the **there is** appears before the subject, the writer frequently fails to anticipate the number of the subject and change the *is* to *are* when necessary. (Note that *there is* or *there are* may be placed before the subject in a dependent clause, as in the second example below.)

Examples

WRONG

There is millions of people who are out of work.

The historian thinks that *there is* secret tunnels under the old city.

CORRECT

There are millions of people who are out of work.

The historian thinks that *there are* secret tunnels under the old city.

(See page 261, **Removing "It is" and "There is."**)

COLLECTIVE NOUNS

Collective nouns are words that name *groups*. Collective nouns are *singular* when the writer means "the group as a whole," but they are *plural* when the writer means "the individual members." Whenever possible, most writers treat collective nouns as if they are *singular*—they refer to the entire group. Thus, they would change "The *army* **are** well trained" to "The *army* **is** well trained." On the other hand, a collective noun sometimes sounds awkward when it is singular. Therefore, "the *police* **is** unable to solve the murder" might be changed to "The *police* **are** unable to solve the murder." Then, too, the writer can add a word like **members** to avoid awkward use of either the singular or the plural. For example, "The *team* **are signing** their contracts one by one" could be changed to "The *team members* **are signing** their contracts one by one." "The *police* **is** baffled" could become "The *police force* **is** baffled" or completely changed to "**Police** *investigators* **are** baffled."

Some Collective Nouns

army	faculty	jury
audience	FBI	police
class	fleet	school
committee	flock	swarm
crew	group	team
crowd	herd	troop

AMOUNTS

Amounts—measurements, distances, weights, volumes, fractions, times, dollars and cents—are usually considered to be *singular* even when they seem to be plural.

Examples

Thirty-nine and thirty-seven hundredths inches **is** a meter.

Twenty-five miles **is** too long of a hike for a beginner.

SINGULAR NOUNS

Nouns like *mumps, measles, social studies, mathematics,* and *pediatrics* end with **-s** and seem to be plural, but they should be treated as **singular nouns.**

Examples

> *Measles* **is** a miserable illness for a small child who hates to stay in bed.
> *Social studies* **is** my favorite subject this year.

This rule does not hold with every noun ending with **-s**, however. One would not write, for example, "The *acoustics* in the concert hall **is** poor." Instead, one would write "The *acoustics* **are** poor." "The *tactics* **was** brilliant" would be wrong; "The *tactics* **were** brilliant" would be correct.

TITLES

A **title** is always used with a *singular verb.*

Examples

> The *Captains and the Kings* **was** a best-selling novel.
> The episode of *The Rookies* you want to see **is** on tonight.

COMPOUND SUBJECTS

A **compound subject** joined by **and** requires a *plural verb* for a predicate, even when each subject is singular. The *and* shows that the subject consists of more than one thing.

Examples

> *Soccer* **and** *tennis* **are** now big spectator sports in America.
> *Bob* **and** *Pat* **do** not **smoke**.

However, when a compound subject is commonly considered to be a *single unit*, use a *singular verb.*

Example

> *Peanut butter* **and** *jelly* **is** his favorite ice cream flavor.

PREDICATE NOUNS

If the subject and **predicate noun** do not agree in number, the *linking verb* used as the predicate should agree with the subject, not with the predicate noun.

Examples

	SINGULAR	SINGULAR	PLURAL

The scariest *part* of the trip **was** the *rapids* at Roaring Run.

PLURAL	PLURAL	SINGULAR

Poverty and scorn **were** his *fate.*

ALTERNATIVE SUBJECTS

Singular subjects that are joined by **or, nor, either/or,** and **neither/nor** require *singular verbs*. These subjects are *compound subjects*, but at the same time they are *singular*, not plural. Each part of the compound subject—each subject—is to be considered individually as a separate *alternative*.

Examples

Bob or *Betty* **has done** this to us.

Either the beige silk *blouse* **or** the peach wool *sweater* **goes** best with that skirt.

Neither the book *report* **nor** the term *paper* **was** ready.

But what if the subjects are joined by conjunctions such as **or** and **nor** and one of the subjects is *plural*? The verb should agree with the nearer subject, but the sentence may be awkward. Try to avoid this kind of construction.

Example

Neither the book *reports* **nor** the term *paper* **was** ready. (awkward)
[PLURAL / SINGULAR SINGULAR]

Neither the term *paper* **nor** the book *reports* **were** ready. (revised)
[SINGULAR / PLURAL PLURAL]

SUBJECTS FOLLOWED BY MODIFYING PHRASES

A *simple subject* may be followed by phrases that *modify* the meaning of the subject. These word groups do not ordinarily affect the number of the subject. (The simple subject never appears in a *prepositional phrase*.)

Examples

[SINGULAR MODIFYING PHRASE SINGULAR]
The lead **singer** *of the Hawks* **attends** this school.

[SINGULAR MODIFYING PHRASE SINGULAR]
The **teacher,** *as well as the students,* **is** required to take a physical exam.

[SINGULAR MODIFYING PHRASE SINGULAR]
Jim, *accompanied by his sons,* **has** begun to hike the length of the Sierra Nevada from Mexico to Canada.

WHEN THE SUBJECT IS A PRONOUN

Singular Pronouns

Writers may be confused when they see **pronouns** that do not seem to be completely singular or plural. The following *pronouns* are normally *singular*; thus, when they are used as subjects, they require *singular verbs* for predicates.

Singular Pronouns

any	one	anybody
each	anyone	everybody
either	everyone	nobody
neither	no one	somebody
	someone	

Writers can easily remember that these pronouns are *singular* because they mean "one of a group." The focus is on *one* person or *one* thing in the group.

Examples

> *Each* **has** its own characteristics.
> *Everyone* **works** a full year before getting a vacation.
> *No one* **was** there.

Often the *singular pronoun* is followed by a *phrase* that contains a *plural noun or pronoun* (as is frequently the case after singular nouns followed by modifying phrases). Ignore that plural noun: the *simple predicate* must agree with the *simple subject,* not with the noun in the phrase.

Examples

Simple Subject	Plural Noun	Simple Predicate	
Each	(of the *colleges*)	**has**	a soccer team.
Neither	(of the *answers*)	**was**	correct.

Plural Pronouns

The following *pronouns* are **plural**. When they are used as subjects, they must be used with *plural verbs* for predicates.

Plural Pronouns

both	few	many	several

Examples

> *Both* **were** mistaken
> *Several* of the houses in the neighborhood **are** abandoned.

Pronouns That Can Be Singular or Plural

When the pronouns **all, most,** and **some** refer to things that can be counted, they are **plural**.

PLURAL   PLURAL
All of the *wolves* in this area   **are**   gone.

PLURAL   PLURAL
Some of the *students* **commute** from Plymouth.

When these same pronouns refer to quantities that cannot be counted, they are **singular**.

Examples

SINGULAR   SINGULAR
All of the *real estate* here   **looks**   good to me.

SINGULAR   SINGULAR
Most of the leftover *food* **is** thrown out.

The pronoun **none** can also be either singular or plural, depending on the context in which it is used.

Examples

SINGULAR   SINGULAR
None of the *contracts*   **is**   legal.
     (Not *one* is legal.)

PLURAL   PLURAL
None of the *contracts*   **are**   legal.
     (Not any group of contracts is legal.)

PLURAL   PLURAL
None but *those* **have been approved**.
(**Those**, the antecedent of the pronoun *none*, is always plural.)

Pronouns Used As Modifiers

Pronouns are often used as **adjectives**. Adjectives that modify the simple subject must also agree in number with both the subject and the predicate.

Examples

WRONG	CORRECT
These root *beer* **is** sour.	**This** root *beer* **is** sour.
Each women **are** welcome.	**All** *women* **are** welcome.

AGREEMENT IN DEPENDENT CLAUSES

The *verb* in a **dependent clause** must agree in number with the *subject* of the dependent clause. Moreover, the entire *complex sentence* should make sense in terms of number.

WRONG	CORRECT
After *John* **do** his homework, he **watch** television.	After *John* **does** his homework, *he* **watches** television.

When the **signal words** (relative pronouns) *that, which,* and *who* refer to singular words, use singular verbs; when these signal words *refer* to plural words, use plural verbs.

Examples

PLURAL

The gang is one of the toughest groups *that* **have** caused trouble in the area.

SINGULAR

The gang is the only one of the tough groups *that* **has** caused trouble in the area.

In such cases, the *plural verb* following the pronoun shows that the word referred to is one of several or one of many. The *singular verb* following the pronoun tells the reader that the word referred to is unique or outstanding in an individual sense.

Agreement—Pronoun and Antecedent

A **pronoun** must agree in number with its **antecedent**.

Examples

SINGULAR   SINGULAR
Anyone can claim *his* or *her* right to settle in the newly opened territory.

SINGULAR   SINGULAR
Each of the women had made *her* fortune investing in real estate.

PLURAL   PLURAL
Damon and *Harold* bought *their* tickets.

Although colloquial, a plural pronoun is sometimes used in conversation to refer back to a singular antecedent.

Example

SINGULAR   PLURAL
Everybody was trying to find *their* lockers. (acceptable in conversation only)

In writing, however, one of the following should be used:

SINGULAR   SINGULAR
Everybody was trying to find *his* locker.

SINGULAR   SINGULAR
Everybody was trying to find *his* or *her* locker.

Often the best solution is to recast the sentence:

PLURAL   PLURAL
All of the students were trying to find *their* lockers.

(Also see *Person: Sexism—Third-Person Masculine*, p. 243.)

When one of the antecedents is singular and the other is plural, the pronoun should agree with the nearer of the two antecedents.

Example

> Neither the *teacher* nor the *students* could forget *their* embarrassment at what had happened.

When possible, avoid placing the singular antecedent after the plural one. The resulting sentence may be awkward and unclear.

Example

> Neither the *students* nor the *teacher* could forget **his** embarrassment over what had happened. (awkward)

Collective antecedents are matched with the pronoun that best shows whether the antecedent should be considered as a single body or a collection of individuals.

Examples

> The *committee* has submitted **its** report. (Single body)
> The *committee* have submitted **their** reports. (Group of individuals)
> The committee *members* have submitted **their** reports. (Group of individuals)

Awk Awkward Sentences

Sentences can be awkward for many reasons. The general label "*awkward*" offers an easy way for an instructor to point out a bad sentence—one that does not read well. Awkward sentences should be rewritten.

Examples

AWKWARD	The reason for legalizing off-track betting is on the grounds of lost tax money.
REVISED	Off-track betting should be legalized to prevent tax money from being lost.
AWKWARD	This statement was about the only one which all of the Indians who fought in the Battle of Little Bighorn agreed.
REVISED	This statement was one of the few about which all of the Indians who fought in the Battle of Little Bighorn agreed.

AWKWARD	Mr. Byer's algebra class is much more difficult than Mr. Miller.
REVISED	Mr. Byer's algebra class is much more difficult than Mr. Miller's.

Capitals

CAPITALIZATION RULES

Capitalize the following:

1. Persons, races, nationalities, languages

Examples

George	Indian
William B. Smith, Jr.	Native American
Afro-American	American
But: blacks, whites	Chinese

2. Specific places

Examples

Boston	Appalachian Mountains
North Carolina	Lake Tahoe
Mexico	in the West (*section of the country*)

3. Specific organizations

Examples

the Sierra Club	*But*: the government
the National Aeronautics and Space Administration	the state government
NASA	the federal government
the House of Representatives	the legislature
Congress	

4. Historical events, documents, and periods

Examples

the French Revolution
World War Two
Declaration of Independence
Magna Carta
the Gay Nineties
the Dark Ages

5. Days, months, holidays

Examples

Monday	*But*: spring
April	summer
Christmas	fall
Memorial Day	winter

6. Titles of courses

Examples

The West as an Idea in American Literature
Spanish
Math 101
Anthropology 2

But: math
anthropology

7. Titles of books, magazines, newspapers, movies, plays, poems, songs, record albums, articles, chapters, speeches, papers, and other publications.

Capitalize the first word and all other words in the title except

—articles (*a, an, the*)
—prepositions (*in, on, over* . . .)
—conjunctions (*and, but, or*)

Examples

Catcher in the Rye (book)
Time (magazine)
New York Times (newspaper)
The Godfather (movie)
Hamlet (play)
"Stopping by Woods on a Snowy Evening" (poem)
"American the Beautiful" (song)
Nashville Skyline (record album)
"Automakers Urge Mandatory Belts" (newspaper article)

8. Official titles

Examples

>Dr. Robert Lee, Jr.
>Professor Johnson
>President John F. Kennedy
>The President (of the United States)
>Secretary of State
>Mr. Fong
>Mary B. Jorgenson, Doctor of Pharmacology
>The Chief Justice of the United States

But: Mary B. Jorgenson, the pharmacist on duty
>James Johnson, a chemistry teacher

9. Religious names, terms, titles, followers

Examples

God	Saint John	the Bible
Christ	Holy Communion	the Koran
Allah	Christianity	Christians
He	Hinduism	Hindus

10. In addresses

Examples

>1215 Park Street
>The (*or* the) University of the Pacific
>Claims Department, Pacific Mutual Life Insurance Co.
>Mountain View, California

11. Names of buildings, ships, airplanes, automobiles, brand names

Examples

>Empire State Building (building)
>Titanic (ship)
>IBM Selectric (brand name)
>Ford Pinto (brand name)
>Jif peanut butter (brand name)
>Spruce Goose (airplane)

But: German shepherd
>oak
>roses

12. Outlines

Example

  I. The Farallon Islands
    A. Appearance of the islands
    B. Intruders on the islands
  II. What has happened on the islands and why
    A. First European visitor
    B. Fur traders
      1. Extinction of fur seal
      2. Sea elephants

MM   Misplaced Modifiers

Avoid the **squinting modifier**, one that can modify either the sentence part before it or after it.

Example

	Adverb
SQUINTING	She asked the salesman *tactfully* to express his opinion.
REVISED	She *tactfully* asked the salesman to express his opinion.
OR	She asked the salesman to express his opinion *tactfully*.

Also avoid placing a modifier in the wrong part of a sentence. **Misplaced modifiers** can be confusing and occasionally embarrassing.

Example

MISPLACED	The president and vice-president of the company were forced to show the memo to the board of directors
	Adjective Clause
	that implicated them in the plot.
REVISED	The president and the vice-president of the company were forced to show the memo *that implicated them in the plot* to the board of directors.

Be especially careful not to write a **dangling introductory word, phrase or clause** that does not modify the subject of the independent clause immediately following it.

Example

	Adjective Phrase
DANGLING	*Naive and innocent,* the intrigues of politics amazed him.
REVISED	*Naive and innocent,* he was amazed by the intrigues of politics. (Note that *he* has been added.)

In *non-technical writing* or writing that is not highly statistical, spell out numbers that can be said in one or two words—except for dates, addresses, times followed by a.m. or p.m., pages, or dimensions.

Examples

The book cost *eighty-five* cents.	July 12, 1883
He knew *three* effective methods.	10:30 a.m.
The dam would cost *seven million* dollars.	
They ordered 575 chairs.	p. 185
	3 x 5 inch index cards

Never begin a sentence with a numeral.

WRONG

25 new colors were added.
$7000 is too much to pay for tuition.
27% were defective.

RIGHT

Twenty-five new colors were added.
Seven thousand dollars is too much to pay for tuition.
Twenty-seven percent were defective.

Large numbers—billions, trillions, etc.—may be written as follows:

five million   623 million   fourteen billion   210 billion

For the sake of appearance, numerals should be used consistently in a sentence, paragraph, or composition.

Examples

The state legislature has approved a 7.5 percent increase in pay for all state employees, which is lower than the 9 percent increase granted last year.
At the conference she paid $45 for a hotel room, $32.60 for meals, and $5 to park.

Do not convert numbers in quoted passages to words. If *Newsweek* magazine uses 27 percent of $14,000,000, leave Arabic numerals.

Parallel Construction **Paral**

Parallel construction—or parallelism—is achieved by repeating grammatical constructions. The basic technique in achieving parallelism is to use the same kinds of words, phrases, clauses, or sentences in pairs or series.

Examples

1. Three Adjectives—Predicate Adjectives

His tie is ‖ red
 ‖ white, and
 ‖ blue.

2. Three Verbs—Compound Predicate

The cornered mountain lion ‖ snarled,
 ‖ snapped, and
 ‖ lunged.

A breakdown in parallelism occurs when an item in a pair or series is not the kind of construction the reader expects. Sentences lacking parallelism lack balance and rhythm—they do not flow well, and they should be revised.

Example

For breakfast John had two scrambled eggs, a mound of fried potatoes full of bacon bits, three pieces of buttered toast, and *drank coffee until he finished the whole pot.* (not parallel)

In the above example, the reader is thrown off balance upon encountering "and drank coffee until he finished the whole pot." That part of the predicate should be revised to read, "and a potful of coffee." Here are some general suggestions about parallel construction:

CORRELATIVE PAIRS

Be on the lookout for these **correlative conjunctions**—they work in pairs.

either . . . or
neither . . . nor
both . . . and
not . . . but
not only . . . but also
first . . . second . . .

Place each conjunction in the pair next to the sentence part being correlated.

Example

NOT PARALLEL	PARALLEL
Either automation is one of the major enemies of the American worker *or* the means to provide future employment and prosperity.	Automation is *either* one of the major enemies of the American worker *or* the means to provide future employment and prosperity.

TEAM MODIFIERS

When separated *modifiers are* **teamed**, fewer words are needed and parallelism is improved. Use similar grammatical constructions, such as two adjectives, and place them together either before or after the word or word group being modified.

Example

NOT PARALLEL	PARALLEL
The *gusty* north wind, *which was cold,* blew steadily for three days.	The *cold, gusty,* north wind blew for three days.

PHRASES IN A SERIES

Try to use similar grammatical constructions in a series of phrases—a succession of *coordinate* phrases.

Example

NOT PARALLEL	PARALLEL
For many, college is a time filled *with* constant mental strain, with feeling *physically fatigued*, and *by periodic depression.*	For many, college is a time filled *with constant mental strain, physical fatigue,* and *periodic depression.*

Note that the preposition *with* in the example above has not been repeated in the "PARALLEL" version.

with ‖ constant mental strain,
physical fatigue, and
periodic depression.

Unless special emphasis is desired, the introductory word—an adjective, a preposition, or a pronoun—need not be repeated in each phrase in a series of short phrases. But when one or more of the phrases in the series contains *five* or more words, repeat the first word at the beginning of each phrase.

Examples

> *to* investigate, prosecute, and publicize (single words and short phrases)
> *to* investigate, *to* prosecute, and *to* publicize (special emphasis)
> *to* the store near his aunt's house *and to* the Mercury Cleaners on Broadway (more than five words)

DEPENDENT CLAUSES IN A SERIES

When writing a series of dependent clauses, keep them parallel. The first clause in the series ordinarily can be used as a model for the rest.

Examples

NOT PARALLEL	PARALLEL
Jimmy believes *that* the lost continent of Atlantis is below the Bermuda Triangle, *and* an underwater civilization flourishes there.	Jimmy believes that the lost continent of Atlantis is below the Bermuda Triangle *and that* an underwater civilization flourishes there.

As can be seen in the example above, the signal word "*that*" is repeated in the second dependent clause to make the two clauses parallel. Also note that it is the missing signal word that makes the example "not parallel."

In a series of long dependent clauses beginning with the same *signal word*, repeat the signal word in each dependent clause. (A *long* dependent clause is one that contains *five* or more words.)

Example

After she spent two days finding a topic for her term paper

and after she spent all day Saturday in the Library locating sources for her working bibliography,   she was ready to begin taking notes.

If, on the contrary, the dependent clauses are short (fewer than *five* words), there is usually no need to repeat the signal word.

Examples

Although Frank lost his ring

and Jamie became seasick,   everyone else had a good time sailing on San Francisco Bay.

Those students *who* studied daily

and completed every exercise   finished the course before those who tried to take shortcuts.

Passive and Active Verbs

When the subject of a sentence performs an action, as in the sentence "Bertie mashed the garlic," the verb is **active**. The writer is using the "active voice." When the subject of a sentence receives an action, as in the sentence "The garlic was mashed by Bertie," the verb is **passive**. Whenever possible, use active verbs to give sentences force and clarity. Avoid passive verbs when they make writing wordy, unclear, impersonal, evasive or dull.

Example

> EVASIVE   It *has been decided* that you are not ready for graduate school at this time.
>
> HONEST   The Dean of Admissions has *decided* that you are not ready for graduate school at this time.

In some situations *passive verbs* are more desirable than *active verbs*, as when the subject is perfectly obvious or when the subject is not known.

Example

> PASSIVE   The huge old jade plant *was stolen* from the front porch during the night. Only a forlorn pile of broken leaves *was left* scattered in the street. It was as if a member of the family *had been abducted, forced* into a car, and *spirited* away to some unknown fate.
>
> ACTIVE   Someone *stole* the old jade plant from the front porch during the night. Only a forlorn pile of broken leaves *lay* scattered in the street. It *seemed* that someone *had abducted* a member of the family and *spirited* him away to some unknown fate.

Using the active voice in the second version caused problems. Since the abductor is not known, the word *Someone* has been inserted, taking away emphasis from where it should be, on the jade plant, as in the first version. Furthermore, the next sentence is not as accurate in the second version as in the first, since, strictly speaking, leaves do not "lay" anywhere. And then in the last sentence, the intrusive *someone* has been employed again, and because there is no alternative, the awkward sounding *him* has been used. A "family member" could not be referred to as *it*, but a jade plant is customarily an *it*, not a *him* or a *her*.

Person—First, Second, and Third

Everything is written in **first, second,** or **third person**, depending upon the writer's purpose and audience. "Person" is the perspective used to distinguish between the writer and those to whom or about whom the writer writes. *First person* is used when the writer or the character in the writing is speaking. *Second person* is used when someone is addressed. *Third person* is used when someone or something is written about. The writer must choose one of these three perspectives—first, second, or third person—and then use it consistently, avoiding **shifts in person**, which can be awkward or confusing.

FIRST PERSON

First-person writing is characterized by the use of the pronouns *I, my, me, we, our,* and *us.* Either the author or a character in the writing is speaking first-hand.

Example

My earliest memory is of a false spring day on the Texas plains. *I* was standing on a wooden porch, clutching a doll with one arm, surveying *my* world. There were no houses close enough that *I* could see into *our* neighbor's windows, nor could *we* hear them talking when they were in their houses. While *I* was standing on the porch deciding what to play that day, a sick dog crawled between some broken palings underneath *our* porch and went mad.

First person is commonly used in narratives, descriptions, anecdotes, fiction, and autobiographical essays. As a rule, first person is to be avoided in explanatory and argumentative essays.

SECOND PERSON

Second-person writing is characterized by the use of the pronouns *you* and *yours.* The writer is speaking *to the reader.*

Example

After *you* have formed the mold in the sand, melt the paraffin. *You* can use one of *your* old coffee cans to heat the paraffin in until the wax is liquified. As it is melting, mix pieces of crayon in with the wax until the color is right. *You* can also add a few drops of scented oil at this stage.

Second person is used in directions and textbooks, but it is generally not acceptable in academic writing.

Often the second person pronoun *you* is understood although it is not actually stated.

Example

Mix the ingredients well. Shake the dressing before use.

THIRD PERSON

In **third-person** writing, people, places, and events are referred to objectively by name or description. Third-person writing is characterized by use of the following pronouns:

| he | his | him | it | its | she | her | one | they | their | them |

The writer is writing *about someone or something*.

Examples

Three hundred years ago in London during the plague, the city was not a very sanitary place to live. *Londoners*, both rich and poor, bathed infrequently. Most *families* bought a limited amount of water daily from *waterbearers*, and there were no private baths. *Samuel Pepys* wrote in *his* secret diary that *his wife* actually dared to wash *herself* all over at a public "hothouse" and that a few days later *he* bathed also, an unusual event. The city had no underground sewer system. Instead of sewers, kennels (open gutters) were used for waste liquids from chamber pots and wash-up water.

Most academic writing—essays, reports, and tests—should be written in the third person. However, a few problems should be avoided when using third person.

Impersonal Use of "One"

In converting first or second person writing to third person, resist the temptation to use the impersonal **one**. When *one* is overused, the writing becomes boring and wordy.

Impersonal

One never knows where forest fires will occur. Many times *one* finds the hottest spots are in difficult places, deep in a box canyon or similar area—difficult to fly into and even more difficult to fly out of—places where maneuverability and good rate of climb absolutely must be there when *one* pulls up after *one's* fire retardant drop. *One* can do just that with the S-2 aerial tanker.

Revised

Forest fires never seem to break out where they can be reached easily. Many times the hottest spots are deep in a box canyon or similar area—tough to fly into and even tougher to fly out of—places where maneuverability and good rate of climb absolutely must be there when the *pilot* pulls up after *his* fire retardant drop. The *S-2 aerial tanker* can do just that.

Sexism—Third-Person Masculine

It has been traditional in academic writing to use the **third-person masculine** *he* and *his* instead of the wordier phrases *he or she* and *his or her*.

Example

SINGULAR
Everyone must turn in *his* test now, or *it* will be marked down one-half grade.

Now, however, due to the increasing concern over sexism in the English language, often the *plural* is used to avoid exclusively third-person masculine pronouns or the phrase *he or she*.

PLURAL

All students must turn in *their* tests now, or *the tests* will be marked down one-half grade.

When plurals cannot be used, the best alternatives are to use the somewhat wordy *he or she* or to revert to the traditional *he*.

Some writers insist on using *he/she* or *s/he*, but the practice is not widely accepted.

SHIFTS IN PERSON

Some shifts in person are subtle and do not jar the reader. In a first-person narrative, for example, third person may be used in general descriptions.

Example

My earliest memory is of a false spring day on the Texas plains. The day was not warm enough for little *girls* to roll up *their* long cotton ribbed stockings. I was standing on a wooden porch, clutching a doll with one arm, surveying my world.

Although it is acceptable as is, the sentence in third person could be rewritten using the first-person point of view:

The day was not warm enough for a little girl like *me* to roll up *my* long cotton ribbed stockings.

On the other hand, however, shifts in person that disrupt the sentence and grate upon the readers should be corrected. Most often these shifts are from first or third person to the second person *you* or *your*.

Examples

SHIFT	REVISED
I got up early the next morning, and *you* wouldn't believe how deep the snow was.	I got up early the next morning, and *I* couldn't believe how deep the snow was.
Most people have learned that *you* have to change the oil in *your* cars regularly.	Most people have learned that *they* have to change the oil in *their* cars regularly.

Pro Pronouns

POSSESSIVE FORMS

Most **pronouns** change their forms to show *possession*—to indicate owner-ship.

244

Some Possessive Pronouns

REGULAR FORMS		POSSESSIVE FORMS	
Subject	Object	As Modifiers	As Nouns
I	me	my	mine
he	him	his	his
she	her	her	hers
it	it	its [not it's]	its [not it's]
we	us	our	ours
you	you	your	yours
they	them	their	theirs
who	whom	whose	whose
whoever	whomever	whosever	

When a pronoun is used as a *modifier*, usually an adjective, the possessive form must be used. This rule causes no problems with pronouns that become possessive with the addition of an -'s ending.

Example

> *Everybody's* feelings were hurt.

But when a pronoun from the preceding list is used as a modifier, the *possessive modifier* form must be used. And, vice versa, the possessive modifier form must not be used where a *regular form* belongs.

Example

WRONG	CORRECT
When *her* came out of Montgomery Ward, *her* could not find *she* car.	When *she* came out of Montgomery Ward, *she* could not find *her* car.

The right possessive form of the pronoun must also be used when the pronoun showing possession functions as a *noun*.

Examples

> SUBJECT
> *Ours*   was the last empty lot on the tract.

> DIRECT OBJECT
> We want   *ours*   now.

Use the "Possessive" form of the pronoun placed before a *gerund* (a verb used as a noun).

Example

> The board of directors did not like *his* hiring four new managers. (gerund *hiring* acts as direct object—use "*his*" not "*him*")

SUBJECT AND OBJECT FORMS

Different forms of some pronouns are used for **subjects** and **objects**. Use the "Subject" form (see the preceding chart) when the pronoun is used as the *subject* of a sentence or clause, even when the clause as a whole functions as an object. Particular attention must be paid to pronouns followed by parenthetical expressions, pronouns following *than* or *as*, pronouns paired with appositives, pronouns in compound subjects, and pronouns used as predicate nouns.

Examples

We are moving soon. (subject of verb phrase)

We contacted the people *who* had attended the conference. (subject of independent clause and subject of dependent clause)

Marty is the classical guitar player *who* they think will be very famous some day. (parenthetical *they think* does not affect the subject *who*)

George can run faster than *I*. (elliptical dependent clause meaning "than *I* can run")

Mr. Koski and *I* will demonstrate the experiment. (compound subject)

We girls all want to go to the dance. (pronoun *We*, paired with appositive *girls*, is subject)

It is *I* who must take the responsibility. (*I* is predicate noun, modified by the dependent clause beginning *who*—formal English)

It is *me*. (informal English)

Use the "Object" form when the pronoun is used as an *object*. (Also use the object form for the subject, object, or predicate noun of an *infinitive*.)

Examples

Charles visited *him* last night. (direct object)

Two of *us* were sent to the conference. (object of preposition)

Two of *us* girls were invited to the dance. (object of preposition paired with the appositive *girls*)

The telephone call was for *me*. (object of preposition)

Seeing *them* was a lot of fun for Kathy and *me*. (direct object in participial phrase and compound object of preposition)

Wilma will be able to help you sooner than *me*. (means "sooner than she will be able to help *me*.")

Whom did you want to see? (objective of infinitive—formal English)

Who did you want to see? (informal English)

I want the winner to be *me*. (predicate noun following infinitive linking verb)

APOSTROPHE

Use an apostrophe:

1. To show where letters have been omitted in a contraction (when two words are combined, leaving out one or more letters).

Examples

aren't (are not)   I'm (I am)   shouldn't (should not)

2. To show possession. With singular words, use an apostrophe followed by an "s." If adding an "s" to a singular noun sounds or appears awkward, add only an apostrophe. (Note that in some cases either form is correct.) With plural nouns that end with "s," add only an apostrophe.

Examples

Singular	Plural
the company's pension plan	the companies' pension plans
Kansas's legislature	the judges' opinions
Socrates' teaching methods	three years' records

Note: The possessive form of *it* is *its*, with no apostrophe. The word *it's* is a contraction of *it is*.

Examples

The dog licked *its* wounds. (POSSESSIVE)

It's too late to go to the show. (CONTRACTION)

3. To form the contraction of dates, i.e., to replace the two numbers that specify the century. (Do not replace these numbers with the apostrophe unless you are sure the reader will know the century to which you are referring.)

Examples

Spirit of '76   The student unrest of the '60s.

4. To separate the "s" from plural abbreviations with periods, and letters used as nouns. (The use of an apostrophe is optional for plurals of numbers or dates and abbreviations without periods.)

Examples

| V.I.P.'s | *A*'s | *x*'s and *y*'s |
| GIs (*or* GI's) | the 1700s (*or* the 1700's) | |

247

COLON

The colon may be used to introduce a series or a list.

Example

> This semester Martha will take the following subjects: English, History 17, algebra, and physical education.

In academic writing the portion of the sentence that introduces the series is usually an independent clause.

Example

> Historians found that the ancient Central American civilization's decline was caused by three factors that seem ominously contemporary: inflation, deterioration of the work ethic, and environmental mismanagement.

Never place a colon after a verb or a preposition. A colon in such instances is redundant.

Example

> We will be traveling **to** Honolulu, Tokyo, Kyoto, Peking, Hong Kong, and Singapore.

COMMA (See Chapter One, pp. 12-22, and Chapter Two, pp. 29-37, 44-47.)

HYPHEN

Use the hyphen:

1. To divide a word into syllables at the end of a line when the whole word will not fit on that line. Always place the hyphen after a complete syllable (check a dictionary for syllable divisions). Do not carry over only two letters to the next line. Do not divide so that only one letter is at the end of a line. If you are not sure of the correct division, it is better to leave a ragged right-hand margin.

Example

> Because travel to these islands is so difficult,
> they are frequently labeled remote and for-
> gotten by most people who hear of them.

2. To connect compound numbers (when spelled out) from twenty-one to ninety-nine, fractions used as adjectives in front of nouns, and the decades.

Examples

> *twenty-five* customers
> a *two-thirds* majority
> the *nineteen-seventies*

When a fraction is used as a noun, do not use a hyphen.

Example

Two thirds of the voters turned out on election day.

3. To connect the words in a compound modifier (two words acting as a single adjective) that is placed before the noun it modifies. Do not use a hyphen when the compound modifier follows a verb or when the first word is an adverb that ends with "*ly.*"

Examples

an *ill-timed* move	the move was *ill timed*
a *third-story* office	the office was in the *third story*

4. To connect compound words. (Consult a dictionary when in doubt.)

Examples

cease-fire	cross-examine
court-martial	great-grandmother

5. To connect certain prefixes. (Consult the dictionary when in doubt.)

Examples

anti-British	*pan*-American
mid-Atlantic	*pro*-Israeli

6. To prevent confusion about spelling, pronunciation or meaning.

Examples

semi-invalid
She will *re-form* the clay model.

SEMICOLON (See Chapter Two, pages 32-34)

UNDERLINING

When papers are handwritten or typed, underlining is used instead of italics. Underlining (or italics) is used in the following situations:

1. The titles of newspapers, magazines, books, plays, movies, book-length poems, long musical compositions, record albums, television series, works of art, ships, and airplanes.

<u>New York Times</u>	<u>The Nutcracker Suite</u>
<u>Roots</u>	<u>The Iliad</u>
<u>Hamlet</u>	<u>Bob Dylan's Greatest Hits</u>
<u>Star Wars</u>	<u>The Mary Tyler Moore Show</u>
Da Vinci's <u>Mona Lisa</u>	Bible (Do not underline.)

2. Foreign words and expressions.

Examples

our <u>raison d'être</u>   <u>non sequitur</u>

3. Words referred to as words and letters referred to as letters.

Examples

She always misspelled the word <u>separate</u>.
She put an <u>e</u> instead of an <u>a</u> after the <u>p</u>.

Ref Pronoun Reference (Also see *Agreement—Pronoun and Antecedent*)

Since a **pronoun** is a word that takes the place of a noun, the reader must be able to refer back to the noun for which the pronoun is acting as a substitute — its **antecedent**. If the antecedent is not clearly stated, either an antecedent must be added or the faulty pronoun must be removed.

AMBIGUOUS PRONOUN REFERENCE

Do not let a pronoun seem to point to more than one antecedent, or the reader may not know immediately which word is referred to by the pronoun.

Example

AMBIGUOUS   The doctor experienced difficulty talking to her patient because *she* knew *she* was late for an appointment.

REVISED   The doctor experienced difficulty talking to her patient because *her patient was worried about being late for an appointment.*

GENERAL PRONOUN REFERENCE

Avoid using the following pronouns to refer *generally* to what was said previously.

which   this   it   that

Remember that a singular antecedent should be *one word* that can be pinpointed. If the antecedent is not that clear because of the general manner in which one of these pronouns is used, rewrite the sentence containing the general pronoun.

GENERAL   He cheated on all of his tests, *which* irritated the rest of the class.

                                          Antecedent

REVISED   He cheated on all of his tests, a *habit* **which** irritated the rest of the class. (Singular *antecedent* has been added)

GENERAL   In *The Jungle* Upton Sinclair writes about unsanitary meat processing and poor working conditions in the meat packing industry at the turn of the century. *This* has not been entirely eliminated today. (Pronoun "*this*" is vague and does not agree)

REVISED   In *The Jungle* Upton Sinclair writes about *the unsanitary meat processing* and *poor working conditions* in the meat packing industry at the turn of the century. **These problems** have not been entirely eliminated today. (Compound antecedent: plural pronoun plus transitional word "*problems*")

INDEFINITE PRONOUN REFERENCE

When an antecedent exists only in the writer's imagination or when the writer mistakenly thinks that a word is an antecedent, the **indefinite pronoun reference** must be corrected.

Example

                                    ADJ

INDEFINITE   She reached for the *elevator* door, but *it* whooshed right past her floor. (Indicates that the *door* whooshed past)

REVISED   She reached for the elevator door, but *the elevator* whooshed right past her floor.

Verb Forms   VF

Each *verb* has **five forms**, or "principal parts," as they are sometimes called. Since a writer is expected to use the correct forms, knowing the characteristics of each is necessary.

LEARN THE CHARACTERISTICS OF EACH VERB FORM

Form One of the verb is the "plain" form of the verb—the *base form* from which the other forms are made. It may tell what happens in the *present*, what happened in the *past*, or what will happen in the *future*. It is used alone or with one *helping verb* when telling about the present; it is used only with the helping verb **did** when telling about the past; it is used with a helping verb when telling about the future. These helping verbs can be followed by *Form One* of the verb:

do	shall	may	would
does	will	must	could
did	can	should	might

Form One may be used with *singular* or *plural nouns* and with the pronouns **I, they, we, you, all, some, which, that, these, those, who**, and others. The first form is also used with **to** in *infinitive phrases*. FORM ONE NEVER ENDS IN -S OR -**ING**.

Examples of Form One

> I *run* every morning.
> John and Mary *run* every Saturday.
> You *should run* every day.
> The shuttle bus *will run* every fifteen minutes.
> They *love to run* in the sand.
> *Will* you *lend* me fifty cents?

Form Two of the verb ends with **-s** or **-es**, and except in a few cases, *Form Two* is made by adding **-s** or **-es** to *Form One*. (The *Form Two verbs* **is** and **has** are exceptions.) Form Two usually tells what happens *presently*; it is never used with *helping verbs*. It is used after *singular nouns* and the *singular pronouns* **he, she, it,** and other *singular pronouns* such as **each, everyone, this, that,** and **yours.** (DO NOT CONFUSE FORM TWO VERBS WITH PLURAL NOUNS THAT END IN -S OR -**ES**.)

Examples of Form Two

> John *runs* every morning.
> The shuttle bus *runs* from the parking lot to the grandstand.
> He *runs* every Wednesday.
> She *has* a horse that *runs* like a kangaroo.
> Clara always *chooses* the most expensive item on the menu whether she *likes* it or not.

Form Three of the verb is often called the "past" form of the verb because it always tells what happened *earlier*. Also, *Form Three* is never used with *helping verbs*. It may be used with *singular* and *plural nouns* and *pronouns*.

Examples of Form Three

> John *ran* every morning.
> He *ran* every morning.
> The shuttle bus *ran* every fifteen minutes.
> She *chose* the necklace that she *wanted*.
> They *hung* a huge fern from the living room ceiling.

Form Four of the verb, often called the "past participle" form, *must* be used with one or more *helping verbs*. (In some cases the only difference between *Form Three* and *Form Four* is the presence or absence of a helping verb.) When *Form Four* tells what happens *presently*, it is often accompanied by the helping verbs **am, is,** and **are.** When it is used to tell what happened in the *past*, it is often used with the helping verbs **has, have, having, had, was, were,** or combinations of helping verbs such as **has been, have been, having been**, and **had been**. When it is used to tell what will happen in the *future*, it is used with combinations of helping verbs like **will have, shall have, will have been, shall have been**, and **will be**.

Various combinations of helping verbs are also used with Form Four when it is used to speculate about things that *are not certain* or to declare *opinions*.

can be	cannot be
could be	could have been
may be	may have been
might be	might have been
must be	must have been
should be	should have been

Form Four is used with both *singular* and *plural nouns* and *pronouns*.

Examples of Form Four

The doughnuts *are fried* fresh each morning.
Saul *has run* every evening for the last two months.
The shuttle bus *will run* on propane.
They *must have chosen* these wild colors.
How *could* anyone *have known* the terrible truth?

Form Five of the verb always ends with **-ing**. None of the other four verb forms ends with -ing. As is the case with Form Four, *Form Five* must be accompanied by one or more *helping verbs*. The helping verbs and combinations of helping verbs that can be used with *Form Five* are the same ones used with *Form Four* verbs. Here are some examples:

am	is	are
was	were	were *not**
has been	have been	had been
can be	could be	could *never* be*
will be	will have been	will *not* have been*
must be	should be	might be

Negative adverbs such as **not** and **never** are often a part of the helping verb combination for Forms *One, Four* and *Five*.

Form Five can tell what happens in the *present, past,* or *future;* and it can be used with *singular* and *plural nouns* and *pronouns*.

John *is running* every morning.
He *will be running* every morning.
They *are running* every morning.
The shuttle bus *has not been running* regularly.
When *will we be choosing* our classes?

SOME TROUBLESOME VERB FORMS

In particular, it is the **irregular verbs** that are most often misused. They must be memorized because the spellings of the different forms are not always predictable. Forms *Three* and *Four* of **regular verbs** usually end with **-d, -ed,** or **-t**.

Examples of Regular Verbs

Form 1	Form 2	Form 3	Form 4	Form 5
ask	asks	asked	asked	asking
borrow	borrows	borrowed	borrowed	borrowing
bury	buries	buried	buried	burying
shoot	shoots	shot	shot	shooting

Irregular verbs, on the other hand, do not form their *third* and *fourth* forms by adding these endings.

Examples of Irregular Verbs

Form 1	Form 2	Form 3	Form 4	Form 5
begin	begins	began	begun	beginning
draw	draws	drew	drawn	drawing
freeze	freezes	froze	frozen	freezing
swim	swims	swam	swum	swimming

Dictionaries list the irregular verb forms.

- *Form One* is always listed.

- *Form Two* is never listed (add **-s** or **-es**).

- *Form Three* is always listed.

- *Form Four* is listed only when it differs from *Form Three*.

- *Form Five* is always listed.

The *five verb forms* are used in certain ways to show the **time** at which an action or condition occurs. The time designations given to the verb forms used are known as **tenses.**

THE SIX BASIC TENSES

1. *Present Tense*

The **present tense** is used to show that an action or condition is occurring now.

Examples

> They *grow* tomatoes in that field.
> She *is* ill.

In academic writing the *present tense* is used regularly to summarize the content of an article, book, story, play, poem, or film.

Examples

> Hill *says* that each student *has* a different learning style.
> As the story *begins*, Dick Dagger *checks* his spy kit.
> The rebels *destroy* the "Death Star" satellite.

Probably the most common method of forming the present tense is to use the *helping verb* **am**, **are**, or **is** with *Form Five* of the verb.

Examples

> I *am writing* a paper.
> They *are moving* to Chicago.
> The north wind *is blowing*.
> He *is planning* to write a novel.
> Carl *is doing* better in math.

In these verb phrases it is the helping verb—**am, are,** or **is**—that tells that time is *present*, not the *-ing* verb.

The writer can form other verb phrases in the *present tense*. What is needed is an appropriate helping verb plus either *Form One* or *Form Two* of the verb. Some verb phrases are in the present tense, but they do not seem to be because they tell about an action or condition that *can* be, *would* be, *ought* to be, *should* be, or *must* be.

Examples

> He *can go* to the party.　　　　　I *may be* late.
> You *do* not *need* to study.　　　*Would* you *like* a cold drink?
> Everybody *must pass* through customs.

255

2. Past Tense

The **past tense** is used to show that an action or condition occurred at some definite time in the *past* — at an **earlier** time. The action or condition did *not* continue into the present.

Examples

He *repaired* the artery.
I *was* there.
We *were* really tired.
The stubborn mule *would* not *move.*
We *did* not *know* the man.
Did we *cook* enough lasagne?

By using **was** or **were** plus a *Form Five* verb, the writer can show that an action was *in progress* at a certain time in the past.

Examples

Tony *was watching* the championship tennis finals.
They *were listening* to one of the most remarkable performances in the history of rock music.

3. Future Tense

The **future tense** of the verb is used to show that an action or condition will occur in the *future*. The action or condition has not happened yet — it will happen later than now.

Examples

I *shall ask* for advice.
I *will win* that race.
They *will graduate* this June.
I *may visit* you Friday afternoon.

Shall or Will?

These two helping verbs are now used interchangeably. Both are correct, although *will* has become the more popular form, as in the sentence "I *will* do my best."

The helping verb **shall** or **will** is used with *be* and *Form Five* of the verb to state future tense.

I *shall be leaving* soon.
They *will be searching* for the real story behind the cover-up of the scandal.

4. *Present Perfect Tense*

The word **perfect**, as it applies to verb tense, means "finished," or "completed." The **present perfect tense** may be used to show that an action or condition occurred sometime in the past. The action or condition that was begun sometime in the past has already been completed. (Use **has** or **have** + *Form Four* of the verb.)

Examples

He *has seen* the doctor already.
They *have flown* to Dallas twice.
Maurice *has completed* all of the work.

The *present perfect tense* also may be used to show that an action or event occurring in the past is continuing into the present.

Examples

Elaine *has baby-sat* for us many times.
The Cabrillo brothers *have hauled* fresh produce for years.
I *have lived* here longer than any of my neighbors.

The helping verbs **has been** or **have been** are used with *Form Five* of the verb to state *present perfect tense*.

Examples

He *has been delivering* the mail since 1958.
They *have been remodeling* the apartment.
I *have been dating* Sue for three months.

5. *Past Perfect Tense*

The **past perfect tense** is used to show than an action or condition was completed sometime in the past *before some other action or condition that occurred later in the past*. In other words, past perfect tense is used to designate the *earlier* of the two past actions. Whereas the *present perfect tense* is formed with **has** or **have**, the past perfect tense is formed with **had**. (Use **had** + *Form Four* of the verb.)

Examples

PAST   PAST   PAST PERFECT
I *fired* and *ran* up to the fallen animal. I *had shot* a cow by mistake.

      PAST   PAST PERFECT
They *were camping* in Pine Creek Gorge. They *had camped* in Miner's Run the night before.

PAST   PAST PERFECT

Then I *knew* that I *had forgotten* my lunch.

Past perfect tense may also be stated by using **had been** plus *Form Five* of the verb.

Examples

PAST PERFECT   PAST   PAST

I *had been dating* Tony for a year before I *discovered* that he *was married*.

Infinitives

Infinitive phrases are used as *nouns, adjectives,* and *adverbs*. When the simple predicate of the sentence or dependent clause refers to the same time as the infinitive phrase, the infinitive phrase should be written in the *present tense*.

Examples

Simple   PRESENT
Predicate   TENSE
I **was shocked** *to see* you with another new husband.

Simple   PRESENT
Predicate   TENSE
George found Mary **had** the will *to continue*.

When the infinitive phrase refers to a time before that referred to by the simple predicate, the infinitive phrase should be written in the *present perfect* or *past perfect tense*.

Example

Simple
Predicate
Now that I have lived in the city for awhile, I know I **am**

PRESENT PERFECT
TENSE
fortunate   *to have lived*   in the country when I was young.

---

6. *Future Perfect Tense*

The **future perfect tense** is used to show that an action or condition will be completed in the future *before some other action or condition*.

The *helping verbs* **shall have** or **will have** and Form Four of the verb may be used.

I *shall have learned* the answer by then.

They *will have thrown* away all of the worn-out toys.

    FUTURE PERFECT   FUTURE

Jerry *will have completed* his junior year when he *transfers* to the University of Michigan.

Future perfect tense may also be stated by using the helping verbs **shall have been** or **will have been** with *Form Five* of the verb.

Example

    FUTURE PERFECT   FUTURE

They *will have been preparing* for the wedding for weeks when we *arrive* next Saturday.

The Subjunctive "Were"

The subjunctive **were** is used instead of **was** in two situations: 1) after *if* or *as though* in a dependent clause stating a condition contrary to fact and 2) after *that* in a dependent clause stating a *wish*.

Examples

If Sam **were** not such a liar, he would be a great salesman.

He talks *as though* he **were** an expert on everything.

I *wish* he **were** more like Larry.

Verb Tense Shifts

VTS

Tense shifts are changes, for example, from *past tense* to *past perfect tense*.

Example

    PAST   PAST   PAST PERFECT

After he *left* home, he *remembered* that he *had shut* the dog in the family room.

By shifting tenses, a writer can communicate very complicated time relationships.

Example

FUTURE
Tonight Ronald Hammersmith *will discuss* the actions Franklin Delano

PAST   PAST
Roosevelt *took* during his first one hundred days in office, as he *attempted*

PRESENT (INFINITIVE PHRASE)
to implement emergency measures against the depression which

PAST PERFECT
had brought America to the brink of disaster.

These kinds of tense shifts are necessary and, therefore, must be mastered by every writer. However, unnecessary tense shifts should be avoided. Even experienced writers sometimes forget—especially in stories and plot summaries—to keep writing in the same tense in which they started.

Example

AWKWARD   PRESENT
SHIFT   Later in the story Mona *runs* into trouble with the law.

                     PAST   PAST
         She *smuggled* a boa constrictor past customs but *was caught*

                           PRESENT
         when the snake *crawls* onto a woman's lap.

REVISED   PRESENT
         Later in the story Mona *runs* into trouble with the law. She
PRESENT   PRESENT
         smuggles a boa constrictor past customs but *is caught* when
                       PRESENT
         the snake *crawls* on to a woman's lap.

Weak   Weak Verbs

WEAK "IS'S" AND "WAS'S"

Look for weak **is**'s and **was**'s that can be eliminated. Often a weak linking verb can be replaced by a strong action verb, or an extraneous helping verb can be removed. As in the case of passive verbs, though, the *is* or *was* may be preferable to the action verb alternative. Each situation must be carefully studied.

Examples

NO   The story *is* the result of a great deal of research *that was con-*
ACTION *ducted* in the Amazon jungle.
VERBS

ALL ACTION VERBS	The story *resulted* from a great deal of research *conducted* in the Amazon jungle.

SAY-NOTHING "HAS'S," "HAVE'S," AND "HAD'S"

Too often these verbs say nothing to the reader. They do little more than mark time and take up space. Replace these weak verbs with strong verbs that more accurately describe the action involved.

Examples

WEAK	Rocky *had* a four-wheel-drive Ford pick-up truck.
STRONG	Rocky *owned* a four-wheel-drive Ford pick-up truck.
STRONG	Rocky *drove* a four-wheel-drive Ford pick-up truck.
WEAK	Farida *has* trouble with punctuation.
STRONG	Punctuation *confuses* Farida.
STRONG	Farida *does not know* where to use commas and semicolons.

Wordiness   Wdy

Edit each sentence for **unnecessary words**. There is a difference between helpful, supportive details and useless verbiage. Often a wordy sentence can be revised to say the same thing better in half the words.

Examples

WORDY	High school, college, and university students have the knowledge now more than they ever did in the past that a degree from an institution of higher learning can be the key leading down the trail to jobs that are better and lives that are richer. (45 words)
REVISED	Students know more than ever that a college degree can lead to better jobs and richer lives. (17 words)

Removing "It Is" and "There Is"

For more concise, livelier sentences, cut out unnecessary *it is*'s, *there is*'s, and related forms such as *it was*'s and *there were*'s.

Examples

At present the world population is approaching four billion, and *it is* doubling every thirty to thirty-five years. (wordy)

At present the world population is approaching four *billion and doubling* every thirty to thirty-five years. (revised)

There are numerous problems caused by overpopulation. (wordy)

Numerous problems are caused by overpopulation. (revised)

It is the intention of the grand jury to investigate auditing procedures in the Assessor's office. (wordy)

The grand jury intends to investigate the auditing procedures in the Assessor's office. (revised)

Redundancy

Some revising may be needed to eliminate **redundancies**. Within the sentence, redundancy is a kind of wordiness, the use of superfluous words whose meaning is approximately the same as that of other words in the sentence.

Examples

REDUNDANT	In [the month of] April a young man [of eighteen] is apt to daydream [in fantasies during the day] about [the beauteous physical charms and attributes of] lovely [feminine] women. (35 words)
REVISED	In April a young man is apt to daydream about lovely women. (12 words)
REDUNDANT	The tiny [little] [spherical] balls were supposed to roll [downward] to a lower level [below]. (15 words)
REVISED	The tiny balls were supposed to roll to a lower level. (11 words)

Index

CORRECTION SYMBOLS

Plag   Plagiarism (source not credited)

Pn   Punctuation faulty

Pro   Pronoun case not correct

Ref   Pronoun reference unclear

R-O   Run-on sentence

Sp or ⬭   Misspelled

Struct   Paragraph strategy not clear or inadvisable

TS   Topic sentence faulty

Trans   Transition faulty

Usage   Word usage unacceptable

Var   Sentences lack variety

VF   Verb form wrong

VT   Verb tense wrong

VTS   Unnecessary verb tense shift

Weak   Weak verb choice

Wdy   Wordy

WW   Wrong word